BRAIN
DAMAGED

Two-Minute Warning for Parents

Kimberly Archie

Jo Cornell

Faces of CTE Families
Foreword by Daniel Carcillo

USA Sport Safety Publishing LLC
Brain Damaged: Two-Minute Warning for Parents

For more information, please contact:
Faces of CTE
info@facesofCTE.com

Jacket design by Paul Enea Brighton
Interior design by Heather UpChurch

Paperback ISBN: 978-1-7336778-2-0
Hardcover ISBN: 978-1-7336778-0-6
E-book ISBN: 978-1-7336778-1-3

Printed in the United States

To Isiah Robertson, a fierce competitor both on and off the gridiron.
Your work on behalf of athletes from kids to the pros lives on.

August 17, 1949 – December 6, 2018

CONTENTS

PRAISE

"This book is a testament to the devastating toll that head trauma can take on the lives of survivors and their families. The problem with the faces of CTE is that we are currently unable to recognize them until it's too late. As researchers, we have a lot of work to do. Congratulations to these brave authors and advocates for sharing their compelling stories. This work ensures that the next generation of contact sport athletes won't be finding themselves in doctors' offices saying, 'I wish I had known.'"

- Kristen Dams-O'Connor, PhD, Director, Brain Injury Research Center of Mount Sinai, Principal Investigator, Late Effects of TBI Brain Donor Project, Associate Professor, Departments of Rehabilitation Medicine and Neurology, Icahn School of Medicine at Mount Sinai

"So often, the conversation surrounding CTE focuses on policies and procedures. *Brain Damaged* puts the personal impact of the degenerative brain disease front and center, where it should be. It is a moving, informative, and important resource for anyone who is invested in sports safety – a category that everyone should be a part of."

-Lindsay Gibbs, sports reporter for ThinkProgress

"When I was kicking the tires on writing a story on outdated football equipment, I asked a friend for an expert to be quoted in the article. The first person my friend suggested was Kimberly Archie. *Brain Damaged* lays out a meticulous case to show us all that a lack of oversight regarding concussions and CTE is a real thing."

- Evan F. Moore, digital content producer for news, Chicago Sun-Times

"This informative book puts a spotlight on sports that are associated with brain damage. The factual information presented is clear and illustrated by poignant, personal stories of tragedy. The face of CTE is a face any of us might know and love. An important read for anyone concerned about safety in sports, from childhood through professional athlete."

**- Shana De Caro, Esq., and Michael V. Kaplen, Esq., adjunct professor at
George Washington Law School, brain injury lawyers and advocates**

"Brain Damaged is a must-read before your child suits up for any sport, not just football. Kimberly Archie enlightened me and our Public Television audience in the award-winning profile "Nothing to Cheer About" – a revealing look at the inherent dangers of what can seem like the benign activity of cheerleading. Now, it's the frightening effects of the head-banging game of football that's front and center in this powerfully enlightening book. It's meaningful. It's memorable. It's straight-up truthful. It's a book that belongs on your bedside table – even if it keeps you up all night."

**- Angela Shelley, winner of Emmy and Edward R. Murrow
awards as producer of "Nothing to Cheer About"**

"Brain Damaged is a thought-provoking book that provides the reader with science-based information concerning repetitive-hit sports that affect our youth. This book is a necessary must-read for all parents, who are contemplating allowing their children to play any youth sport, so that they will be equipped with facts about the risks involved."

**- Darcy Keith, award-winning public speaker and author,
traumatic brain injury survivor, and board member
of the Brain Injury Association of Indiana**

"It's one of society's great dilemmas! What the heck are we going to do with tackle football with all that we already know? Kimberly Archie has long been one of the leading champions of youth sports safety. Fighting through personal tragedy, Kimberly has become a leading advocate, activist and educator in the world of brain trauma, injury and CTE related to football. With emphasis on the players and families affected by it, *Brain Damaged* is powerful and timely!"

-Dr. Bob Weil, sports podiatrist, host of "The Sports Doctor" on bbsradio.com, and co-author of "#HeySportsParents: An Essential Guide for any Parent with a Child in Sports"

"These stories of young tackle football players who died with proven chronic traumatic encephalopathy should be a wakeup call to schools that sponsor this sport. Schools are for educating brains and for cultivating lifelong interest in physical well-being. Schools can do without tackle football. The price of junior and high school tackle football is too high."

- Steven Miles, MD, Professor Emeritus, Department of Medicine, University of Minnesota

"Kim Archie was a tenacious advocate for young athletes long before her own son was found to have CTE. This is the powerful story of a mother, a warrior, a clear-eyed observer of the dangerous game of football."

- Steve Delsohn, Delsohn Strategies, former ESPN investigative reporter, New York Times best-selling author

"*Brain Damaged* needs to be read by every politician, every parent, every coach, every person who believes the lie that sports are "safer than ever." It is a choice to listen to the cover up, the propaganda, the white lies and equivocation churned out by those who personally benefit from youth sports, or to listen to the 8,000 hours of research done by Kimberly Archie, who is fighting to put 'brains before games.' Listen to the heart-breaking stories of many families who have lost a loved one to CTE and who are now joining forces to ensure other children aren't sacrificed to a rigid system that privileges a game and knowingly sacrifices children to it."

- Jen Fraser PhD, author, founder, End Bully & Abuse Academy

"This book is a tour de force of tragedy and heartbreak, but it shines a necessary light on a devastating disease that is needlessly killing our loved ones. The authors make their mission clear – they want to save lives, not by being 'alarmist' but by being realistic. The game at the youth level must change, and this book highlights what will happen if we maintain the status quo."

- Paul Anderson, attorney, adjunct professor of law at University of Missouri-Kansas City, and founder of NFLconcussionlitigation.com

"This book is about loss. Loss of the gravest kind but it is also a book about perseverance and activism. The game of football inflicts a great harm on the mind and body and this book is a testament to this suffering. Parents who consider football for their kids would pause before doing so upon reading this book and this is of great value!"

- Nadav Goldschmied, Ph. D., Associate Professor, Department of Psychological Sciences, University of California San Diego

"*Brain Damaged* is a collection of firsthand accounts of the lives and deaths of their loved ones. The common thread that connects these stories is that their loved ones were athletes - youth, collegiate, or pro - who were lost due to CTE or other brain damage. Told with fierce love, these stories are deeply important, because the changes they should inspire have the capacity to ensure that future athletes and their families won't suffer the same tragic fate."

- Michael Kasden, IP attorney, adjunct professor NYU Law, special projects co-ordinator Good Men Project

"Brain Damaged is an account of families who have been touched by the devastating effects of brain injuries. After their lives were changed forever, this group of laypeople have become experts, educators, and advocates to make the public aware of their struggles with CTE so others won't have to. The Faces of CTE group have done the brain injury community a huge favor by sharing these accounts. Prevention is a huge goal of brain injury advocates. However, when someone is actively facing a hardship, one of the biggest comforts to many is knowing you are not alone. This collection allows families to know that they have others who have walked in their shoes who are willing to help. As a brain injury survivor, I applaud this group and highly recommend this book they have provided."

- Mat Blankenship, firefighter, founder, Firefighter Concussion Protocol

"If you are seriously interested in protecting your children from long-term harm, you should read this book from cover to cover. Football is bad for anybody's health. Even more so for kids and adolescents. And they cannot give informed consent. Their parents are responsible and should only make well-informed decisions."

-Jürgen Kalwa, writer and US correspondent for German Public Radio

"This jolting book on the cause and effect of repeated trauma to the head from childhood sports in younger children, principally playing football, is a cautionary warning to parents who encourage the joy of sports for their children. It contains some grim results. The stories contained here, told lovingly, but shockingly by parents and loved ones, portray children and adults whose lives were damaged and destroyed by CTE. Our godson was one of these tragic suicide victims from this condition. The world has become different since then."

-Ralph Mitchell, PhD

"Brain Damaged hits us where it hurts most: With how we care for our children. This series of devastating portraits from families whose lives have been upended by brain trauma in contact sports tries to both explain and give meaning to these senseless CTE deaths. Any parent who reads these stories can't help but shudder at the thought of something similar happening to their own child - and can identify with the guilt so many of these survivors feel, wondering what they could have done differently. If these families' grief can be channeled to bring positive change in safety in youth sports, then their loved ones' deaths will not be in vain.

- Reid Forgrave, author, "The Concussion Diaries: One High School Football Player's Secret Struggle with CTE"

FOREWORD

Kimberly Archie and I met online. At the time, I was reaching out to her in a search for answers amid the hysteria surrounding chronic traumatic encephalopathy (CTE).

I was in my early 30s and having thoughts of suicide due to my brain injury symptoms, and my best friend from the game, Steve Montador, already had died at the age of 35.

I played 12 seasons of professional hockey, appeared in more than 750 games, and won two Stanley Cups with the Chicago Blackhawks in 2013 and 2015.

My nickname during my NHL career was "Car Bomb." When I say I used hockey as an emotional release, I'm not joking. I have always been intrigued by different rules. Rules in life, in school, within your own household and family. I also liked to test those rules and push boundaries. Hockey appealed to me because, all of a sudden, I had an avenue to express all of this frustration, confusion and anger I had built up within me from a very young age.

Physical contact was allowed in hockey. In fact, it was encouraged! If you had possession of the puck, you could be hit. Let me repeat that. If you are gliding along with a black rubber puck, I can put my shoulder through you as hard as I can, and separate you from said puck. It was a big draw for me.

But it exacted its terrible price.

I retired from the game at 30 years young because of post-concussion syndrome. Amid many injuries to my back, shoulders, hips and knees, I lost three teeth, suffered a broken nose twice and had seven documented concussions.

I'm now 33 and make my way in this world a changed man.

I am well equipped and prepared to live out my life with all of the lingering pain that wasn't going to kill me. What almost killed me were the concussions that were misunderstood and uncared for in a professional league that continues to deny a link between repetitive head trauma and CTE.

The NHL killed my best friend.

Steve Montador suffered 17 diagnosed concussions in 614 NHL games over 11 seasons. By those numbers, he was receiving (and being cleared for) a diagnosed concussion at a rate of one every 36 games. I was his teammate and was a first-hand witness to concussions numbers 14, 15, 16 and 17.

In my heart of hearts, I know that is what eventually led to his death. On February 15, 2015, Steve was found dead in his home in Canada. His brother was quoted as saying, "He just stopped breathing or his heart went." Four days later, Steve's girlfriend, Chantel, gave birth to their son, Morrison. Steve's brain was studied after his death and he was found to have CTE.

In Steve's last year on this earth I could hear the pain and anguish in his voice. He tried to disguise it as best he could by asking me what was going on in my life, but deep down I knew he was suffering and deteriorating.

I wish I knew more then. I wish I had the courage to say something to him and ask him if he was OK. I harbored a lot of guilt for a very long time because I wasn't completely honest with him. Because I felt like I didn't try my best to help my friend.

I have since let go of that guilt. I can't help someone identify signs and symptoms of a disease that I was unfamiliar with at the time.

As my life went on and I read more of the biased studies, the thoughts of killing myself became stronger and with more frequency. I'd think that maybe I could justify my suicide by knowing that it would help in further brain research. That's when I was scared enough to seek care for my brain damage.

Through the Carrick Institute and Plasticity Brain Center, I had a profound awakening, and I am excited to make my way in this world free from neck pain, headaches, suicidal thoughts, depression, anxiety, uncontrollable blood pressure and heart rate spikes, as well as substance abuse.

I am grateful that I didn't act on my suicidal thoughts, and that Kimberly was there for me on social media. She helped me navigate this concussion/brain injury landscape.

As in most fields, there are good and bad apples. Kimberly's knowledge alleviated my anxiety and depression. There was anxiety because I wanted to be sure I wasn't supporting the bad apples and furthering their CTE hysteria for personal and financial gain. The depression came when I realized that many of the symptoms I was experiencing were, in fact, from a brain injury. I will be forever indebted to her, the Faces of CTE, and to Jo Cornell, one of the leaders of the brain injury awareness movement.

When we met in Los Angeles for the first time, Kimberly handed me the draft of this book. She said she had one request: that I read it and consider doing the foreword. I boarded a flight from Los Angeles to New Orleans and began to read. I was punched in the gut by the CTE/brain injury timeline. It upset me, made me furious. Then I began to read the story of Kimberly's son, Paul Bright Jr. I barely got through the opening description without breaking down into tears. It was a full flight, and people were probably wondering what was going on. I didn't care.

I powered on through tears and sweating as I read. My worst fear as a parent would be losing a child. I cannot fathom the pain. I kept reading because I wanted to get to know Paul. I wanted to understand him. About halfway through his story, I began to see the person he was. I only played football for two seasons in Canada because it overlapped with hockey, but I understood his symptoms, his impulsivity, his pain, his suffering. I understood all too well his anxiety and depression and his personality changes. I too have battled through those same mental health complications while trying to put on a brave mask for my loved ones.

Sadness and remorse were replaced by anger and passion. I will do everything in my power to spare other parents this kind of anguish. I can't imagine having to watch the deterioration of a young adult. Much less a son or daughter. My grandmother passed away from Alzheimer's, so I have some experience with dementia, but this is different. This is more hurtful and disrespectful because it could have been prevented if certain people put kids' interests before a sport's interests.

I moved on to Jo's story about her son, Tyler. Again, many of the same feelings boiled up as I read through tears. I've felt these changes in myself and watched them overtake Steve Montador. I felt that I needed to use my platform as a professional athlete to help these two women and their families ensure history doesn't repeat itself.

My life's mission is to align with those who are like-minded, passionate and want change, and to reject those who simply want to line their own pockets. The people who tell their heartbreaking stories in this book have been directly affected by the loss of loved ones. We will not accept this. I stand with Kimberly Archie and Jo Cornell and Faces of CTE and vow to do everything in my power to help change laws and hold those accountable for these unspeakable losses.

–Daniel Carcillo

CHAMPIONS FOR CHILD ATHLETES

Kimberly Archie, collaborator with Mt. Sinai and Mayo Clinic Brain Banks; former officer, Oregon PTA Board of Directors; former chapter president of Young Republicans; 1994 Volunteer of the Year, College of the Desert; former member of the President's Advisory Board at College of the Desert; 2010 Safety First Child Abuse Prevention Award recipient; 2015 PinkConcussions PINK State Award; 2014 Teach Believe Inspire Award from Brain Injury Law Center; former board member of the California Brain Injury Association; known by former NFL players as the "Mother of Youth Sport Safety"; social justice engineer of child rights in sports; co-founder of National Cheer Safety Foundation, Child Athlete Advocates, Save Your Brain and Faces of CTE; expert witness and legal consultant.

Kathleen Bachynski, M.P.H, PhD; postdoctoral fellow in medical humanities at NYU Langone Health; author of forthcoming book based on her dissertation, "No Game for Boys to Play: Debating the Safety of Youth Football, 1945-2015."

Sharon Bates, founder of the Anthony Bates Foundation; co-founder Parent Heart Watch; 2016 Healthcare Hero Award; member of advisory panel of Child Athlete Advocates.

Kevin Beineik PhD; former research fellow at Mayo Clinic-Jacksonville, Fla.; associate professor at the University of Texas Health Science Center San Antonio.

Solomon Brannan, cofounder Child Athlete Advocates, former professional football player, former board member of the NFLPA and Atlanta chapter president. Black History Achievement Award Honoree, Save Your Brain Advocacy

Award 2018, Solomon was inducted into the Greater Savannah Sports Hall of Fame in 1999.

Shana De Caro, attorney; officer and member of Board of Directors of Brain Injury Association of America; former chair of American Association for Justice, Traumatic Brain Injury Litigation Group; member of Board of Directors of New York State Academy of Trial Lawyers; first vice-president of the American Academy of Brain Injury Attorneys; New York Super Lawyer; Top 25 Brain Injury Attorney by the National Trial Lawyers Association.

Rachel Denhollander, attorney; educator; gymnast; victim's advocate; leader of army that brought down Larry Nassar; Time Magazine 100 honoree; 2018 Glamour Woman of the Year.

Gary Dordick, attorney; owner, Law Offices of Gary A. Dordick; Board of Governors, Consumer Attorneys of California Gary Dordick, nominated for CAALA Trial Lawyer of the Year 1994, 1996, 1998, 1999, 2006, 2007, 2009, 2010, CAALA Trial Lawyer of the Year 2001, CAOC Trial Lawyer of the Year 2009 and the Bernard Jefferson Award 2003.

Enrico Esposito, DC, AT; retired professor and former Sports Medicine Chair at the United States Sports Academy.

Lorena Gonzalez Fletcher, California state lawmaker; attorney; former cheerleader; cheerleading coach; union leader; chair of California Latino Legislative Caucus.

Rhonda Fincher, heat illness prevention advocate; founder of Kendrick Fincher Hydration for Life.

Bob Geffner PhD, ABN, ABP; pioneer in prevention of violence and abuse; founder, Institute on Violence, Abuse & Trauma; co-chair of National Partnership to End Interpersonal Violence Across the Lifespan (NPEIV); president, American Academy of Couple & Family Psychology; editor of five professional journals (including the Journal of Child Sexual Abuse, Journal of Family Violence, and the Journal of Child & Adolescent Trauma).

Thomas Girardi, LLM; attorney; founding partner, Girardi Keese; associate professor at Loyola Law School since 1976; 2005 "Champion of Justice," Loyola Law School; 2018 Trial Lawyer of the Year, Consumer Attorney of California; member of Trial Lawyer Hall of Fame; member of Inner Circle of Advocates, Top 100 Lawyers in California; president, Litigation Counsel of America; trustee, Library of Congress; radio host of Champions for Justice; 2018 "Lawyer of the Decade," International Association of Top Professionals; past president, International Academy of Trial Lawyers; member of the California Judicial Council.

Hayley Hodson, child and amateur athlete advocate; former Division I volleyball player at Stanford; Pac-12 Freshman of the Year; Volleyball Magazine Freshman of the Year; AVCA All-America second team; brain injury survivor and filmmaker.

Derek Howard, attorney; adjunct professor; California Consumer Attorney of the Year finalist; member of Consumer Attorney of California Board of Governors.

Michael Kaplen, attorney; chair of NYS Traumatic Brain Injury Services Coordinating Council; professorial lecturer in law at George Washington University Law School; teaches only course on traumatic brain injury law in nation; served three terms as president of the Brain Injury Association of New York State; chaired the Traumatic Brain Injury Litigation Group of the American Association for Justice; New York Super Lawyer; Best Lawyers of America, New York.

Larry Mallory, director of Faces of CTE's "Flag Under 14"; Dallas chapter president of the NFL Players Association; former NFL player for the New York Giants.

Ed O'Bannon, lead plaintiff, O'Bannon v. NCAA; athletes' rights activist; author; member of the UCLA Athletics Hall of Fame; and NCAA champion.

Krista Robinson, owner of PT Squared physical therapy and personal training center; gymnast; cheerleader; physical therapist; TBI survivor; and executive director of the National Cheer Safety Foundation.

Bill Simpson, retired race car driver, author, pioneer in race car driver safety, founded Simpson Performance Products, member of the Motorsport Hall of Fame, designer NASA's umbilical cords, invented first fire suit in racing, invented first light weight Kevlar football helmet that doesn't trap heat, and developed over 200 racing safety products.

Katherine Snedaker, LCSW; founder of PINKConcussions and SportsCAPP; co-founder, Save Your Brain; breast cancer survivor; child athlete advocate; and VA brain bank collaborator.

Victor Vieth, JD, MA; attorney; founder and senior director of Gundersen National Child Protection Training Center. He has served as senior director since its in inception in 2003. Mr. Vieth has trained thousands of child-protection professionals from all 50 states, two U.S. Territories, and 17 countries on numerous topics pertaining to child abuse investigations, prosecutions and prevention.

BRAIN DAMAGE TIMELINE

1893 U.S. Naval Academy football player was told by his physician that another hit would cause traumatic insanity.

1914 A physician with interests in nervous and mental diseases hypothesizes that trauma to the nervous system can create both organic and functional changes and furthermore hypothesizes that this explains the remote effects of head injuries.

1916 A physician who is also a pathologist hypothesizes that a head injury creates, what he terms, a locus minoris resistentiae (a point of less resistance to injury) in the brain which he predicts makes patients more vulnerable to subsequent head injuries.

1927 Pathologists Onsato and Giliberti raised the possibility that traumatic encephalopathy might occur in young men knocked out in football and other games.[1]

1928 Harrison Martland introduced the term "punch drunk" into medical literature.[2]

1933 NCAA medical handbook for member schools stated, "There is definitely a condition described as 'punch drunk' and often recurrent concussion cases in football and boxing demonstrate this." It also stated, "If symptoms of headache, dizziness, blurred vision, vomiting continues over 48 hours, individual should not be permitted to compete for 21 days or longer, if at all."[3]

---

1   Michael Osnato, Vincent Gilberti, Post-Concussion Neurosis-Traumatic Encephalitis, 18 Achieves Neurology & Psychiatry 181; 1927
2   Dr. Harrison Martland, "Punch drunk," 91 JAMA 1103; 1928
3   "National Colligate Athletic Medical Handbook for Schools & Colleges," July 1933, accessed January 26, 2019 http://nflconcussionlitigation.com/wp-content/uploads/2016/06/NCAA-1933-CTE-Admission.pdf

1940 The term "Chronic Traumatic Encephalopathy" was first used by Bowman & Blan in describing a case of a 28-year-old boxer.[4]

1943 Martland explains CTE/dementia pugilistica may be seen in wrestlers and football players.

▪ Physicist produces a model of concussive injuries that expresses the injuries in biomechanical terms, resulting in the now accepted view that concussions are impact acceleration and deceleration injuries, that the damaging forces are caused by rotational acceleration, and that these forces create shear strain across the brain. A. H. S. Holbourne performed an experiment in which he created a gelatin model of the brain. The figure reproduced here is his diagram of a parasagittal section of the brain showing shear-strains produced by rotational force by a blow on the occiput. The gelatin was made in such a way that shear-strains would produce colors making the effect of the force visible.

1957 The American Academy of Pediatricians (AAP) releases a consensus statement saying no children under 13 years old should play tackle football. [5]

1968 Pathologists showed that permanent damage can be inflicted on the brain from a concussion and concluded that such injuries, if repeated, would result in progressive, cumulative loss of tissue and of nervous function.

1969 The National Academy of Science report to Congress on football injuries, testifying that plastic hard-shell football helmets cause brain damage and increase the risks of injury.

---

4   Bowman K.M., Blau A. Brock S., editors, "Injuries of Skull, Brain and Spinal Cord: Neuropsychiatric, Surgical, and Medico-Legal Aspects." Baltimore, MD: Williams & Wilkins Co; 1940.

5   SportsCAPP, "Why did AAP reverse its policy against youth tackle football?" March 25, 2016, SportsCAPP. com, Accessed January 26, 2019 http://sportscapp.com/wp-content/uploads/2015/12/1957-page-2.jpg

1973 Corsellis et al. describe in detail the neuropathology of 15 retired boxers and a pathologist using autopsied brains from boxers found chronic traumatic encephalopathy in those new samples and noted the presence of tangle formations. He predicted that while not every punch need visibly alter the structure of the brain, one or many of them to the head would eventually leave a mark, which would initiate the early stages of the degenerative nervous disease and become exaggerated with repeated injuries.[6]

1974 Neurosurgeons hypothesize that shearing takes place in head injuries, including concussion, and they produce a flow chart of the mechanics of head injury and the areas where sufficient experimental research has been done to formally test. They also identify areas where further research is still needed. They hypothesize that the biological response to cerebral concussion is post-traumatic sequelae, but note further observation work needed to be done to clarify whether primary lesions lead to the formation of secondary lesions, initiating degenerative changes.

1981 Authors of a prospective study of 538 hospital admissions with head injury find noteworthy persisting difficulties and say that these observations lend weight to the observation that the effects of concussion, however slight, might not be completely reversible.

1983 A neurosurgeon at a conference on car accidents argues that the evidence gathered from many studies fit, a) the biomechanical model of concussion, b) the connection between concussion and more severe injuries, c) the fact that neuropsychological sequelae follow concussions and in cumulative ways, d) neuropathological evidence, and e) population data.

1986 A neurosurgeon reviewed the trends of concussion research and hypothesized that the reversal of neural dysfunction normally seen following concussion is due to the unexcitability of axonal membranes following primary mechanical strains. He observed that it was unknown why some dysfunctions persisted but suggested it may be due to permanent structural changes in axons or neural networks.

6   Corsellis J.A., Bruton C.J., Freeman-Browne D. (1973). "The aftermath of boxing." Psychol. Med. 3, 270–30310.1017/S0033291700049588 [PubMed] [CrossRef]

1989 A pathologist described the pathology of repeated head trauma using boxers as an example; confirms the presence of tangles but absence of amyloid plaques, and observed that current advanced imaging techniques cannot show the incipient disintegration of living fiber pathways or groups of neurons.

2003 Forensic pathologist Dr. Bennet Omalu confirms extensive brain damage and CTE in former Pittsburgh Steeler offensive lineman Mike Webster.[7]

2008 The National Cheer Safety Foundation is founded and creates the first "Rehearsed Catastrophic Emergency Plan for Youth Sports" and "Heat Illness Prevention Guide," cited by experts in the wrongful death case of high school football player Max Gilpin, as the legal standard of care.[8]

2009 The National Cheer Safety Foundation releases the first international guidelines for a seven-day return to play after a concussion.[9]

2010 The National Collegiate Acrobatics & Tumbling Association creates the first "safety official," whose duties included spotting possible brain injuries, with the authority to stop a meet.

2011 Plaintiff attorney Jason Luckasevic files brain damage lawsuit on behalf of former NFL players against the NFL and Riddell helmets. He later teams up with attorney Tom Girardi, who enlists brain injury survivor and sport risk management expert Kimberly Archie to educate players on brain injuries.

2012 Junior Seau commits suicide and is later found by the National Institute of Health to have CTE and other brain damage. He is the most recognizable former player to have brain damage from football, confirmed via brain autopsy, and becomes *the* face of CTE.[10]

---

7   Omalu B.I., Dekosky S.T., Minster R.L., Kamboh M.I., Hamilton R.L., Wecht C.H. (2005). "Chronic traumatic encephalopathy in a National Football League player," Neurosurgery 57, 128–134; discussion 128–134.10.1227/01.NEU.0000163407.92769.ED [PubMed] [CrossRef]

8   www.nationalcheersafety.com/emergencyplan

9   http://www.nationalcheersafety.com/concussionr2pguidelines.pdf

10 Pauline Repard, Debbi Baker, Kristina Davis, "Junior Seau, hometown icon, takes his life," *San Diego Union-Tribune*, May 2, 2012, accessed November 6, 2018 "https://www.sandiegouniontribune.com/sports/chargers/sdut-report-of-shooting-at-seaus-home-2012may02-htmlstory.html

2014 Longtime Peabody award-winning investigative journalist Karen Hensel runs a story on WishTV in Indianapolis, informing the public that youth football helmets have no youth manufacturing standard and had never been tested for children.[11]

- Former National Hockey League players sue the league for brain injuries.

2015 Debbie Pyka files, on behalf of her son Joseph Chernach, the first lawsuit for CTE versus Pop Warner football.[12]

2016 The NFL's top health and safety officer acknowledges there is a link between football-related head trauma and CTE. It is the first time a senior league official has conceded football's connection to the devastating brain disease. The admission comes during a roundtable discussion on brain injuries, convened by the U.S. House of Representatives' Committee on Energy and Commerce. Jeff Miller, the NFL's senior vice president for health and safety, was asked by Rep. Jan Schakowsky, D-Ill., if the link between football and neurodegenerative diseases such as CTE had been established.[13]

- Kimberly Archie and Jo Cornell filed the first class action lawsuit versus Pop Warner for brain damage on behalf of their sons, Paul Bright Jr., and Tyler Cornell. The case is set for trial in January 2020. It will be the first case to go to trial in the 90-year history of Pop Warner. They are represented by Thomas Girardi and Robert Finnerty of Girardi Keese in Los Angeles.[14]

---

11   Sean Murphy, "Youth football helmets – What are the standards?" November 21, 2014, accessed January 21, 2019 https://www.safetyfirstsports.com/blog/youth-football-helmets-what-are-the-standards/

12   Ken Belson, "Family sues Pop Warner over suicide of player who had brain disease," *New York Times*, February 5, 2015, accessed November 5, 2018 https://www.nytimes.com/2015/02/06/sports/family-of-player-with-cte-who-killed-himself-sues-pop-warner.html

13   Sam Farmer, Nathan Fenno, "NFL executive acknowledges a link between football-related head trauma and CTE," *Los Angeles Times,* March 14, 2016, accessed November 4, 2018 https://www.latimes.com/sports/sportsnow/la-sp-nfl-cte-jeff-miller-20160314-story.html

14   Ken Belson, "Pop Warner is facing a class-action lawsuit over concussions," *New York Times*, September 2, 2016, accessed November 5, 2018 https://www.nytimes.com/2016/09/02/sports/football/concussions-pop-warner-class-action-lawsuit.html

2017 At Super Bowl LI in Houston, sports families unite and launch Faces of CTE to collaborate with Mayo Clinic and give families more choices for brain donations to further science. Faces of CTE also begins the first national "Flag Under 14" program, overseen by former NFL player Larry Mallory.[15]

2018 The first CTE case goes to trial in Dallas, Texas, against the NCAA. The case was filed by Deb Ploetz, the widow of former Texas Longhorn football player Greg Ploetz. It is settled for an undisclosed amount after three days of trial.[16]

- Darren Hamblin files a wrongful death lawsuit in Ohio against Riddell and Schutt helmet companies on behalf of his son, Cody Hamblin for fraud and selling helmets, during the time his son played that were not made or tested for children, while having known design defects that increased the risks of brain damage.[17]

- Faces of CTE collaborates with attorneys and researchers to form the first global open access model for brain donation.

---

15   Brian T. Smith, "While NFL parties, women raise awareness for CTE," *Houston Chronicle,* January 30, 2017, accessed November 5, 2018 https://www.houstonchronicle.com/sports/columnists/smith/article/While-NFL-parties-women-raise-awareness-for-CTE-10895702.php

16   Mike Finger, "As first CTE trial begins, former players finally get a voice," *San Antonio Express-News,* June 2, 2018, accessed November 2, 2018 https://www.expressnews.com/sports/columnists/mike_finger/article/As-first-CTE-trial-begins-former-players-finally-12962995.php

17   Josh Kosman, "Father sues football helmet makers over son's CTE-related death," *New York Post,* May 31, 2018, accessed November 1, 2018 https://nypost.com/2018/05/31/father-sues-football-helmet-makers-over-sons-cte-related-death/

INTRODUCTION

by Kimberly Archie

"As long as the fox is watching the henhouse in youth football, he will continue to sell the eggs and keep all of the profits — to the detriment of our children." [18]

Kimberly Archie, Huffington Post, January 30, 2018

This book was the brainchild of the CTE families in our Facebook group called "Save Your Brain." [19] We saw story after story about research, or former pro athletes with CTE using the same old "two sides of the story" rationale. It looked like a phony WWE match, with each side having a preconceived role and scripted outcome, rather than what was actually happening at the grassroots level.

As a group who paid the ultimate price of seeing our loved ones die, we've watched the sports industry keep kicking the "safer than ever" can down road and feel compelled to tell our stories to help ensure this would be the last sports safety crisis, rather than the third safety crisis in a series of never ending ones.

Our book is not intended to be just a collection of sad stories, or to be a scare tactic, or promote CTE hysteria. We are families pouring out our most private moments, no matter how embarrassing or uncomfortable, with the hope of sparing even one family the hell we have endured. It's to open hearts and minds to know what we know, before it's too late.

---

18   Kimberly Archie, "The NFL must listen to football moms if it wants to survive," *Huffington Post*, January 30, 2018, accessed January 1, 2019 https://www.huffingtonpost.com/entry/opinion-archie-cte-football_us_5a6f87a2e4b00d0de222f3cc

19   "Save Your Brain sports families launch Faces of CTE awareness campaign," PR Newswire, January 30, 2017, accessed January 18, 2019 https://www.prnewswire.com/news-releases/save-your-brain-sport-families-launch-faces-of-cte-awareness-campaign-300398533.html

It's to save lives.

Jo Cornell, a fellow Faces of CTE mom, and I were talking recently about a brain donation we were coordinating, and she mentioned she had seen a website with newly confirmed cases of football players with CTE who had never played past high school.

When I scrolled down the list, one kid's photo jumped off the page at me. The polo shirt he wore looked like it had the logo from my son Paul's high school, Bishop Manogue Catholic High School, in Reno, Nevada. I quickly googled his name, "Dylan Rutherford," found a memorial website and began to read about him. He did indeed go to the same school as Paul and played Pop Warner in the same area.[20]

There was another chilling similarity. Dylan and Paul had the same death date – September 1 – only three years apart. But what took my breath away was seeing those haunting words, "Chronic Traumatic Encephalopathy research study donor." (It was determined that Dylan had brain damage, but not CTE.)

I stared at the screen for so long, just frozen. Tears streamed down my face as I sobbed, mascara and eyeliner everywhere. Damn. My son's is the first high school in the country to have two former athletes die off the playing field, but related to brain damage.

Even 8,000 hours of research working on the NFL lawsuit couldn't prepare me for this.

Two kids from one high school die three years apart on the same exact day – one by reckless driving, the other by suicide. Both irrational, erratic and involving risks increased by brain damage. What are the odds?

Dylan and Paul never played past their freshman years of high school. Yes, you read that right. They played only until 15 years old – their time of participation in tackle football coming in the years we're told that kids don't even hit hard enough to really get hurt.

---

20   "Honoring the Life of Dylan," accessed January 20, 2019 https://dylanrutherford.com/

Parents are not warned of brain damage exposure, much less CTE risks. So-called experts claim we don't know the prevalence, as if that's a legitimate argument for kids to keep playing. So we can see how many will be damaged? How illogical and cruel is that?

Let's have kids entertain us, be crash dummies for the development of helmets not designed for them, lab rats of brain injury, and see if 1 in 100 get CTE, or 1 in 1,000 or 1 in 10,000? How many will get brain damage that never escalates to CTE, or another neurodegenerative disease?

How many is okay? How many moms and dads will bury their children and donate their brain before we stop exposing children who don't have the physical readiness to sustain hundreds of hits a year and thousands over a childhood?

To us, it's more than a question about brain injuries. This is about long-term cumulative exposure.

Football doesn't want to talk about that part. It's the age of entry (earlier equals higher risk), number of hits, number of years played, additional occurrences of traumatic brain injury, and the known defective design of helmets that all add up to one's cumulative brain trauma.

The Long Road to Here

I began my adult work career as a manager for the first black owner of a McDonalds franchise in Reno, Nevada. Luther Mack wasn't your average business owner. He had a commanding presence that everyone noticed immediately. He was tall, smart and extremely successful. He not only owned a number of McDonalds, but other businesses, including a television station. He also served on the Nevada Boxing Commission.[21]

Between the intense and well-versed business training given by corporate headquarters for McDonalds, and gleaning whatever nuggets of wisdom I could from

---

21   Steve Carp, "Second Nevada HOF Class called an amazing group," Las Vegas-Review Journal, February 12, 2014, accessed January 21, 2019 https://www.google.com/amp/s/www.reviewjournal.com/sports/second-nevada-boxing-hof-class-called-an-amazing-group/amp/

Luther and his then-wife Genie, I had a solid foundation that's served me well in the three decades since. During that time at McDonalds, I also met Tiffani and Paul's dad, and we married in 1988.

After we divorced, I moved to Rancho Mirage with our two kids. I worked in retail management for various companies such as San Francisco Music Box, Bullock's and Macy's. But the long hours and not-so-great salaries drove me to enroll in college. It was then that I became involved in college clubs and activities, including student government and being president of Young Republicans.

I had the honor and pleasure to work on the campaign for Congress by then-Palm Springs Mayor Sonny Bono. For someone who grew up in a small town with modest means, the experience exposed me to a side of life I hadn't seen. Many of those life lessons still come in handy today.

One of them worth mentioning is learning public relations from the perspective of the Republican Party and what many called the "Ronald Reagan Spin Room." It was there I came to understand that offense is the best defense, as well as other invaluable tools our group uses today to further child rights in sports.

During this time I also remarried and had my youngest daughter Janaye in 1994.

Later, after suffering huge personal setbacks due to my own health issues with a traumatic brain injury I sustained at 9 years old, I moved away from the Palm Springs area to live near my brother Tony, an F/A-18 pilot and Navy officer stationed at the Naval Air Station in Lemoore, California.[22] With my brother's support I was able to put the pieces of my life back together, piece by piece. I began working for a division of Nestle that sold goods and services to schools and non-profits to help raise money. I spent the next four years working for them until my daughter Janaye was diagnosed with Stage IV cancer. She had a condition called Wilm's tumor, a childhood cancer that spread to her left kidney and both lungs.

---

22   Jessica Press, "How one woman found relief after decades of chronic pain," Oprah.com, undated, accessed January 17, 2019 http://www.oprah.com/health/what-weight-loss-has-to-do-with-chronic-pain-relief

I took off just over a year to nurse her back to health. During that ordeal, I learned more about healthcare than I ever imagined. Janaye went into remission after 10 weeks of treatment, and 10 years later her doctors declared her to be cured. At the time they removed her kidney, her father and I agreed to donate it to cancer research for children.

I eventually went back to fundraising, this time for a smaller distributor who allowed me have my own territory and business. By then, my daughter Tiffani was in high school and began helping me with data entry and other computer or technology related tasks. We didn't know at the time it was the beginning of a blending of old-school business and millennial technology that would change the landscape of child rights in sports.

Blowing the Whistle

In 2002, Tiffani came home from school and declared she wanted to try out for her high school junior varsity cheer team. She cheered for one season of Pop Warner when she was ten, and I cheered in high school, so it wasn't a complete surprise. But being new to the Medford, Oregon, area that year, I knew it wouldn't be easy for her to make the team. But she did make it, and what seemed like just another childhood event ended up changing the trajectory of our lives.

After Tiffani broke her arm at practice so badly it required surgery, an insurance company denied paying the claims for more than $10,000 worth of medical bills. The reason given for rejecting our claims: child maltreatment due to improper supervision. That prompted me to research cheerleading injuries and child rights in sports.[23]

To my shock and horror, there really wasn't any such thing. I kept saying to myself, "How could this be possible?" The more I dug into it, the less I found. Adults in the workplace had more protection and rights than children in sports. Sports are a huge business, woven into the fabric of society. Many kids play one or more sports, so it seemed highly unlikely that there were no regulations to protect them.

---

23   Tammy Asnicar, "Mom on a mission," *Medford Mail Tribune*, October 5, 2017, accessed November 28, 2018 http://mailtribune.com/news/top-stories/mom-on-a-mission-04-24-2018

In the end, I spent what little savings I had to pay the medical bills related to Tiffani's cheerleading injury.

Like most parents, my first thought was to meet with administrators at school, and then the school district, to see how I could help improve safety at the local level. As a longtime volunteer to the schools my daughters attended – from going on field trips, being in their classrooms, serving as the PTA/PTO president and cheer booster club president – it wasn't a big deal to call the athletic director or district office. As the year passed, I wasn't getting anywhere. The typical answer was, "We're following the current national guidelines."

Tiffani continued to cheer at North Medford High School. She made the varsity team, was the co-captain, and helped lead her squad to a second-place finish at the Oregon state cheerleading championships in the co-ed division. They notched the highest score in school history.

Unfortunately, injuries to Tiffani, as well as her teammates, continued to pile up.

I was determined to get to the bottom of why kids had little or no protection in sports. By the middle of Tiffani's senior year, before another competition season began, and after a laundry list of injuries all considered by the school as "accidents," Tiffani hung up her pompons for good.

A friend who was aware of my newfound research project gave me a book called, "Raising the Bar." It was about Supreme Court Justice Ruth Bader Ginsburg's career of fighting for women's rights. This was long before she became known as the "Notorious RBG," and a darling of today's media. After reading the book, I had an epiphany about civil rights.

It was clear Justice Ginsburg was the legal engineer of women's rights in the United States. It was clear Thurgood Marshall was the legal engineer of civil rights, in general. Who was the legal engineer of children's rights in sports? Again, it was a question for which I couldn't find an answer.

After years of research and searching for answers, in 2008 I enrolled in paralegal classes with Tiffani, thinking that if no one was willing to take a stand for children in sports, why not us?

With a year of legal coursework behind us, we began working on cheerleading cases, starting with Ashley Burns, a young cheerleader from Massachusetts who died on the way to the hospital after rupturing her spleen at a high school cheer practice.[24] This work lead to one case after another. Things began to ramp up in 2012 when I became a legal consultant for the law firm Girardi Keese, (made famous in the Oscar award winning movie "Erin Brockovich") on the most talked about legal case in sport history, now referred to as, the "NFL concussion case."[25] I continued to work on youth sport cases in dance, cheer, gymnastics, football, and even helped create the legal strategies used in mediation with US Soccer to remove headers for kids under eleven, and limit headers for kids eleven to thirteen.[26]

But the case that hit closes to home wasn't a cheerleading injury, it was when I was asked to consult on the first CTE lawsuit against Pop Warner the year after my son Paul Bright Jr. died.[27] At that time I could hardly get out of bed most days, sometimes I could lose track of time with thoughts just swirling around asking myself, "how could I work so hard all these years to protect kids in sports and still lose my own son?" After getting Paul's brain autopsy, I had to figure out how to go from victim to survivor again.

There were times I felt alone, screaming into a hurricane and no one could hear me. We started a monthly coping group called, Tackling Grief. Helping others who belong to a club no parent ever wants to be in, I found my tribe. I never wanted to be here, but here I am. I am grateful to know other people who want to be healed, who want to get justice, who want to unleash their pain. Who want

24 "Cheerleader's death a mystery," *ABC News*, August 10, 2005, accessed December 30, 2018 https://abc-news.go.com/Health/OnCall/story?id=1025150&page=1

25 Maryclaire Dale, "The NFL drops appeal over dementia claims in concussion case," *Associated Press*, January 9, 2019 https://apnews.com/2f71ae228e6f4c04bdeac4256f8376e6

26 Scott Stump, "No more heading: U.S. soccer out with new youth guidelines," *Today*, November 10, 2015, accessed December 18, 2018 https://www.today.com/parents/no-more-heading-us-soccer-out-new-guide-lines-youth-soccer-t54971

27 *Pyka vs. Pop Warner Little Scholars, Inc.* http://footballandbraindamage.com/wp-content/uploads/2015/02/Complaint-Chernach-v.-Pop-Warner-Signed.pdf

to be a voice for the voiceless – our sons, brothers, fathers and husbands who were lost to the game they loved, but didn't love them back.

Thank God for our grief support group, so that we no longer had to suffer alone in silence; we don't have to stuff our pain away; we no longer have to scream in a hurricane. We can channel our enormous loss to help the greater good, so that our loved ones who are gone too soon didn't suffer or die in vain.

It has been said that you die twice; the first time when you take your last breath, and again when your name is said for the last time. It's my job as Paul's momma, the one to whom he was attached to by an umbilical cord, to ensure his name is said long after I'm gone.

To score a win for Paul and the others like him who suffered, we want to be a beacon of light that's so intense that there's no way the propaganda of football and the sports industry can continue to fool the American public that football is "safer than ever." No one should be allowed to play Russian roulette with children, whose minds house their God-given intellect and spirit – the very things that make us human, and set us apart from all things on Earth.

Yet, despite the grief, I dug deep down for strength to pull myself together because that's what you do when you're a warrior for justice.

Our decade of legal work taught me two things: the losses teach more than the wins, and in all fifty states we have to prove gross negligence in order for a coach, or school, or sport organization to be held liable for preventable injuries of a child athlete. Gross negligence is the standard for criminal cases, so like in the murders of Nicole Simpson and Ron Goldman, OJ was found not guilty by criminal standards, but was found liable for civil damages. That's how tough of a standard gross negligence is. Kids hurt by the wrongdoings of corporations, coaches and a system stacked against them, have a long, uphill battle on the road to justice. And like other civil justice crusades it wouldn't happen overnight but will take decades to even the playing field.

In order to win a negligence case, the plaintiff (the person injured) must prove the following four elements to show that the defendant (the person allegedly at fault) acted negligently. The first element is to show that the defendant owed a legal duty to the plaintiff under the circumstances. The second element that must be proven is that the defendant breached that legal duty by acting or failing to act in a certain way. The third element required of the injured party is to show it was the defendant's actions (or inaction) that caused the plaintiff's injury, and the forth element that must be shown is that the plaintiff was harmed or injured as a result of the defendant's actions or inaction.

The harm must be a substantial factor, but doesn't have to be *the* substantial factor, or the *only* factor. A substantial factor can be five percent, twenty percent, fifty percent, or ninety percent in contributing to the harm.

So when the trolls, or so-called experts, or those with deep financial ties to sports, contend that tackle football isn't "the cause" of the deaths, they don't understand how our legal system works, or perhaps even more misleading is that they may know and want to convince the public otherwise.

The Sport Health & Safety Administration is Born

After years of involvement in the research of injuries, testifying in lawsuits, and doing media interviews, it became crystal clear that while all three of those endeavors – combined with grassroots efforts and social media – were necessary to drive change, regulation would still be required to protect children from maltreatment.

In the summer of 2010, while having drinks one night in Hollywood with an old friend DeAndre Adams and the then-CEO of Ticketmaster, Sean Moriarty, I shared how vulnerable kids are in sports and my passion to protect them.

We started brainstorming, and before the night was over the Sport Health & Safety Administration was born.[28] I explained to them how it was much like tobacco, asbestos, lead, and sugar, except sports held a sacred place in society.

---

28   Kimberly Archie, "'Concussion' is not the NFL's two-minute warning CTE families hoped for," December 15, 2015, accessed January 25, 2019 https://goodmenproject.com/arts/concussion-is-not-the-nfls-two-minute-warning-cte-families-hoped-for-gmp/

Taking the institution on wasn't your ordinary David vs. Goliath battle to change the balance of power.

Sean looked at me and said, "I think your challenge is also your strength. I think Ticketmaster might even be interested in being the hero of the story. What's better than making sports safe for kids? What if I present to our board to add a fee on every ticket sold to fund a non-profit to protect kids in sports?"

Well, that was eight years ago, and like many other Hollywood stories, promises are made, deals are hatched, and all too often they don't become reality. In those eight years, the idea went from a napkin, to a business proposal and PowerPoint presentation, to language to introduce a federal bill.

The idea has been proposed to folks such as Jeff Miller, then-Vice President of Government Relations for the NFL (now the league's VP of Health & Safety). We spoke in his Washington, D.C., office, and at the time he didn't say yes or no, though I didn't really leave him the chance to say no. My pitch to him was quite simple: If I could show you a way to make sports reasonably safe for kids, and it makes you even more money while being the hero, would you be interested?

All the NFL had to do was take the lead by, say, allocating a dollar for every ticket sold to fund youth sports protection while allowing child maltreatment professionals to oversee the fund. They could go to their pals at the NBA, NHL, MLB, MLS and the NCAA to do it, too.

What fan would begrudge a dollar for keeping kids safe? As amicable as Jeff was in the meeting, he never followed through.

This was before my son, Paul Bright Jr., died with Chronic Traumatic Encephalopathy (CTE), so I wasn't recognized as the "threat" I'm seen as now in the industry. In fact, most would have considered me an insider of sorts. I had mentors such as Fred Mueller, a professor and founder at the National Center for Catastrophic Sport Injury Research; Herb Appenzeller, who wrote the first sport risk management guide and more than 30 other books since; and Dr. Thomas Rosandich, who was the founder of the United States Sports Academy in 1972.

These men of influence in sports took me under their wing and opened doors that were once locked. It was through my friendship with Dr. Rosandich that I met NFL Hall of Fame cornerback Mike Haynes, who I consider a great friend and astute businessman. I value Mike's opinion greatly, especially when it comes to sports. He's a pretty damn good golfer, too.

Faces of CTE

Faces of CTE was launched at the Super Bowl in Houston, Texas, on January 30, 2017. We held a press conference at the St. Regis Hotel with sports families who donated the brains of their loved ones who were confirmed to have CTE from repetitive hits in sports.[29]

Families came from all over the country and represented youth, college and pro players. Larry Mallory, a former NFL player and president of the Dallas section of the NFL Players Association, attended and addressed the media. He offered a former player's perspective and shared that he would lead the new initiative by our group called "Flag Until 14." As the first program of its kind, the effort is to encourage kids under fourteen years old to play flag football, then transition to rookie tackle, and later tackle football. It has since been adopted or mimicked by other organizations.

The second component to our new group was to promote brain donations. The more brains acquired, the more research can be done to further the science, improve health care, and discover a method to diagnose neurodegenerative diseases – especially CTE – in the living. We announced our collaboration with the Mayo Clinic Brain Bank, based in Jacksonville, Florida.

We also declared January 30 to be CTE Awareness Day to help spread information about the mind-robbing disease. We were thrilled when the print edition of the Houston Chronicle sports section headline the next day read, "Grief Overshadows Super Bowl," with a picture of Faces of CTE co-founder Cyndy Feasel.

---

29   Brian T. Smith, "While NFL parties, women raise awareness for CTE," *Houston Chronicle,* January 30, 2017, accessed November 5, 2018 https://www.houstonchronicle.com/sports/columnists/smith/article/While-NFL-parties-women-raise-awareness-for-CTE-10895702.php

Our fight for justice was off and running.

The following year, our group decided to focus on establishing recognition of CTE Awareness Day at the state level. We contacted our local lawmakers and were able to have resolutions announced in California, Indiana, Pennsylvania, Texas and Iowa. In Ohio, it was introduced as a bill named Cody's Law, in honor of former youth football player Cody Hamblin, and later in December of 2018, Governor John Kasich signed it into law![30]

With CTE Awareness Day taking off quickly, we rolled up our sleeves to do the very difficult work of assisting families in donating their loved one's brain. As of this book's publication, we have attempted to acquire dozens of brains and have successfully assisted with brain bank collaborators in brain donations, including that of six-time NFL Pro-bowler, and Los Angeles Rams legend, Isiah Robertson.[31]

I thought my daughter having cancer would be life's biggest challenge for me. Later, I thought it was giving my son's eulogy in front of hundreds of people. Then came time to contact families for brain donations.

Everyone in our group has donated a loved one's brain, and we all feel enormously compelled to acquire as many brains as we can to help researchers learn more about brain damage in sports, the military and domestic violence.

When we began our collaboration with the Mayo Clinic, we had lofty goals and got busy immediately, reaching out to medical examiners and role-playing what we would say when we contacted families. We knew first-hand what it felt like to get the call no parent wants. We know how horrifying a thought it is to donate a brain.

---

30   "Kasich signs bill named for Miamisburg athlete into law," *SWDTN*, December 19, 2018, accessed January 27, 2019 https://www.google.com/amp/s/www.wdtn.com/amp/news/local-news/kasich-signs-bill-named-for-miamisburg-athlete-into-law/1667229531

31   "Rams star leaves legacy in ETX, *CBS 19*, January 25, 2019, accessed January 25, 2019 https://www.cbs19.tv/mobile/video/sports/rams-star-leaves-legacy-in-etx/501-e491a604-8bf0-461f-951a-5bb790d3d27d?utm_campaign=trueAnthem%3A+Trending+Content&utm_content=5c4c59e304d3015a784b50c5&utm_medium=trueAnthem&utm_source=facebook?utm_campaign=trueAnthem%3A+Trending+Content&utm_content=5c4c59e304d3015a784b50c5&utm_medium=trueAnthem&utm_source=facebook

Then we see a tragic headline like the one about Tyler Hilinski, the promising quarterback at Washington State who committed suicide by shooting himself in January 2018.

Debbie Pyka, our brain acquisition coordinator, made a call to the medical examiner to suggest a donation. The Hilinski family agreed. When the results came back, the Mayo Clinic diagnosed Tyler with CTE and cumulative damage so bad that his brain looked like that of a 65-year-old. Tyler was 21.[32]

The cover-up of brain damage in football didn't begin in 2002 when Dr. Bennet Omalu performed the autopsy of Pittsburgh Steelers center Mike Webster and diagnosed him with CTE. That *was* the beginning of unraveling the decades of fraud by the NFL, NCAA, Pop Warner, and helmet manufacturers.

It also didn't begin in the 1990s, like ESPN journalists reported in "League of Denial," with the now-defunct NFL mild-traumatic brain injury committee created by rheumatologist Elliot Pellman.

It began decades earlier, at least as early as 1969. Not only is there extensive research that proved that hits were causing brain damage, but football increased these risks with hard, rigid, heavy plastic helmets not designed or tested for kids. Artificial surfaces added even more risk, and techniques for tackling were taught by trial and error.[33]

Known Helmet Defects

To understand football helmets and their design and defects, we have to look at their manufacturing standard, and how they test helmets to measure whether they meet this voluntary standard.

---

32 Scott Stump, "Parents of college quarterback Tyler Hilinski reveal son had CTE when he died by suicide," *Today,* June 26, 2018, accessed September 10, 2018 https://www.today.com/health/college-football-player-tyler-hilinski-who-died-suicide-had-cte-t131843

33 Josh Kosman, "Ex-NFL players sue Riddell for hiding concussion info," *New York Post,* April 13, 2016, accessed January 22, 2019 https://www.google.com/amp/s/nypost.com/2016/04/13/ex-nfl-players-sue-riddell-for-hiding-concussion-info/amp/

First of all, there is only one standard for which helmets are tested – whether you're a 300-pound NFL lineman or a 35-pound 5-year-old playing your first season in football. The standard was set by the National Operating Committee on Standards for Athletic Equipment (NOCSAE) – an organization created by the NCAA, National Federation of High Schools, Junior College Athletic Association, National Athletic Trainers Association, Athletic Goods Manufacturers Association, and the American College Health Association. In an NCAA newsletter dated June 1970 and titled "Committee to Set Equipment Standards," it is stated, "Besides the desire for greater safety in competitive athletics, an important reason for the formation of the committee is the number of lawsuits being contested today based on substandard equipment." I mean, wow, let's just admit we're doing this to cover our buns.

Just a few years later in 1973, NOCSAE introduced standard and licensing agreements with manufacturers that allowed their seal on helmets for child athletes, knowing they did not have a standard specific to children.

It has become fairly common to see such headlines regarding football helmets like the one in the Washington Post on September 11, 2017, that proclaimed, "High-tech helmets designed to lower risks of concussions make NFL debut."

Nothing could be further from the truth.

Modern football helmet designs were created to reduce the severity and frequency of skull fractures and facial injuries. They were not designed to prevent concussions or brain injuries. In fact, the consequences of the helmet's design to prevent skull fractures, while not considering such important factors such as weight, trapped heat, and vibration, that actually increase the risk of brain injury, brain damage and disease.

A more accurate headline should read, "New helmets fail to correct design defects known for decades to increase the risks of brain injury."

The tackle football helmet presents an unreasonable risk of harm to the children because it was not designed for them; there are known design defects; fitting instructions are inadequate; and adult manufacturing standards are applied to a vulnerable population – child athletes.

Currently, there is not a mandatory or funded central database for football injuries, or any sports injuries for that matter. That is despite studies funded by the NCAA and the National Federation of High School Sports, such as those conducted at the National Center for Catastrophic Sports Injury Research at the University of North Carolina, that have shown that football injuries, including death, make up 90 percent of all high school catastrophic injuries tracked in male sports in the United States since 1982.[34] Football historian Matt Chaney at Four Walls Publishing also tracks football injuries and lists considerably more data than any other database on catastrophic injuries and death. His blog is a great resource for information on football history, safety and injuries.

The Federal Center for Disease Control has a National Electronic Injury Surveillance System that monitors emergency room visits. It has reported that among athletes ages 18 and under, overall football injuries from 2009 to 2015 were down 14 percent. Yet head injuries increased by 38 percent and concussions by 59 percent during the same time period.

California case law says, "A manufacturer, distributor, or retailer is liable in tort if a defect in the manufacture or design of its product causes injury while the product is being used in a reasonable way." There is compelling evidence that the failure to establish and use a specific youth standard for child athletes, and a failure to provide reasonable and adequate protection from child maltreatment, exposes children to an unreasonable risk of catastrophic injury and death.

The potential risks of helmets present a substantial danger when used in a reasonably foreseeable way, that ordinary consumers who are minor children, and who are not be able to recognize the potential increased risk.

The current helmets sold and worn by children ages 5 to 17 have a sticker saying that the helmet "meets NOCSAE standards," even though there is not a standard for helmets intended for children to wear, misleading the consumer.

---

34   Ron Maxey, "Why high school players lead the way in football fatalities," *Memphis Commercial Appeal,* August 27, 2018, accessed January 25, 2019 https://www.google.com/amp/s/amp.commercialappeal.com/amp/1113674002

Manufacturers erroneously use age to instruct the user on which helmet to wear between adult and youth – not height, weight or proper performer physical readiness to carry more than four pounds of extra weight. In general, football players before high school are instructed to wear the youth model, while the adult model is suggested for those fourteen and older. There is no available science to back that 14-year-olds can reasonably wear safety equipment designed for adults. The law is plain that we owe a greater degree of care to children because of their lack of capacity to appreciate risks and avoid danger. It is highly probable that the adult manufacturing standard applied to child athletes creates an unreasonable risk of catastrophic injury and death, and to make matters worse parents would be shocked to know that the testing of helmets does not mirror live play.

Helmets are only tested from helmet to surface, not helmet to helmet, and, of course, helmet to helmet is a common way players are injured. The helmet also is tested without the face mask and only uses a head form with neck, not full crash dummies that would be more reasonable to predict human collisions. With a head form only, in a helmet with no face mask they drop helmets from different heights straight down and test the linear force (A force that always acts in a particular direction, such as weight - which always acts vertically. The continuation of this line is the line of action of the force. For example, a person's weight has a line of action that passes vertically through the center of their body).

That's it.

So even though we know brain injuries or concussions are primarily caused by rotational force, helmets were not tested for it.

NOCSAE founding members claimed the need to create their own organization because the American Society of Testing Materials was "too slow" in developing a testing method. Yet, since 1973, the only substantive change to the pass/fail severity index used by NOCSAE was lowering the pass/fail threshold from 1600 to 1200 in 1997. Helmets with lower Severity Index or SI were grandfathered in and never removed from the market.

In its own newsletter in 2005, NOCSAE admitted the "SI number was not designed to be a qualitative data point. There is no reliable data from which it can be concluded, for example, that a helmet with an average SI of 300 is measurably better at preventing any particular injury than a helmet with an SI of 400 or 500. The number simply is not designed to make that qualitative measurement."

SI scores are not made available to the public.

By the 1960s, experts knew that hard plastic shells, without further exterior padding, would be used by players to hit their opponents, whether purposely or due to the inability to choreograph the violence of the sport. Yet NOCSAE didn't make any effort to create a standard that required a soft outer layer, even though the technology and materials were available as early as NOCSAE's formation.

By their own admission, NOCSAE knowingly passed off helmets as reasonably safe when they had no standard specific for minors, based on their unique anatomy, or a system with which to measure effectiveness of the product.

A NOCSAE press release in June 2016 states, "NOCSAE has been researching the potential benefits of creating a separate standard for helmets designed for youth. At this time, there is insufficient data to suggest a distinct helmet mass limit for youth or other similar performance changes would provide more injury protection or protect against injury risks not already addressed."

https://sgbonline.com/nocsae-says-data-does-not-yet-justify-youth-helmet-standard/

Meanwhile NOCSAE continues to collect fifty cents for every youth helmet sold for kids with their label claiming it meets this standard that still doesn't exist.

The actions on the part of the football helmet industry and related entities is reckless, and puts the safety and well-being of minor children in danger. As such, it departs from the standard of care owed to young football players for safety equipment in a collision sport, and that is directly linked to an increased risk of brain injury, damage and disease.

To say football helmets prevent concussions or brain injuries is false advertising.

Trolls, Grief & Tenacity

How does one even begin to describe trolls on the internet, much less those who seek to poke at the wounds of a grieving parent? It's truly difficult to put into words.

I have always been a strong person by nature. As a kid I stood up to bullies who made fun of classmates for their glasses or braces or not having the "cool" brand of clothes or shoes. As president of Young Republicans in college, I personally went to the university president to make the case for the gay and lesbian club to be recognized on campus for the first time and was successful. In the workplace, I have fought for women, single moms, those who speak English as a second language, and giving second chances to those deemed to have made too many life mistakes to be eligible for hire.

None of that prepared me for what I refer to as the "Sandy Hook Truthers of Football." Much like those who attacked the parents of the children who died in the tragic killings at Sandy Hook Elementary School, our trolls have no limits, no boundaries, no decorum. Nothing is off limits in their quest to "save" youth tackle football.

"Your son was dumb, that's why he died," was one tweet I've received.

Others:

"He was driving a motorcycle you dumb bitch."
"He chose to be reckless."
"You use your son's death to make yourself relevant in football."
"You dig up his grave for attention."

One former NFL player, Jeff Nixon even posted this on Facebook:

The trolls say anything to protect the game, and buy time. They throw shade daily in hopes we will give it up, pack our virtual bags and stop telling our sons' stories. They know if moms and dads know what we know, they won't let little Johnny play at age 5 or if at all.

When California lawmakers decided on their own – for the record, we NEVER lobbied for it – to introduce a bill to ban tackle football before high school, and I decided to get involved in the process, the trolls came out in force.[35]

When I say trolls, I'm not referring to anyone who opposes my perspective, I'm talking about nasty, evil, trash-talking, people often using phony social media accounts.

---

35   Madeline Ashmum, "California bill would limit tackling during youth practices. Why it has leagues' support," *Sacramento Bee*, January 15, 2019, accessed January 25, 2019 https://www.sacbee.com/news/politics-government/capitol-alert/article224331020.html

The save youth football crowd was brutal. Here are just a few screenshots of real posts from trolls.

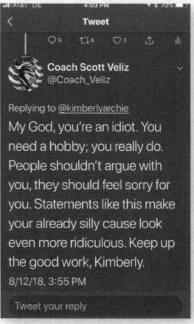

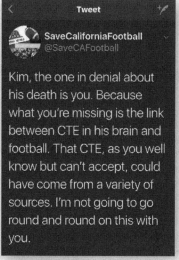

After we pulled our support before the billed died, the trolls lived on to troll.[36] After almost a year of intense attacks about my son and how he died, I had to face the toll it took on my mental health. As a brain injury survivor, I am already at increased risk for depression. Add the grief of losing a child, and that would be enough to break the average person. But to be attacked almost daily became

---

36   Ryan Kartije, "Law to ban tackle football for California youth falls short of committee," *Orange County Register,* April 27, 2018, accessed January 22, 2019 https://www.google.com/amp/s/www.ocregister.com/2018/04/27/law-to-ban-tackle-football-for-california-youth-falls-short-of-committee/amp/

more than even I could handle. I began to limit my social media time, muted borderline accounts and blocked the worst of them.

Ironically, football, as an industry, is a bigger enemy to itself than any of us grieving families will ever be.

Much to the contrary of how the save youth tackle football crowd might view it, this book isn't intended to be only a bunch of sad stories, or to provoke hysteria.

It's about shining a bright light in dark places and exposing the fraud perpetuated for decades by the sports industry.

It's about fostering the change required for stopping preventable injuries, such as paralysis, damaged organs, or exposure to repetitive hits that make brain damage not just possible, but even highly probably, depending on the number of years of exposure and the age it began.

It's about protecting kids, putting brains before games, loving kids more than sports, while not having to love sports less.

In this book, we don't want our loved one's lives to have played out in vain. We want to be examples of what not to do and hope to provide wisdom through excruciating loss to future generations. Rather than dwell on our grief and loss, we are focusing on: advocacy, research, passing laws to protect children, providing a no-cost grief support conference call once per month, and telling our stories so families will hopefully choose to delay putting their kids in repetitive-hit sports.

We insist that youth sport equipment including football helmets be designed for kids, that hit counts and hit limits be implemented, like pitch counts in baseball.[37]

We are turning tragedy into triumph. We are giving back every step of the way. That's what this book is all about: Sharing our stories to save other families from enduring the hell we have, because we didn't know then, what we know now.

We're looking on the bright side. When you know better, you do better.

---

37   "Pitch Count," *Wikipedia,* accessed January 21, 2019 https://en.m.wikipedia.org/wiki/Pitch_count

YOUTH ATHLETES

CHAPTER 1

Paul Bright

Paul Bright Jr.

July 28, 1990 – September 1, 2014

Paul Bright Jr. was a phenomenon. Most boys wouldn't even consider playing high school football if they were only 5-feet-2 and just over 100 pounds as a freshman. But Paul never considered his size to be a detriment. How could they keep a kid off the field with such an enormous heart and bottomless tenacity? Paul loved football, and from the time he was 7, each fall was filled with the satisfying rituals that come with practices and games on frosty Fridays and Saturdays. His family cheered, not knowing each hit he delivered or took was slowly creating irreparable damage to his brain. With a mom and sister heavily involved in the youth sports safety movement, Paul became aware of the dangers of football after he'd stopped playing. His behavior was erratic enough to cause concerns, but it wasn't until a fatal motorcycle accident in which he was driving far too fast on a city street, that the true nature of Paul's brain injuries were clear: He was diagnosed with Stage I chronic traumatic encephalopathy (CTE). Paul was the very person his family was fighting for, and they didn't know it.

"Why can't you fight for me?"
By Tiffani Bright

As life happens, you have no idea what thoughts or conversations will end up holding enormous meaning after the death of a loved one.

"No dying."

Unsettling laughs filled the air, though they seemed to mean nothing at the time. It wouldn't be long before I'd know how much the words would ring true, or how often I'd think back on it.

"I love you. I'll see you next time."

"I love you, too."

Last sentiments are easy to attach meaning to when they seem to be merely a coincidence.

"No dying."

Paul hopped on his green donor-cycle that he'd been so proud of fixing up himself. He put on his helmet that cost more than he paid for the bike.[38] "He's being

---

38   Zach Helfand, "Death comes from motorcycle accident, but was CTE really to blame?" Los Angeles Times, August 13, 2016 accessed January 17, 2019 https://www.latimes.com/sports/sportsnow/la-sp-cte-death-20160813-snap-story.html

smart about having good equipment, at least," I thought. One last nod and off down Burbank Boulevard he went.

They say hindsight is 20/20, but sometimes we're seeing so clearly in the moment and simply don't act. I knew Paul could be another crash statistic. I knew he could become quadriplegic. I knew he could be one of the many motorcyclists who become spare parts for someone in need of a new liver or kidney. I knew the dangers, and yet all I said was, "No dying."

In the months after Paul's death, I kept a note on my phone so that every time I had a memory of my brother I could jot it down, no matter how insignificant. There was the last time we spoke, or watching the movie "Rudy" too many times to count, or Paul attempting to unsuccessfully sing in tune in the car on the way to class.

There was an overwhelming fear that, someday, I wouldn't be able to picture his smile or hear his laugh. How do I make sure he doesn't just become a name in stories we tell, a lost spirit of the past? Someone asks me now about something Paul said or did that I can't remember, and my breath gets stuck in my throat, my body tenses, my brain freezes. I should *know* this; I should *remember* this; how can I *not* remember this? I had no idea I should've been making mental notes of our conversations about CTE and football.

Five months before the fatal motorcycle accident that ended Paul's life, the idea that Paul was exposed to brain damage from football made its way into conversation. Paul met me at Mom's house to help retrieve some miscellaneous item from the attic while she was out of town for the White House Summit on Concussions.[39] On a recent trip to a sports equipment standards meeting in Indianapolis, she was interviewed by a television reporter about the lack of a youth standard for football helmets.[40] A small comment referring to my brother stood out: "How could it be that my son took more hits than a Hall of Famer?"

39 David Jackson, "Obama to host concussion conference," *USA Today*, May 16, 2014, accessed November 6, 2018 https://www.usatoday.com/story/theoval/2014/05/16/obama-concussions-football-white-house-summit/9178645/

40 Jason Navia, "Sitting on the bench: The failure of youth football helmet regulation and the necessity of government intervention," accessed January 24, 2019 http://www.administrativelawreview.org/wp-content/uploads/2014/04/Sitting-on-the-Bench-The-Failure-of-Youth-Football-Helmet-Regulation-and-the-Necessity-of-Government-Intervention.pdf

Paul was excited that Mom talked about him on TV. I told him I thought he could have CTE. Not that he was so depressed that he was going to kill himself tomorrow, but that he was slowly beginning to show some effects of brain trauma. The exact words of our conversation have escaped me now, but I won't forget that after we talked, we both thought that while he might not have CTE, there was definitely a chance he did.

At 14 years old, my brother, Paul Bright Jr., stood a mere 5-feet-2 and weighed 108 pounds. As kids, we were taught we could be anything we dreamed. Paul dreamed his future career would be as an NFL player. Never mind statistics that indicate otherwise, every game night Paul would head out onto the field with such passion. He may not have been the biggest player, but he played with the biggest heart. He had a sincere love for the game and his football family. If he were still with us, even knowing he had CTE and other brain damage, he'd still love football.

Our parents divorced when I was 2 and Paul was still a baby. When we grew older he went to live with Dad, so my brother and I spent the school year separated. Summer vacations we spent together, split between each parent. First, Paul would come to Mom's for six weeks, while the last six weeks we always stayed with Dad to make sure Paul wouldn't miss the start of football season.

"Eat. Sleep. Football. Repeat."

He started Pop Warner football in first grade at the age of 7 and played every season but one through his freshman year of high school. "Eat. Sleep. Football. Repeat." It's the routine for those who live and breathe football. Youth sports had been a way of life at Dad's house. Each year, all of my brothers played every season of football, basketball, baseball, and, later, wrestling. Every summer, five days a week for two hours, I watched as my brother tackled and got tackled in an attempt to reach Pop Warner's version of the Super Bowl in Orlando, Florida.

I'd sit on the sidelines, watching as these little warriors, their tiny heads poking up out of bulky shoulder pads, lined up for stretching and warmups. They'd split up into offense and defense – off to learn drills, new plays and how to hit. At home, my brothers practiced together in the backyard. Paul would even write out his own plays on lined paper and give them to his coach. Thanksgiving vacation was sometimes interrupted, depending on if one of my brother's teams made it to regionals. If they did, it meant leaving our home in Reno, Nevada, to face one of the California teams. The other team always seemed to have a bigger team, bigger players, and nicer equipment. We always had heart and grit.

One of the occasions Paul's team made it to regionals, and we drove to see him play. Bundled in scarves and pocket warmers, we sat on frosty metal bleachers, ready to cheer for the unlikely victory.

The team huddled up. Coach Jesse yelled, "Who are we gonna play?"

"Who cares?!" the team shouted back.

They were true underdogs, playing with determination and hustle.

In Paul's first home high school game, he was so pumped for the season to start. Mom and I traveled to Reno from Oregon to watch as he started the next phase of his football life. Friday night lights blasted down to the field. Paul stood at the end of the line of players, farthest from us. He stuck out like a sore thumb. He wouldn't hit his growth spurts until after he'd left the game. He was at least a full head shorter than the rest of the players.

The national anthem rang through the stadium. The kickoff started the game and the minutes ticked down. The halftime show came and went. The fourth quarter was coming to an end and Paul had yet to even be put in for a single play. His team won by 11 points, and though he tried to hide it, the disappointment could be seen on Paul's face from across the field.

That freshman season of little opportunity on the field led to Paul quitting football. At 6-feet-1 and 195 pounds in his senior year, we joked that all those years he did play he was tiny, and now that he was finally bigger, he didn't want to play anymore.

There was not even a second thought that after my brother died that his brain would be donated to determine if he'd suffered brain damage.

Fighting for Child Safety

For the previous five years, Paul watched as Mom and I tirelessly worked to bring awareness to youth sports safety. When I was in high school, I was at a tumbling practice with my cheerleading team. Another girl was allowed to practice her back handspring on the tumble track at the same time I was completing my last flip. Playing on a backyard trampoline, even school children know you can create tension in the trampoline by bouncing right before another person, giving them extra height in their bounce. As I jumped backwards for a final time, my left arm hit the trampoline first and a loud snap made everyone in the gym freeze.

When my body finally managed to get back upright, my forearm looked like it had an extra elbow bending my wrist away from me. Mom dropped the pen she was using to sign a check for that month's membership fee and ran over to me. No one had a clue what to do. The mouths of the other athletes and coaches gaped open at the sight of my gruesome injury. There were no slings, no first-aid kits, no emergency plans. Someone grabbed a piece of carpet and cut a strip to wrap around my arm. A rope found its way around my head and arm to create a sling as Mom picked me up and rushed me to the hospital.[41]

The incident started a journey of more than 10 years of fighting for the safety of children by Mom and me. After my injury, we started the National Cheer Safety

---

41 Teresa Ristow, "Cheerleading safety in its infancy," Medford Mail Tribune, December 24, 2012, accessed January 24, 2019 http://mailtribune.com/news/education/cheerleader-safety-in-its-infancy

Foundation in 2008 to help bring awareness and better safety standards for cheerleaders. Early on, our collection of data was featured in the annual report from the National Center for Catastrophic Sport Injury Research. Our research showed the staggering amount of serious injuries occurring to high school and college cheerleaders across the country.[42]

After the annual report was published, it created a lot of media attention, with hundreds of stories produced by various news outlets, including *People*[43] magazine and the *Washington Post*,[44] Mom and I decided to enroll in paralegal classes to learn about more child athlete rights. Soon after, Paul moved to Southern California to live with Mom and me. Having recently graduated from high school, Paul wasn't sure what he wanted to do for the rest of his life. Still, he knew it was imperative that he go to school. So he signed up for classes at the same school Mom and I were attending.

Paul would help us whenever he could with the foundation. He volunteered at heart screenings or ran out for midnight snacks because we were pulling another all-nighter. One of the many things he undertook was to visit Patty with us. Mom was an expert for Patty's injury case, but as with a lot of the cases, we became more than simply advocates for her. Patty suffered a form of cardiac arrest, commotio cordis, during an acrobatic maneuver with her cheerleading team.[45] Oxygen deprivation to her brain resulted in a traumatic brain injury and Patty became quadriplegic. She could only communicate with her eyes. One blink for "yes." Twice for "no." Three times for "maybe." Paul never hesitated to take time out of his day to talk to Patty about new music or bring her new DVDs.

During one of our paralegal classes, a teacher played the movie "Erin Brockovich." The story of Ms. Brockovich fighting to bring down a power company polluting a city's water supply inspired us to write the law firm, Masry & Vititoe, where

42   Frederick O. Mueller, PhD, "Cheerleading & Safety," Nov. Dec. 2009, Journal of Athletic Training, NCBI, accessed January 27, 2019 https://www.ncbi.nlm.nih.gov/pmc/articles/PMC2775356/

43   Nicole Weisensee Egan, "Is cheering safe? *People,* January 19, 2009 https://people.com/archive/is-cheering-safe-vol-71-no-2/

44   "Cheerleading can be risky," Denver Post, September 10, 2008, accessed January 27, 2019 https://www.google.com/amp/s/www.denverpost.com/2008/09/10/cheerleading-can-be-risky/amp/

45   "Cheerleading: Nothing to cheer about," Real Life Productions, accessed January 26, 2019 https://vimeo.com/119392162

Ms. Brockovich worked, to see if they could help us. We thought it was a long shot, but they actually wrote back. The relationship later led me to getting a job there and Mom becoming an expert in the concussion case against the NFL.[46]

During the concussion case, Mom took trips across the country, meeting with players about CTE and the effects of repetitive hits to the head. As a huge football fan, Paul wanted nothing more than to be by her side. There was an exuberance that came over him when he told people where Mom was or which player she met that week. He couldn't wait for the chance to meet some of the players he'd grown up watching each Sunday. Both of us had our hearts set on going to a Super Bowl together, preferably in a year it wasn't in a city that was freezing. We thought there would be so many future opportunities.

After one of her trips, Mom brought back a helmet manufactured by SG. She'd recently met with SG's owner, Bill Simpson, and he gave her a sample so players could see the difference between his helmets and those considered the industry standard. Paul walked her out to the car to retrieve her luggage. She opened the trunk and handed the helmet to Paul. He immediately had that exuberance come over him.

"Oh yeah, if only I had worn this," he commented, grinning madly.

He held it by the face mask, eagerly observing every angle as he turned it. The inner padding, the new material. This shiny new technology was sleek.

In the days after Paul died, many people expressed vivid memories of his animated behavior when talking about what we were doing in sports. He was obsessed about us being involved in such a monumental thing happening in football. He was proud we were fighting for a good cause.

---

46   Robert Silverman, "The mom winning the fight to save kids' brains from football," Daily Beast, June 15, 2018, accessed January 16, 2019 https://www.thedailybeast.com/the-mom-winning-the-fight-to-save-kids-brains-from-football

Celebrity Chef

When it came to his own job, Paul was a dedicated and hard-working employee. He had a passion for food that rivaled his childhood love of football. He moved up to be a manager at Cricca's Italian Deli not long after starting. By the time the owners decided to sell the deli and focus on their catering company, Humble Pie, Paul was part of their family. Fulfilling a promise made earlier to train Paul to be a chef, they negotiated for Paul to transition with them if he stayed for a few months to help the new owner. He worked every day that he could, sometimes putting in 16-hour days for weeks at a time. He often missed family get-togethers because he never wanted to take a day off.

Paul was the kind of employee and person you could always count on. He wasn't just someone you could ask for favors. He went out of his way to be helpful. One of his co-workers was unfortunate enough to have his car break down at a time when he didn't have any savings to replace it. Paul offered to give him rides to and from work every day for several months. His co-worker was undeniably grateful for the kindness Paul showed him.

As children, our stepmom suffered from a parasite that fossilized in her brain and caused her to have seizures. Dad was a full-time member of the Air National Guard and went away on trips overseas for extended periods of time. As the oldest son, Paul took charge of helping our stepmom and looking out for his little brothers. At the age of 10, he learned what needed to be done when she was having a seizure, including giving her a shot of Diazepam. As he grew up, that protection Paul showed for the women in his life was always a part of who he was.

Because he was such a helper around the house, Paul had the skill of throwing together whatever ingredients we happened to have on hand and making it into a delicious meal. He loved the feeling he got from seeing people enjoy his food. He also could display a flash of smugness when showing off how great he could cook. He had a habit of calling to boast about the new celebrity he'd cooked for that day.

A memory that brings the biggest grin to my face is what he said after he'd prepared a meal for Jennifer Lopez. "I helped JLo keep up her curves today," he said.

"What are you talking about?" I replied.

"She loved my crème brûlée so much she came back for seconds. She said it was the best she had ever had!"

The last time we ever spoke, Paul was working at the site of a Pizza Hut commercial. He called to say how much Blake Shelton loved what he prepared for him. I could hear the smile in his voice as he described what he cooked. There was such excitement about having one of our favorite country artists go out of his way to compliment Paul's food. The call wasn't long. He was still at work. But he could barely contain his happiness.

Some of those who have been found to have CTE, like Paul, have died being reckless, whether it's car accidents or drug overdoses. Early signs of CTE from brain injury can include sleep disturbances, impulse control issues, memory problems, lapses in judgment, and headaches. But the symptoms of brain injury and Stage I CTE are often not glaringly obvious in such an early part of the disease. Sometimes, symptoms seem to mask themselves within someone's personality. That's the difficult part when you don't know you have brain damage. You don't understand what's wrong.

Red Flags

Looking back at one of the last times I saw him, there were red flags. He called to tell me he bought a used motorcycle off some guy who was selling it because he had already had the unfortunate experience of falling off of it. Red flag.

Paul had no fear, no idea that he would experience the same thing. He had such pride in his voice as he described all the things he was going fix, doing it with his own two hands. The bike needed a lot of work: a new body, new seats, new brake lines, new headlights. He couldn't wait to start riding it.

When he brought it over for the first time, Paul pulled up in front of my house with a beat up-looking bike. He hadn't taken the motorcycle class to get his license. Red flag. He hadn't got insurance for it. Red flag.

Yet, here he was, taking off his helmet to reveal a huge grin. He hopped off and went right into describing the bike, what he had done so far, what else needed to be completed.

"Mom doesn't know I bought it and I'm not going to tell her," he said. Red flag. "Well, yeah," I said, "she'd come find it and throw it off a bridge." Sticking together as siblings do, I had no intention of telling on him. He told just about everyone he knew that he bought it, and the news was met with the same reluctant nervousness from each of us. But Mom was the only one who would have blatantly taken action to make sure he didn't ride it, and he knew that.

My own anxiety was not calmed when we noticed a long cord dangling from the back of the bike. Red flag.

My already worried mind immediately jumped to him speeding down the street and the brakes not working. Paul was undeterred. He said he'd let us know he made it back to his place safely. Luckily, he did.

A few weeks later, I was visiting my boyfriend's family for the Fourth of July weekend I got a text from mom because she couldn't get ahold of Paul. I silently freaked out. She still didn't know about the motorcycle. I called and texted him, but hours went by with no response. I was in a panic. We didn't know where Paul was and didn't have contact information for the people he recently moved in with. I asked him in a text to at least let us know that he was alive. A little after midnight, I finally received, "I'm fine!" All the anxiety melted away.

As different things occurred in Paul's life, we didn't think they were the signals that would later flash in our minds as risky and reckless behaviors. That dedication for his job didn't always transfer to other areas of his life. On Paul's 21st birthday, he was giving a friend a ride home and was pulled over. He admitted to the police that he smoked marijuana earlier that day, and he was cited with a DUI. When it came time to go to court, Paul was inconsistent with his appearances even though the charges had been changed to wet reckless. Multiple times, this resulted in warrants for his arrest.

Paul barely played football in high school. He never played in college or the NFL.

My brother wasn't suicidal. He didn't suffer from depression or at least he never shared that with any of us. He never had a diagnosed brain injury in the nine years he played. He did, however, suffer from painful migraines for most of his life. By middle school, his knees were already suffering from overuse. He'd have me walk on his back to help ease his lower back pain. He used prescription marijuana regularly to help with his difficulty falling asleep. With all of this, how could his brain be in proper working order?

The knowledge that came with Mom being a brain injury survivor herself, and years of working with former players in the NFL brain injury lawsuit, and being aware of CTE, we knew he had at least been exposed to brain trauma.

Upon receiving the medical report of his brain autopsy, the neuropathologist indicated the signs of Paul's CTE weren't in the part of the brain she sees for boxers, hockey players or soccer players. The protein tau had formed in a cluster, precisely where she would expect one in a football player.[47]

There were many times when Paul voiced his frustration of feeling left out. He once said to Mom after getting his DUI, "You fight for everyone else. Why can't you fight for me?" We gave up a lot to help our sister fight cancer. We gave up a lot to help fight for better safety standards in cheerleading, and for my rights as an athlete. We gave up a lot to help fight for gas pipe safety.[48] Where was Paul's crusade?

His crusade comes now. Now that we know Paul had CTE. Now that we know years of repetitive hits can cause degenerative brain damage. After years of Paul feeling like he wasn't part of our fight to help youth athletes, in the end, we were fighting for him all along and didn't know it yet. Our mission is still the same. Our passion simply burns brighter than ever.

---

47 Zach Helfand, "Death comes from motorcycle accident, but was CTE really to blame?" Los Angeles Times, August 13, 2016, accessed January 17, 2019 https://www.latimes.com/sports/sportsnow/la-sp-cte-death-20160813-snap-story.html

48 "CBS2 Investigates: Experts say decaying gas lines are a ticking time bomb below city streets," CBS 2, January 8, 2016, accessed January 17, 2019 https://www.google.com/amp/s/newyork.cbslocal.com/2016/01/08/new-york-gas-main/amp/

CHAPTER 2

Tyler Winston Cornell

February 18, 1989 – April 3, 2014

Tyler Cornell and his family got an early taste of the heady buzz football can produce. When he was only 12 years old, Tyler's Pop Warner team made it to the national championship in Orlando. He would stick with those teammates through high school, enjoying a bond that no one outside of his circle could possibly understand. He was a gifted student in school, sensitive, athletic and socially outgoing – the "perfect" kid in so many ways. After a high school football career in which he earned all-league honors as an offensive lineman, Tyler moved on after graduation to college. But the kid who formerly had no problems with his studies began having to struggle with schoolwork and fell into bouts of deep depression that required hospitalization on numerous occasions. Though his family tried desperately to help him in every way, Tyler committed suicide at the age of 25. A brain study revealed he had Stage I chronic traumatic encephalopathy (CTE).

Get Mad Mama
By Jo Cornell

My son always loved hearing the story of how he came into the world. Tyler Winston Cornell was born at the stroke of midnight on Feb 17, 1989. In the moments after he arrived, the doctor gave us options for his birthday: Do you want February 17, the last minute of the old day, or the 18th, the first minute of the new day?

We chose a new day for a new life.

What can I tell you about my one and only child? He was a beautiful, perfectly healthy baby boy. He was easygoing, a joy, and stole my heart at first glance. His nursery room was wall-papered in primary colors with an alphabet border. I like to think that was the reason he read three grades above his own level all through his school days (please forgive a proud mom's boast) because, perhaps, that border from so long ago gave him his lifelong love of reading.

When Tyler was 4 years old, we moved from the La Crescenta area of Los Angeles to Carlsbad. He loved places with magical names like Moonlight Beach and Stagecoach Park. When people asked his name, he would proudly answer: "My name is Tyler Winston – Ghostbuster!" while adjusting his plastic backpack with the bright yellow hose capable of taking down any ghosts foolish enough to present themselves.

The summer before Tyler turned 5, we moved into a two-story house in Rancho Bernardo, a few homes down the hill from Chaparral Elementary. He had a wonderful imagination. He drew, created elaborate vehicles and buildings with Legos, and would lose himself in books. (The "Goosebumps" series and Michel Creighton novels were early favorites.)

He also was supremely physical: tall, athletic and passionate about team sports such as baseball, basketball, and, of course, Pop Warner Football, which he started when he was 8. When his Raptors won the Wescon regionals in Arizona, he jumped into the hotel pool ... wearing his full uniform!

Just months before the horrors of September 11, 2001, and by virtue of their undefeated season, he and his teammates earned a cross-country flight to Orlando, Florida, to play at the Disney Wide World of Sports Complex for a chance to compete in the Pop Warner Super Bowl. It was a powerful moment for an impressionable 12-year-old. That memory was beyond special for Tyler. Those Raptors were his brothers for life and the team photo from that season sits in his room to this day.

Pop Warner football helped define my son, helped shape his identity. He was dedicated, disciplined, and driven, and not just in sports. He tested into his school's "gifted and talented" program as a third-grader. (I bring this up not so much to brag, though to this day I'm beyond proud of him, but to provide context for what happened later.)

On his first day of middle school, he noticed a plaque bearing the names of students who maintained a high grade-point average. He vowed to get his name on that plaque. And he made good on it. Tyler had an especially strong grasp of math and began tutoring his fellow students in that subject as a fifth-grader, a practice he kept up through high school.

He was a natural athlete who loved his ball sports, of course, but also snow and water skiing. He took tennis lessons and, after high school, became a very good golfer. More than all those pastimes, he loved football. God, how I wish that were not so.

Did We See Early Signs?

It's hard to answer that question, but here's what I can say: Tyler was happy, outgoing, and social as a child. He had lots of great friends. In school, he participated in every class and outside clubs. My sister-in-law, Susan, liked to embarrass me by asking, every so often, "How did you raise a perfect child?"

Of course, once the ravages of brain damage started to manifest themselves in my beautiful boy, he was far from perfect. He was, too often, perfectly miserable.

Tyler played football and basketball for Rancho Bernardo High School. Truth be told, he probably had more natural talent at hoops. To hone his basketball skills, he trained in La Jolla at 7:30 on Saturday mornings with ex-NBA player Jim Brogan. He'd set a goal, to make the basketball team and was willing to sacrifice his Saturday mornings to make it happen. And it did – he made the team. He earned that roster spot.

He was happy playing both sports and was named as a first-team offensive line-man for the *San Diego Union-Tribune's* All-Palomar League squad. His future seemed so bright.

Not long after, his hoops coach at Rancho Bernardo told Tyler he needed to choose between the two sports. Tyler chose football.

The *brain trauma* had already begun its stealthy work on Tyler's brain, I believe.

In his senior year of high school, my son was 6-feet-1, 190 pounds, with an athletic build, hazel eyes, and a deep dimple to mark his smile. However, *how* Tyler viewed himself was beginning to change.

There was a time when he removed household mirrors, or draped them so he wouldn't have to see himself at all. To this day, his bedroom mirror remains covered. Despite having so much going for him, he suffered from anxiety. To quell that anxiety, to give himself a feeling of control over his life, he would rearrange paintings and decorations in our home. My husband and I would go out to dinner, come home, and items would be in completely different places. Tyler believed he was "helping us". I would ask him not to do that. It reflected an instability I hadn't seen in him before. It was disturbing.

Once, on New Year's Eve, Tyler was getting ready to go out with his close friends. Something triggered him, and he ended up leaving the house at 10:30 p.m. and walking 19 miles from home, without his cell phone. He finally called me from the guard house at the front of a gated community. He asked me to come pick him up. He didn't celebrate New Year's Eve with his friends that night.

Tyler graduated in 2007, but never bothered to pick up his diploma. That summer, he shared with us the complaint we would hear more and more often, until we never heard it again: *I am depressed.*

That Fall, he enrolled at UC Santa Barbara, one of the gems of California's UC system. It's about a four-hour drive from where we live, on the far side of Los Angeles. He went off to college with two of his closest friends, Chris Barry and Alex Ryden.

There were problems straightaway. We started flying Tyler home for appointments with his psychologist. He went on meds, but continued to battle depression. Then came a terrible, triggering event.

One of Tyler's Pop Warner buddies, a close friend named Richard Caldwell, drove an SUV recklessly through a residential neighborhood. Intoxicated, he rolled the car, in the process passenger, childhood friend, and another Pop Warner teammate, Charles Amaro II, dies on his 20th birthday.[49]

---

49 "Teen who rolled SUV, killing passenger, sentenced to 4 years, 8 months," *San Diego Union-Tribune"* March 3, 2009, accessed September 1, 2018 https://www.sandiegouniontribune.com/sdut-bn03caldwell-sentenced-2009mar03-story.html

That news left Tyler understandably and deeply upset. But when he later learned that Richard was convicted of gross vehicular manslaughter and sentenced to prison, something snapped inside him. He basically destroyed his off-campus apartment in Goleta, adjacent to UCSB. After a night in the emergency room – I slept by his side between two metal chairs – he was taken by ambulance to a San Diego psychiatric hospital, Sharp Mesa Vista.

Tyler would later write this poem to honor Charles on the fifth anniversary of his death.

Monuments stand at attention,
stride over fresh cut grass as a man with apprehension

White athletic tape woven on my palm and wrist,
same look in my eyes as having my face mask clenched,
the sweat of suicides and two-a-days has my faith drenched

I retrace my steps amidst windmill rainbows,
my soul is soaring as old pains grow
Four steps to the southwest,
I am at your doorstep; there is no doubt left

I carry you in my heart forever, Charles; you made me laugh,
momentary rage to see your face covered with severed blades of grass,
I scoop handfuls of death as I toss them aside

I see you look fresh with fire in your eyes,
I lowered flat on my toes and fingertips,
I use my breath until everything is perfect

In my new Raider shirt I pull the Chargers keychain from my pocket,
I place the circle on your heart and the dark blue helmet on the acrostic

I rise as the wind grows calm,
I slam my right fist against my chest and stay strong

Change

Tyler's mental illness put us on an escalator going down. Thus began a seven-year period of psychologists, psychiatrists, hospitalizations, meds, misdiagnoses, side effects, and self-medication with marijuana.

I now know that suicidal ideation also is an ugly attribute of brain damage sustained by sub-concussive and concussive blows. This was another grim milestone in Tyler's journey. As his depression became deeper and more pervasive, it brought him closer to the edge.

The other side of the depression "coin" was anxiety. As much as he loved his "Bolts," the San Diego Chargers, there came a point where he would go to the game, but then wait in his car in the parking lot until the stadium was nearly full. Only then would he venture to his seat.

He had good days and weeks, and we would get our hopes up. He was accepted as a transfer student to UC San Diego. Then came the day he walked into his psychiatrist's office wearing his board shorts … and nothing else. Later that night he was admitted to UCSD hospital.

Tyler would self-medicate sporadically with marijuana, a drug that affected him differently than it did other people. He didn't just get high, then get silly, start laughing and zone out on couch with a big bag of chips. Weed worked on him much differently; he would spend three or four days with little or no sleep.

He committed to stop using it.

In his application letter to UC San Diego, Tyler mentioned the medical challenges he faced. It was determined that he had a student "disability," which allowed him to take more time on tests. He'd never needed that kind of dispensation before. Something was clearly changing him, something undetected, something from within. And I think my son was starting to figure that out.

For seven long years he made and kept appointments with a battery of medical professionals who did their best to treat his worsening symptoms. Tyler was good about staying on his meds. He truly wanted to get better. I know he took his pills because I watched them like a hawk. I would leave a weekly dose in the dispenser. I knew, at the end of the day, whether he'd taken his meds.

He took the pills despite such side effects as weight gain, tremors in his fingers, and the occasional twitch of his eye. That was tough for him, and for me, as his mom, to see. Later, I would discover mental health treatment is a problem for those with a traumatic brain injury, a brain under attack.

To be a constant in his life, I found it necessary to take 4½ years off my job as a civil litigation paralegal. The sad truth is, despite the fact that he was a young adult by now, he needed me – to help, to guide, to be supportive, to monitor his mood, and drug test him. From time to time he slipped and smoked some weed. This would fill him with remorse. He really didn't want to use marijuana, and on his own accord, wrote me a check for $500 as an assurance and pledge he would not use it. To give some heft to that vow, he agreed to drug testing and attended a Christian Recovery Support group.

A friend of our family who is also a doctor has told us that, by giving our son this care, we probably added years to his life. I know having this time with him was a gift but later there would come a time when *all* I could remember was how awful the journey was for him. *All* I could think about was the awful wreckage, the terrible trauma of his last seven years. I *wanted* the happy joyous memories of my beautiful and precious son, but instead was flooded with memories of the agony Tyler endured as his downward spiral accelerated.

One day, Tyler impulsively boards a train and stays on it for 100 miles, from Solana Beach to Los Angeles. He pays for a 22-mile cab ride to his grandmother s house in West Covina. That night, at a dinner with family and friends, one of his cousin's buddies jokingly says, "F___ your grandmother," and Tyler snaps and punches him in the face. He leaves the scene. The police can't find him. I drive two hours to West Covina to convince Tyler to come home. My sister-in-law, Kris, says I look like "a prisoner of war." I'm sure she's right. I didn't take a change of clothes when I got the call. I took a deep breath and started driving. I didn't care how I looked, I just wanted to bring my son home. A prisoner of war.

That feels about right. Tyler and me and everybody who loves him – we're all at war with this enemy inside his brain, and we aren't winning.

We finally convince him to take a sedative, and he sleeps in the backseat of my SUV for the ride home. But he wakes up angry and hostile. He doesn't want to go home; he wants to be taken back to his UCSD campus apartment. So that's where I take him. It was that or he's homeless.

… One afternoon I'm getting a bad feeling, so I drive to his apartment. His place, usually kept neat, is a disaster. There's a raw steak in his room. He's agitated and tells me he's leaving "to go to Santa Monica," which is 120 miles away. He has no car on campus and starts walking. I walk beside him, frequently falling behind because he's got a longer stride, and is walking fast. I'm talking to him, begging him to grasp that a northbound walk on the Pacific Coast Highway from La Jolla to Santa Monica is not normal behavior. He insists that "everything will be better" when he's in Santa Monica. My husband arrives and follows slowly, two car-lengths behind. I cannot get Tyler to stop for a rest, for food, for a drink of water. At one point he takes my cell phone and throws it into the middle of Pacific Coast Highway. I retrieve it. After we'd walked 13 miles, my husband calls 911. Tyler is admitted to back to Sharp Mesa Vista.

… In normal times, Tyler takes care of his possessions. This morning, in an ag-itated state, he seems intent on destroying the interior of his BMW, pulling out everything he can, ripping off everything that can be torn away. He drives to a local branch of the Bank of America and walks up to random strangers, asking, "Who wants to fight me?" Someone calls the cops, and Tyler leaves, walking to the nearby Vons. We know none of this at the time, and only find out about it when the police come to our home. I tell them Tyler didn't come home the night before and missed his medication. Back at Vons, he's throwing golf balls in the parking lot. Someone else calls the cops. Before they arrive, Tyler drives his trashed BMW to a Chevron. Once there, he takes off his shirt, whips out a lighter and sets his shirt on fire. At a gas station! Later, he tells me that he stopped short of torching his car because his late grandfather, Fred, would not have ap-proved. He loved his grandfather. Thank God, no one was hurt and nothing exploded. Tyler leaves the Chevron station and is arrested within the hour, facing a felony charge. We post his bail.

...Working with an attorney who understood Tyler's issues, and cared about him, we get the judge to reduce my son's sentence to 30 days of psychiatric residential treatment.

Before he starts the Pasadena-based program, he experiences two telling incidents while in the hospital:

He's in ICU with a recovering heroin addict we'll call Kyle, who talks too much for Tyler's taste. Tyler asks him over and over again to be quiet. At one point Kyle calls Tyler a "coward," so Tyler felt he had no choice but to punch him. But Kyle doesn't report him, so Ty doesn't get transferred, or thrown out. Eventually those two hug it out, with Kyle saying of my son, "He punches hard!"

I call early one morning and am told, there was an "incident last night." Tyler is pulling a few leaves off a ficus tree in the hallway. A nurse asks him to stop. It seems like a reasonable request. That's not how Tyler heard it. Agitated, he grabs a free-standing, 5-foot tall blood pressure machine and charges full speed with it toward the nurse's station. The nurse quickly locks the door behind her and Tyler then smashes the nurse's station window with the machinery. Later he would say he was testing the strength of the glass. As if providing a public service.

We worried that these incidents would disqualify him from the only California residential treatment program willing to take him. The magnitude of his serious illness was clearly escalating. That Tyler is striking anyone or anything is a disturbing new sign that his brain is under siege.

After these events and when Tyler is "better," he was finally discharged from the hospital at the end of his 30 days, the entire ICU staff and patients came into the Day Room to clap and cheer him on and wish him continued success in his recovery and residential treatment. I'd been around a lot of ICUs, and never seen anything like that. That was a good day for my son. He had faith, believed in himself, and believed everything would be better.

The Battle, the Warrior

He scrapped and battled. He was a warrior in this fight. In addition to the psychologists and psychiatrists he saw, Tyler visited holistic doctors, became vegetarian, ate raw, tried hypnosis, practiced meditation, read the Bible, spent time in prayer, volunteered at a homeless shelter, attended support groups and participated in excellent outpatient programs.

He fought hard against the looming, enclosing darkness. He fought with courage. He had no chance.

He is trying so hard to do the right things. By this time, he's simply not in control. By now, his friends are graduating from college, attending law school, getting married, beginning their chosen careers, buying homes, starting families. He's giving it his all to try to decide his major. He's 25 years old and still at the end of his junior year. He often felt old, off track.

We loved, supported and encouraged him through all his struggles and good times. There were ups mixed in with the downs. Tyler loved the English language, took classes in linguistics, savored British literature, read and wrote poetry and devoured "The Simpsons" and "Breaking Bad."

He was intelligent, but never made anyone feel less so around him. I once heard one of his coaches' say: "Tyler listened twice as much as he spoke," and I thought: Exactly. That's Tyler.

At UCSD, he was invited to join an honors fraternity, Phi Sigma Pi. That made him feel good, feel included. Before becoming a PSP brother, he'd been self-conscious. Joining the fraternity made him feel like his old self. I think PSP nailed it when they gave Tyler the designation: "Most likely to help a brother with a deep concern."

Unfortunately, one day when he was not well, he decided to quit the fraternity. It was the kind of destructive, impulsive decision we'd warned him against. Still, no amount of discussion or pleading could sway him from his decision.

He found self-expression in poetry and rap. He took the creative process very seriously and spent nearly $2,000 on studio equipment, which of course struck us, his parents, as impulsive and irrational. Two sample verses:

Dad would buy me a pony, if I asked/
Mom had me in a playpen with bubble wrap.

A later passage says, "*He could not blame me.*" I believe he knew there was something intrinsically wrong.

Tyler and I would go to feed homeless at Father Joe's in San Diego. It made him feel good to help others. Sometimes he was cooking fish, washing pots, or serving the men, women and children who lived at Father Joe's. We would come home on a natural high that lasted days. We were truly thankful for a roof over our heads and the light in our home. That he had a special compassion for the plight of the homeless touched my heart, as did the fact that he pro-actively shared of himself. He held a blanket drive for a charity called the Alpha Project, filling an SUV three times with blankets for the homeless. I know 60-year-olds who say that they, too, would like to help the homeless "someday," but it never happens.

On evening of September 8, 2013, Tyler was in Michigan Stadium – the "Big House" – to see the Wolverines take down their longtime rival Notre Dame. His grandfather, Fred, was a Michigan alum, and passed that passion to his grandson.

Even that special experience was marred by Ty's internal battle. He abruptly checked out of the hotel he was sharing with his Dad, then threatened to skip the game altogether. In fact, we didn't know where Tyler was and I called local hotels from San Diego trying to find him. When he did show up at his assigned seat, at the last minute, he'd changed out of his Michigan sweatshirt. Instead, he wore black.

Looking back, I'm grateful for the grace notes, the small moments of happiness we shared, even as he sunk deeper into his personal hell. On the final morning of his life we went on a hike above the Chaparral Elementary School, his first school. As we climbed the hill I told him how much I loved him, and reminded him of all the family and friends who had his back and held him in their hearts. I tried to be encouraging and uplifting. He was quiet and listened. He had appointment with his psychologist, a doctor whom he'd been seeing for years. It was the start of a new term at UCSD. I made him breakfast and before he left he said in a sing-song voice, "I love you Mom." I responded, "I love you Tyler."

He went to the psychologist appointment, and even made a follow-up appointment for the following Thursday. One of the songs he heard, upon getting back in his car, was a Christian hymn called "Going Home." But he didn't drive to the university, for his morning classes. He went to his grandmother's home in West Covina, let himself in, and took his own life. His struggle was over.

My son was 25.

Post-mortem

Suspecting there was a link between football and Tyler's depression and suicide, we made the difficult decision to send his brain to be autopsied, where the majority of CTE study has taken place. Almost a year later, the results came back. Tyler suffered from brain damage including CTE. As of this writing, he is the fifth of eleven youth players diagnosed; however, some of the other families have chosen to remain anonymous.

There are many, many more young men whose brains have not been tested after their shattered lives came to an early and tragic end. I am sharing this account because: CTE is real, it's devastating, and there is no cure.

No game, no winning season, no trophy, is worth a life. Not my son's life, not the life of any young man.

Some 250,000 children play Pop Warner football every year, brain sloshing occurring in helmets that to this day have no child safety standard. This mom has decided the cost is too great. Speaking on brain damage including CTE awareness is worthy of my best effort. I wish CTE had been out in the open in 1997. I wish I knew when Tyler was 8 years old what I know now. Trust me, that boy would never have come near a football helmet. Especially now that I know the helmets were never made or tested when Tyler played.[50]

Read and investigate about sub-concussive hits, brain damage and CTE, mama.[51] Look at the studies that aren't sponsored or funded by the NFL. They have a vested interest, but so do you mama. Yours is breathing; theirs is in the bank.

That's why you'll see me speaking my hard truth. To random moms who happen to be wearing football jerseys. To complete strangers at the park. To a hotel clerk. To friends at a reunion. To an unsuspecting policeman at a community BBQ whose young son is wearing his football jersey.

I tell them about Tyler's sub-concussive hits, brain damage and CTE.[52] I tell them because I should. I simply cannot keep this information to myself. I do not want another child to grow up, suffer and be robbed of everything. I tell them

50 Josh Kosman, "Father sues football helmet makers over son's CTE-related death," *New York Post*, May 31, 2018, accessed November 1, 2018 https://nypost.com/2018/05/31/father-sues-football-helmet-makers-over-sons-cte-related-death/

51 "Blows not concussion cause brain disease, according to new research," *University of Oxford*, January 18, 2018, accessed September 2, 2018 http://www.ox.ac.uk/news/2018-01-18-blows-not-concussion-cause-brain-disease-according-new-research

52 Patrick Hruby, "New Pop Warner lawsuit raises hard questions about the future of youth tackle football," *Vice Sports*, September 6, 2016 https://sports.vice.com/en_us/article/qkyvmp/new-pop-warner-lawsuit-raises-hard-questions-about-the-future-of-youth-tackle-football

don't risk brain injury! It's not a sprained ankle or sore back. It is un-diagnosable, untreatable, degenerative and real. Would you let your five old son play by an open flame? Who would?

The information on brain damage and neurodegenerative diseases like CTE is public knowledge. Knowledge is power, and that power now lies with parents who will be wise and choose their son's brain health over Saturday afternoon touchdowns and sitting on lawn chairs while their son sustains an injury that will cost him everything.

What do I tell football parents? There are other sports, other activities that build character, but don't lead to traumatic brain injury. How crazy is it, knowing what we do about CTE and other brain damage in NFL players (70 percent of which began their football playing days in Pop Warner according to their website) that we willingly put a hard, heavy plastic helmet on a child and have that child run and crash into another child?[53]

I tell them to ask about the helmet. Does the helmet prevent sub-concussive hits, brain damage and CTE? The answer is no. The helmet prevents a skull fracture. It can't prevent CTE, actually, it increases the risk of brain damage and other injuries. Ask your son's coach, "Does this helmet prevent brain trauma, brain damage and CTE?" All levels of football from the NFL to Pop Warner don't want to hear your question, mama.

When you ask, my guess is you won't get a straight answer or assurance that playing football won't cause brain damage. What does that tell you?

The glory of winning the big game and football parents rallying for their son makes for grand memories, but, factor in sub-concussive hits, brain damage and CTE, the eventual cost of a life cut short by 50 years. No rah, rah now. Your son playing tackle football is traumatizing his brain, your most precious son is being slowly sacrificed for a game.

---

53   "Benefits of Pop Warner," Pop Warner Little Scholars, accessed September 5, 2018 https://www.popwarner.com/Default.aspx?tabid=1463862

"Brain Sloshing"

Our human brains are not designed to sustain traumatic impact. Especially useful, for me, is the visual image of a raw egg being forcibly moved back and forth represents the sloshing movement of your son's brain while taking a blunt trauma hit. How many times can *your* son sustain an injury to his brain? The ongoing hits of a long season football season add up. These sub-concussive hits take their toll on a young developing brain. I recently learned a term Pop Warner's top doctor and head of its Medical Advisory Committee uses to describe what happens to a brain while taking a football hit … "Brain Sloshing."[54] As much as I try to forget that, I won't.

How many sub-concussive hits will it take to get CTE? Scientific research is clear, and trauma to the brain is real. Repetitive hits cause brain damage. There is no cure, no treatment for a young man whose brain damage progresses to the eventual level of CTE.

It's awful to think "the game" that gave Tyler his best childhood memories was also the game that gave him a degenerative disease. How sad that brain damage would lead him to *choose* to take his own life, rather than live with Stage I CTE. Upon reflection, I now say that Tyler didn't choose to end his life, brain damage did.

I think he was too kind to admit to us, his loved ones, how very low his low was. He identified as a warrior. He fought hard, with determination. But his foe was silent, invisible. And undefeated.

The truth is, our Tyler was gone *before* he was gone.

Over the years some very smart people worked on his behalf, but they did not see what the real problem was; they could not see it. "It" was a tangled bunch of tau protein within a brain cell that's only visible under a microscope. I made a point to tell all of the doctors who cared for Tyler that he had brain damage. I thought they had the right to know.

---

54   "Going for the jugular," *SportsCAPP.com*, November 17, 2015, accessed September 6, 2018 http://www. sportscapp.com/tag/slosh-theory

I recently read the transcript of an interview Dr. Omalu gave to PBS, in which he defined CTE: Chronic (ongoing) Traumatic (trauma) Encephalopathy (bad brain).[55]

It was football that did this Tyler. Wake up and get mad mama. I am.

Tyler was so bright. So funny. CTE took that away, like taking his soul. By the end of his short life, my son suffered from brain damage including Stage I CTE. His journey was more brutal than anyone could have imagined. He endured misdiagnosis, side effects of medications, numerous hospitalizations – truly, an utter assault on his life.

Get mad mama.

Why aren't our sons in a coliseum with the lions? What we have here is a blood sport. That's what football is. Annually, we have a quarter million boys, *little boys* playing a violent blood sport that gives them a bad brain.[56]

Get mad mama.

It's an ongoing struggle for me to *not* pull my car over and speak to parents about CTE when I see their 8-year-old sons wearing football gear and playing Pop Warner football in the community park. Brain damage is football's dirty secret.[57] Brain damage is in the light of day. Brain damage took Tyler, just as surely as it took my 32-year marriage.

Still, I will never forget the good times.

---

55   Michael Kirk interview, "League of Denial: Concussion Crisis," *PBS Frontline*, March 25, 2013 accessed November 15, 2018 https://www.pbs.org/wgbh/pages/frontline/sports/league-of-denial/the-frontline-interview-dr-bennet-omalu/

56   Mike Florio, "John Madden doesn't believe in Heads Up football program," *Pro Football Talk, NBC Sports*, August 5, 201, accessed September 6, 2018 https://profootballtalk.nbcsports.com/2014/08/05/john-madden-doesnt-believe-in-the-heads-up-football-program/

57   Jason M. Breslow, "Study of former NFL players shows risks for brain from youth football," *PBS Frontline*, August 12, 2015 https://www.pbs.org/wgbh/frontline/article/study-of-former-nfl-players-shows-risks-for-brain-from-youth-football/

Tyler was 23 when his childhood dog, Lucky, passed away. Tyler asked if we could get a puppy. By this time, my boy had been treated for depression, hospitalized numerous times, had his education disrupted, and lost dear friendships while battling his invisible enemy. The world weighed heavily on him, and his time left with us was short.

But on *this* day, the day we brought home Zooey, a black lab mix, I saw Tyler's essence. He was a grown man by then, but as he got down on the floor, frolicking with his new friend, I clearly saw the little boy he used to be and wished with all my heart he could have a do-over. No meds, no psychiatric hospitals, no derailment. I would later add to the list: No Pop Warner Football and no CTE.[58]

Tyler did everything right in the last six months of his life, but his destiny was no longer in his hands. His father describes the disease that claimed our son – he said this before we knew it was CTE – as "a slow-moving avalanche that finally had its way."

We all loved Tyler. He made us proud and he brought us joy.

NOTHING will ever change that.

---

[58] Tod Leonard, "Moms sue Pop Warner for CTE damage," *San Diego Union-Tribune,* January 28, 2018, accessed September 8, 2018 https://www.sandiegouniontribune.com/sports/sd-sp-moms-sue-pop-warner-for-cte-damage-20180128-story.html

CHAPTER 3

Charles Michael "Mike" Jenkins

March 3, 1966 – May 5, 2011

It seemed as if Mike Jenkins was always a champion. From the time he started playing Pee Wee football for the YMCA Packers in Indianapolis when he was 7 years old, he managed to be on a title-winning team. He had a big role in those wins as the star quarterback for years before switching to tight end in high school. Mike never feared a hard knock and truly earned the nickname of "Crash." That would also be how his life would later go – one big "crash" after another. Despite having a wife and two sons that he adored, Mike turned to alcohol to calm the pounding headaches that made him miserable. At 45 years old, he could take the anguish no more, and on a day when he did a good deed by mowing an ill neighbor's lawn, Mike took his own life. He was diagnosed with chronic traumatic encephalopathy (CTE), and doctors said his brain looked like that of a 75-year-old.

Destructive Crash
By Marcia and Kim Jenkins

Son, brother, husband, dad, grandfather, friend, neighbor, coach, co-worker, caring person. This is who Mike was. How do all of these personalities get lost in depression and alcohol? How do they become scary, unpredictable and toxic? Just the sound of his voice would make us tremble. What awful news would be shared today?

Then there were the rare occasions when small windows of the past open, only narrowly, and we'd see the little boy who fell in love with sports. If it had anything to do with a ball, he was all in.

My son Mike started playing youth football in the early 1970s. He was a natural and assigned the duties of quarterback. He led teams to championship games. Of course, there were bumps and bruises. The occasional "ring of the bell" – oh yes, his brain. *You're fine; shake it off; go get 'em; football players don't cry.* My words, my actions. I lived to watch him play. What kind of mother was I? If I had only known about brain injuries, I wouldn't be sharing all this with you.

The first time I know that Mike suffered a brain injury was when he dove into the shallow end of the community pool. A lifeguard saved him, unconscious, from the water. He awoke with a headache and nausea. The doctor said, "He'll be fine, just wake him periodically in the night." End of story or was it just the beginning?

He played every football season in junior high and high school except one, when he wrecked his mini-bike and tore up his foot. Maybe he had hit his head on the way down? Hmmmm.

When Mike started his football career at Warren Central High School in Indianapolis, I was over the moon. He was playing for my alma mater. By now, his position on the team had shifted from quarterback to tight end. Day after day, week after week, through summer camp and all through the regular season, he gave it his all. Mike would complain about having a "crappy" flu. He had headaches, dizziness and would vomit. What do you think that "crappy flu" was all about?[59] One concussion. Another concussion. The beginning of the darkness. His light was so bright, it blinded me to what had begun the addiction to alcohol. We had no idea. Shame on us.

Face Down in the End Zone

Friday nights were filled with cheers, screams from the bleachers from mom, dad and his girlfriend Kim. So it went to the final game. We dreaded to see it come. What would life be without football? As the final pass was thrown in the pouring rain, it was intended for Mike. The ball was intercepted. I stood there in shock. Just like that, it was over. Mike lay face down in the end zone for what seemed like forever. He got up in the now-silent stadium, took his helmet off for the last time, and walked the length of the field with his head down.

Life went on. Mike asked Kim to marry him. On the day of their wedding, he developed one of his many headaches, but this one was different. It was so bad that his brother Rick almost had to carry him to the shower. Mike was almost 20 minutes late to his wedding, but it was still beautiful. It came and went, but the headache stayed for a year. The doctor called it a cluster migraine with no relief until the sunset. "It probably is just stress, new wife and new responsibilities," the doctor reasoned. Now we ask ourselves, "Was it the beginning of his brain trauma journey?"

The 1990s were life enjoyed to its fullest. Mike and Kim became parents to two amazing sons, Kyle and Nick. There were days filled with work, and evenings and weekends packed with coaching all the boys' sports, from football to baseball

---

59   "It's not simply getting your bell rung," *CBS 4 Denver,* September 12, 2014, accessed September 8, 2018 https://denver.cbslocal.com/2014/09/12/its-not-simply-getting-your-bell-rung/

to soccer. But the addiction to alcohol began weaving a web of confusion and disconnect.

As the years went by, the journey became so hard. Mike worked diligently to hide the addiction, giving way to lies and irresponsible behavior. It was strange, as Mike always cared about people and what mattered.

Destructive

One of the first big changes I saw was his lack of respect for Kim. He'd speak to her in a way no one should speak to someone they loved. When we confronted him, he would say nothing was wrong with his behavior. This was not him.

Mike came to hate holidays. He would say to Kim, "Why can't we have fun like everyone else?" The answer was because we never knew who he would be if we were to join in the fun. It was better to just stay home, and so the isolation continued.

Our son Rick said it was like Mike was building walls around himself. One Memorial Day, he spoke of suicide for the first time and went into rehab for a short period. When he got out he went to meetings, and one time Kim went with him. When the meeting was set to start, the counselor said someone smelled of alcohol. They were going to do a Breathalyzer on everyone, unless the person who had been drinking spoke up. Kim was in total shock when Mike admitted it was him. They were asked to leave the meeting.

The depression increased and his self-esteem floundered. He often asked Kim why she stayed, saying he wasn't worthy of her love. But her support continued to be unwavering. He always said she deserved someone better than him. We always believed he would one day get help and come back to us.

Just seeing his name on the caller ID would make me sick to my stomach. The tornado of addiction to alcohol blew powerful and destructive.

During the times we thought Mike was working a 12-step program, his ability to hide drinking came to a crushing reality. He told Kim he was going to a meeting, but sat in his car drinking. He drank so much he couldn't control his blue Mustang. Blocks from the house, he careened into a ditch, hit a concrete driveway, and totaled his car. Mike suffered a broken back, and when the nurse came in to say his blood alcohol content was five times the legal limit, we were shocked and devastated. He talked to us as if he had never drank a drop. That was normal now.

After much pressure he agreed to get help again. He had a great counselor, and they really clicked. We thought this was finally it. It wasn't, and his disappointment was profound. Kim would hold him while he cried and shared his disappointment in himself. He'd point to his head and say, "Something isn't right in here? Why can't I do this? What is wrong with me?

The family was completely falling apart. Kim became very sick, stricken with meningitis and the West Nile virus. I took Mike to see her at the hospital and brought him home. The next night, he didn't answer the phone. I found him unconscious on the floor, unable to wake him. After he finally came to, I convinced him to go back in for treatment. He called Kim from the intake area saying, "It will be different this time, I know, Babe." He so wanted that to be true. Of course, it was only for a while. Again, disappointment and self-hatred.

In November 2010, Mike's son Kyle was having some personal issues, and his dad couldn't handle it. Kim was working upstairs at home, and when she went downstairs, she found Mike lying on the floor with a bloody slit on one wrist. Luckily, the wound wasn't bad enough to hurt him seriously, and he got stitches. Again he went into rehab, and again in no time he was back to drinking again.

Mike's drinking was so out of control that Kim would have to search the house, garage, and his car constantly to see if he was hiding anything. He never drank in front of Kim or the boys; he'd hide vodka around the house, the garage, even in the engine compartment of his car. He'd put the alcohol in water and Sprite bottles. Most people didn't know he had a drinking problem because he covered it up so well.

In February 2011, Mike fell on the ice while working and slammed the back of his head on the ground. When Kim called to tell me, her words – the words so many of us had heard – was that it was just a "mild" concussion.[60] No worries.

The days and weeks that followed are so confusing, overwhelming and sickening. I'm not sure those are the words to adequately express the ugliness of it for all of us.

Mike went back to driving his semi-truck for work. He tried hard to hide the physical symptoms: headaches, nausea, vomiting, dizziness, vertigo, exhaustion, confusion, etc. We made him go to the doctor. Of course, the doctor said, "Oh, you'll be fine; take it easy; it'll go away." Sound familiar? The same message he was given as a boy. On some weekends, he could hardly make it out of bed.[61]

We were all beside ourselves with worry and frustration. No one was helping. I contacted our niece, Daun Weliever, an Indianapolis attorney, to see if she could help find brain injury specialists. There were none to be found.

One day, Mike returned home early from work. "I just got fired," he said very calmly, almost like he was relieved. There was an emptiness to his eyes that was haunting. When you talked to him, it seemed like the words went right through

---

60   David Menon, "What happens in the brain during a concussion?" *BrainFacts.org*, June 11, 2015 https://www.brainfacts.org/Ask-an-Expert/What-happens-in-the-brain-during-and-after-a-concussion

61   Mayo Clinic https://www.mayoclinic.org/diseases-conditions/chronic-traumatic-encephalopathy/symptoms-causes/syc-20370921

him. The physical symptoms continued. The father and coach who never – never! – missed a game, could no longer leave the house.

It is now March 2011. Kim and I went to the theatre for a much-needed escape. When she arrived home she found what she couldn't have expected – the remains of a father-and-son relationship destroyed.

Mike and Nick had gone out to eat at a restaurant, and Mike got into an argument and nearly a fistfight with another guest over putting his peanut shells on the floor (which is common at this restaurant). The manager made them leave. On the drive home, Nick cried and told Mike that he had always wanted to grow up to be just like his dad, but not anymore. He told him he was nothing but an alcoholic. Mike responded like it was nothing and he didn't do anything wrong. You would never have known that Nick had said the things he did, because it was like Mike didn't even hear it.

In the midst of all this ugliness, a small, tiny new light came into the world. Kyle's daughter, Jayda, was born. She would sleep peacefully on Mike's chest next to his heart. He called her his little JJ. It was a bond that would give Mike the joy he hadn't known for a long time.

Close to Easter, we had the occasion for just the four of us – mom, dad and our two grown boys – to go out to dinner. It was good to be just "us." We actually laughed and shared family stories. Mike volunteered to drive home, but halfway there, he didn't know where we were. He had driven those same streets all of his life.

Someone told me to check into traumatic brain injury (TBI).[62] I went online and there it was. Everything he had was right there. Maybe there would be hope. We coaxed him to see the doctor, who checked him again and said he could order a CT scan. "But, Mr. Jenkins," he said, "your problem is your drinking." Feeling defeated, we left, but I still had hope.

On May 5, 2011, Mike came to do some work at our home. Kim was helping out at the school's concession stand. We were away that morning, and Mike called his dad to say there was a man lying in the yard. While still on the phone, he asked, "Are you OK buddy?" Mike then said the man got up and walked down the road. To this day, I don't believe there was anyone there.

After doing some chores for our neighbors, Mike went home and called Kim to see if she wanted him to take the turkey out of the freezer, so they could cook it for Mother's Day. He asked if she needed help with the concession stand. There was nothing out of the ordinary. He sounded just fine. But something was going on in his brain.

"It's Over"

When Kim got home, she couldn't find Mike. She went to see if he was fishing in the pond behind the house, but he wasn't. She went into the master bedroom and happened to look into their closet. There, the storm had come to rest.

There he was, the former light of our world, quiet, still, on his knees, hanging from the clothes rack. Kim got him down and started screaming. Kyle came running to see what was wrong. Kim called 911 while Kyle started CPR. It was

---

62   Brian Resnick, "What a lifetime of playing football can do to the human brain," *Vox*, April 30, 2018, accessed September 8, 2018 https://www.vox.com/science-and-health/2018/2/2/16956440/concussion-symptoms-cte-football-nfl-brain-damage-youth

6:40 p.m. where I was, and in an unexplained tremble, I had to grab a chair. I know that was when he left.

Nick attempted to get home, but the street was lined with emergency vehicles. He asked a neighbor what was going on. He was told the emergency was at his house. He doesn't remember much more after that.

Kim called our son Rick to tell him the news. He arrived later, but there was nothing to be said or done. "It's over." Those were the words he used as he and Krissy came in the door at 10:40 p.m. I don't remember much after that.

How do you pick up the pieces? What will the world be like without him? Then the relief comes, a peace no one should ever try to describe. It was over. No more dreading, wondering about "what" and "when." The disease won.

Early the next morning, our niece Daun called and said, "Aunt Marcia, have you heard about the concussion study?" She told us that she had spoken to the brain bank about its CTE studies, and if Kim and the family consented, Mike's brain could be part of that work.

"Oh my God, yes!" was my response.

Everything was arranged. Off to the brain bank went the puzzle of Mike's life after all the information was taken. The team explained it would be six months before we would have a conference call. The days following were filled with hope, confusion and anxiety.

In November 2011, it was time for the call. Kim, the boys and her family, Jack, Rick and I, as well as Daun, were all on the line.

This is part of what was shared: The neuropathologist said Mike's 45-year-old brain looked like that of a 75-year-old. She reported he lost almost 25 percent of his brain matter. There was evidence of multiple brain injuries.

The Answer

There it was, the answer to all of the questions. The peace was overwhelming. If only he could have known that he was right all along. There was something wrong, something that could not be healed.

Mike's light lives on in his sons and his granddaughter, who knew him and says he was funny.

Up to the last moments of his life, he was still doing for others, making a difference in a way he could never imagine.

As you read these words, be kind to yourself and those you love, because you may never know what you don't know.

He didn't make a big step onto the fields of the NFL, but in the climb of life, Mike was a winner.

CHAPTER 4

Joseph Chernach

July 11, 1986 – June 6, 2012

As a leader in life and sports, Joseph Chernach could light up a room with his personality and sense of humor. On the field and playgrounds, he had a never-quit attitude and was a fierce competitor. He played football from 11 years old through his senior year of high school, and despite all the hard hits he took and delivered, Joseph never once was diagnosed with a concussion or any other head injuries in sports. It was after high school that he began a spiral downward into despair and hopelessness. Joseph died by suicide when he was only 25 years old and was later found to have Stage II chronic traumatic encephalopathy (CTE). His mother has since been on a mission to educate other parents on the dangers of football while also being an advocate for brain donation.

"Look at me Mom, I have nothing"
By Debra Pyka

When he was only 11 days old, my son Joseph had to undergo surgery for pyloric stenosis, a rare condition that blocks food from entering the small intestine.

While he was recovering in his hospital room, I left him for only 30 minutes. When I came back, I was shocked to see him gone and the nurses removing the sheets from his bed. I immediately started to cry, wondering if my son died while I was gone. The nurses were there to reassure me that he was fine and had moved to another room.

This was the most horrible feeling I ever had until June 7, 2012, when my worst nightmare became reality. That's the day Joseph took his own life.[63]

Joseph was 25 years old and had suffered for years with depression and hopelessness. I came to expect something tragic to happen, but a parent never really can accept the possibility of their child dying before them.

The following account is graphic and devastating for anyone to read or imagine, and I do remember all of it like it was yesterday.

---

63   Lindsey Adler, "Youth football, brain disease, and the suicide of 25-year-old man," *BuzzFeed News*, December 6, 2014, accessed January 18, 2019 https://www.buzzfeednews.com/article/lindseyadler/youth-football-brain-disease-suicide

Months before Joseph's death, I stood in his room begging him to see a doctor. I made an appointment, but he refused to go. He got angry and said, "Look at me Mom, I have nothing."

I told him, "You have your family; we all love you; we'll get you back into school and you'll get back on your feet."

No reply.

I said, "You are not going to die before me."

No reply, only a blank stare looking right through me. It was the strangest look I had ever seen.

This was the moment I realized my son was going to die, and I felt helpless. He wouldn't listen to me. Little did I know at the time his brain was being destroyed by chronic traumatic encephalopathy (CTE). No matter how much I tried to help him, I really don't think he could comprehend anything.[64]

I couldn't get mad at him, I knew he was suffering, and I believed I could fix it. How wrong I was. There were days I begged him to get out of bed and go to work. I didn't want him to lose another job. He couldn't even handle a job, but he did try.

Joseph had no hope, only thoughts of dying. Depression, anger, hopelessness and paranoid/suicidal thoughts plagued him. The note he left is one that I will never fully disclose. In it he said he felt abandoned by all. It's heartbreaking for all of us to know that he left this earth feeling that no one cared. Yet we know that his brain was not functioning normally at the end.[65]

Joseph graduated from Forest Park High School in Crystal Falls, Michigan, with high honors. During his years in elementary, middle and high school he participated in many sports, including wrestling, track, baseball, basketball and

---

64 Nadia Kounaug, "Five things to know about CTE," *CNN,* April 26, 2017, accessed September 9, 2018 https://www.cnn.com/2016/02/04/health/5-things-to-know-about-cte/index.html

65 Adam Carlson, "Former football players' suicides tied to concussions," *Atlanta Journal-Constitution,* updated, December 1, 2014, accessed September 10, 2018 https://www.ajc.com/news/former-football-players-suicides-tied-to-concussions/cudUjIuE1rqvKNcpE4HQTI/

football. These sports started at an early age – wrestling and baseball when he was 6, and football at 11. He was an MVP in wrestling and football in high school, and was named the top senior athlete.

Joseph was never diagnosed with a brain injury in sports and never complained of any of the symptoms associated with one. He did have one brain injury in college that wasn't sports related.

His life started to fall apart after high school graduation. His grades in college declined from the first year, as he skipped classes and eventually was suspended. He later enrolled in the local community college, but he again didn't attend classes regularly and eventually quit going. When I questioned him about his grades and why he quit school, his reply was, "Don't worry about it."

I noticed the symptoms of his decline a few years after high school graduation. I thought his depression was the result of all the problems he had in college and feeling like a failure. I never saw him smile the last few years before his death. I had no idea his brain was destroyed before he graduated from high school.[66]

The night of June 6, 2012, Joseph walked out the door of our home and down the long driveway. This wasn't unusual for him to go out for walks, especially when he was angry or upset. When he didn't return after two hours, I tried calling his cellphone, but got no answer. I kept calling, and at some time after midnight I got a recording that the minutes had expired on his Tracfone. I tried calling again, praying the message had been a mistake. But I got the same response. There was no way to reach him.

After a fitful night on the couch, I got up at 6 in the morning and started calling family to see if Joseph had contacted anyone. No one had heard from him. He didn't show up for work either. I asked my daughter and Joseph's half-sister, Nicole, who was 16 at the time, to drive us around to see if we could find him. I remember the car moving down the driveway and me looking in the trees. Thoughts of him hanging already were in my mind.

We drove through the countryside with no success. My husband Fred came home before noon and we sent Nicole on an errand. Fred then went to the shed at the back of the house. When he came back, I knew something was wrong because he was walking rapidly down the hallway. "Call 911," he told me.

I ran out to the shed. The door was open, and I fell back against the wall in shock. My son was hanging from the rope around his neck. I knew he had been dead from the previous night.[67]

"Joseph, no; Joseph, no."

Devastation and sadness took over as I held my son. My husband took me back into the house, and within a few minutes, my son Seth, who is a year younger than Joseph, called. He heard Joseph was missing and wondered if we knew

---

66   Nicole Wetsman, "We have no idea how dangerous football really is," *Popular Science,* February 2, 2018, accessed September 8, 2018 https://www.popsci.com/how-dangerous-is-football-cte

67   Sports Court, *Fox News,* accessed January 18, 2019 https://video.foxnews.com/v/4724240135001/#sp=-show-clips

anything. I had to tell him that his brother was dead. Seth didn't believe me, so I told him again. I told him to find his older brother Tyler, and Jeff, their dad and my ex-husband. I went back to the shed to hold my son until the first responders came. They had to pull me away from Joseph. I kept repeating, "Joseph, no; Joseph, no."

The phone calls started. First, Joseph's dad. Then Tyler, who asked me to send his brother's brain to a brain bank. I had no idea at the time why. Nicole was kept from the house because we didn't want to expose her to such a tragic scene. The coroner arrived, and I requested that Joseph's brain be examined in an autopsy. In September 2012, tissue samples were forwarded to be studied. We waited a year for the results.

I was curious when Tyler gave me an explanation of the recent deaths of former NFL players. What an eerie feeling I had, remembering that Joseph watched the live news reports on the day that retired NFL Hall of Famer Junior Seau, who was later diagnosed with CTE, died from suicide on May 12, 2012. Less than a month later, Joseph was gone.

Joseph was born to his dad, Jeff, and me on July 11, 1986, in Lansing, Michigan. Jeff and I divorced when Joseph was 6 years old. It was difficult for Joseph. He would stay up at night, crying and wondering why we weren't together. He'd later come to understand that the relationship simply didn't work out.

When Joseph was 11 and Tyler 13, they went to live with their dad in Michigan after my dad was diagnosed with a terminal illness, and I moved in to take care of him. Seth, our youngest, was 10 when he also moved to Michigan. The boys came to stay with me during the summer and attended school in the Upper Peninsula of Michigan.

Some of the greatest memories all of us have are of Joseph and his brothers playing sports through high school. Joseph's close family and friends would tell you he also was quite the comedian. He could light up a room and put a smile on your face, no matter the mood you were in. He was compassionate and always willing to hear your story and to be there for you. It would be very hard to find anybody who had anything negative to say about Joseph. A protective brother, he would jokingly tell Nicole to bring her boyfriend over so he could put the fear of God into him.

Joseph was also a leader in life and in sports. No matter what the circumstances, he'd fight to the end and never give up, no matter the score. His accomplishments speak for themselves, but they don't tell you how much of a fighter he really was. The brotherly bond shared was very strong. We think about him every day and will never forget him. He will live with our family forever. We hope one day we can provide more help for people who suffer as Joseph did. To have him gone is beyond tragic.

Donating Joseph's brain was an important decision in finding out what caused his severe depression and suicide. The thought of an autopsy made me sick, knowing every organ would be dissected. I also was afraid of seeing him in an open casket at his funeral if there were rope marks on his neck. When that day came, there were no visible marks on his body.

We decided to have two services – one in Wisconsin, followed by the final funeral and burial in Michigan. Having two services was exhausting and almost unbearable. I felt nauseated and faint throughout, and I experienced daily panic attacks and months of crying. I was more worried about my kids than my own health, because at that point I didn't care if I died along with my son.

Friends and family were stunned and devastated to lose Joseph. It was apparent how much he was loved by the overwhelming outpouring of people at his funeral and the sympathies sent to us. On June 12, 2012, we laid him to rest at Evergreen Memorial Cemetery in Crystal Falls.

In the days and weeks following Joseph's death, I began researching CTE and was stunned to realize he had most of the brain damage symptoms associated with CTE: depression, mood issues, anger, hopelessness, lack of empathy, paranoia, suicidal thoughts and withdrawal from friends and family. Although we waited for the diagnosis that came in September 2013, I was convinced they would find that Joseph had CTE.

We were all shocked by the severity and damage to his brain. In Joseph's CTE results, the most abundant tau was found in the cerebral cortex, with neurofibrillary tangles found in the thalamus, hypothalamus, and substantia nigra. There were dense tangles found in the locus coeruleus.

After receiving the diagnosis of Joseph's brain autopsy, I began writing letters to Congress. I was concerned with children playing tackle football. I didn't want another family to suffer.

I searched for more than a year and contacted close to 30 attorneys in regard to filing a wrongful death lawsuit. No one would take the case. I was about to give up when I read a story quoting Gordon Johnson, an attorney from the Brain Injury Law Group in Sheboygan, Wisconsin. I contacted them and they took my case! I was relieved that someone would finally help and listen to me.

Nearly three years after my son's death, we filed a lawsuit in February 2015 against Pop Warner, and the media came rushing to my door.[68] In pursuing the case, I knew I would be crucified by the public and those who loved the sport. As the news broke, I faced unimaginable anger and hate. On social media, I

---

68   Ken Belson, "Family sues Pop Warner over suicide of player who had brain disease," *New York Times*, February 5, 2015, accessed January 19, 2019 https://www.nytimes.com/2015/02/06/sports/family-of-player-with-cte-who-killed-himself-sues-pop-warner.html

was told that I should kill myself. I was called a greedy bitch, worthless mother, killer, and abuser. I was roasted for trying to get justice for my dead son, and for bringing awareness to the dangers of what could happen to other children.

It was a difficult time for our family as we went through hell – grieving and devastated while being trolled and criticized by the football-loving community. We also had the support of many, those who believed the science and had suffered as we had with their own losses of loved ones to brain injury. In March 2016, the lawsuit against Pop Warner was resolved and dismissed with prejudice.[69]

Brain Injuries and Brain Banks

I began connecting with other families. As a result, many of us joined together with a group of NFL athletes to meet in Washington, D.C., during "Brain Injury Awareness Day." We formed the group "Save Your Brain" and meet each year with members of Congress. We met with the D.C. medical examiner's office and agreed that more brains needed to be donated and studied for us to better understand how dangerous collision sports can be, as well as those brain injuries suffered by those serving the military.

After I read about the Mayo Clinic Brain Bank, a group of us from Child Athlete Advocates traveled to the Mayo Clinic in Jacksonville, Florida, for a tour and to watch the autopsy of brains. We made plans then to collaborate with the Mayo Clinic for brain donations, which generally does not solicit for brains. For the past two years I have asked for the donation of approximately 100 brains. I most often speak with the medical examiners or coroners, but the most difficult calls are to families who are in shock and grieving.

The most publicized result of my calls followed the suicide death in January 2018 of Tyler Hilinski, a 21-year-old quarterback at Washington State. After hearing about Tyler's death, I contacted the medical examiner's office and coordinated his brain donation to the Mayo Brain Bank.

---

69   Ken Belson, "Pop Warner settles lawsuit over player who had CTE," *New York Times*, March 9, 2016, accessed January 19, 2019 https://www.nytimes.com/2016/03/10/sports/football/pop-warner-settles-lawsuit-over-player-who-had-cte.html

In June 2018, Tyler's parents, Mark and Kym Hilinski, appeared on the *Today* show to announce that the Mayo Clinic found CTE in Tyler's brain. Mark Hilinski said doctors told him their son had the brain of a 65-year-old.

"He was the sweetest, most outgoing, giving kid," Mark Hilinski said. "That was difficult to hear."[70]

A Warning to Parents

Six years have passed since Joseph's death and we are all still struggling with it. I have many regrets to this day. I feel that I failed my son. If I could turn back time, I would have followed him out the door the night he left for the last time.

As we look back on Joseph's Facebook page, we only see the smiles and his love for life. This is how we need to remember the son, brother, uncle, cousin, nephew and friend who was taken away from us too early.

What I have to give after Joseph's death is to warn parents on the dangers of collision sports. These sports are not character-building. My son's character was destroyed. He never had a chance. From the first impact his fate was sealed.

I'm waiting for the time when we will be together again, and I look forward to his smiling face. Grief is exhausting and devastating. I don't want any parent to suffer like our family, or a child to go through what Joseph did. The biggest regret in my life is letting my three sons play tackle football. I would have said no, knowing what I know now.

Today, I would tell parents, "Please don't let your young child play collision sports. The repetitive hits will cause brain damage, and your child needs his or her brain for a bright future. No parent should have to bury their child and stand above the grave, shedding tears of sadness and regret."

---

70   Scott Stump, "Parents of college quarterback Tyler Hilinski reveal son had CTE when he died by suicide," *Today,* June 26, 2018, accessed September 10, 2018 https://www.today.com/health/college-football-player-tyler-hilinski-who-died-suicide-had-cte-t131843

CHAPTER 5

Cody Hamblin

June 2, 1993 – May 29, 2016

Cody Hamblin was a reluctant football star. From the time he scored all of his team's touchdown in his first youth football season, Cody was a popular and dominant player. For years before high school in his native Ohio, he was in on almost every play on offense and defense, constantly delivering the most violent hits a 50-pound child could. But, the kind, goofy kid who wasn't shy about asking for pink casts on his legs also showed an introverted side. Through all of his high school years, Cody's letterman's jacket stayed hanging in the closet. It was as if he didn't want to call attention to his achievements. Cody had a football career of incredible highs marred by a constant string of injuries: the dying of bones in his knees; a herniated disc; two broken feet; and a brain injury that wiped out his memory of an entire high school game. Cody was tough, but he couldn't overcome the unseen damage to his brain. Cody struggled with the use of drugs and alcohol, and just as it seemed his life might be turning for the better, at the age of 22, Cody suffered a seizure while standing on a boat, speaking to his mom on his cell phone. He tipped into the water and drowned as his grandfather watched in horror. Months later, a brain study confirmed that Cody was suffering from chronic traumatic encephalopathy (CTE), and in May 2018, Cody's father, Darren Hamblin, became the first youth parent to file a lawsuit against helmet makers Riddell and Schutt. In December 2018, Ohio Governor John Kasich signed "Cody's Law," which designates Jan. 30 as CTE Awareness Day in the state.

"Look, Man, I Don't Know What the Hell Is Going On With You"

By Darren Hamblin

All right. I want to handle this the way I really don't want to handle it. I don't want to say stuff that could change the legacy or the memory of my son, Cody, but I'm going to because I'm hoping that possibly it might help somebody down the line.

This story is about the things that I feel so much guilt about, and about things that we missed, and things that we could've done differently. We always make excuses for our family, right?

So, in Cody, we had this bubbly, funny, zany, goofy kid. Loving as can be. He wasn't a person who was a fighter or mean or anything like that. He was this amazing athlete, the star of his sports teams since he was little.

In his sophomore year of high school, his personality began to change. The outgoing, silly boy became introverted. He still had fun, don't get me wrong. He had girlfriends, and friends, and did all the things a typical teenager does.

But things start happening completely out of the blue, and out of character for Cody.

In his sophomore year of high school, I got a call on a Saturday morning that Cody was picked up for shoplifting. The police said he stole a wallet from a store at the mall. Our kids have never wanted for anything. If Cody needed a wallet, he'd get a wallet. We spoiled our kids like a lot of people do. We didn't hold back anything.

So I just remember talking to him about it, and usually, he would never try to make excuses. He took total responsibility for everything he did until the day he died. But I remember looking him in the eyes and saying, "Cody, why would you do this?" That was the first time I remember looking through him, seeing through him. He didn't have an answer. I could tell he didn't know why he did it. I could just see that deep within his soul that he didn't know. He took responsibility and the punishment, but he couldn't figure out why he did it. It was just such a weird situation.

Later, after the football season started, we got a call at 11 at night from a police officer in another city. He said he'd pulled Cody over for swerving, and Cody told him it was because he was looking at his phone for directions. But they also found an unopened malt liquor can in the trunk of his car. Cody said a friend had thrown it in there, and they eventually let him go.

Then, still that night, Cody had the nerve to ask me if he could stay over at a friend's house because they're going to a campfire. I told him to get his butt home, and though he was argumentative with me, he agreed.

A while later, we get another call from the police telling us that Cody drove off the road. He said he'd fallen asleep. The officer checked him out to ensure he was not under the influence of anything and released him to go.

That always stuck with me. It's just so weird for a young guy who's in the best shape of his life for that to happen to him. Two police officers checked him in the same night.

Around this time I noticed that Cody's speech was changing. I had a hard time understanding him. It used to drive me crazy. I'd said, "Cody, could you please quit being a lazy talker." I just attributed it to him trying to be cool or something. I think now that maybe it had something to do with brain damage. A doctor would need to tell me that, but it's just one of those things that I look back on now.

All through school, Cody never had emotional problems with his girlfriends or friends. He never shed a tear over a girl. He was very cool about it. He never argued. Then he went to college with his high school sweetheart, and he just started falling apart. He'd call us, say that his girlfriend ditched him. He'd call his mom, bawling and really upset.

I said, "Cody, what is wrong with you, man? Get ahold of yourself. Who cares? It's fine." So that was another thing that I look back on now saying, "What is this trigger? What happened?"

His girlfriend did break up with him, and Cody came home. He was working but was still hung up on this girl, and we get a call from her mom, saying "Cody's threatening suicide." It was the first time we'd ever heard of him saying such a thing.

Now, I suspected he might feel that way, talking to him before when he was so emotional. I asked him, "Dude, are you all right? Are you fine? You're not thinking about hurting yourself?" He said, "No, Dad, I'm just really upset."

He was in a really bad place. Really bad. He let it be known that he was going to kill himself. So we took him and had him committed that night to psychiatric care. Come to find out; he'd been using some drugs — another red flag moment. Following that, he got clean and seemed to be doing fine.

We met up at our daughter's house somewhere around Easter of 2016. It was all of the family, and Cody came in and was not acting right. I didn't know if he was on something or drunk. He admitted he'd been drinking, and I got really fed up with him and said, "Look, man, I don't know what the hell is going on with you, but here's what's going to happen. I'm going to come to Ohio University and have you tested for drugs. I'm going to take you personally to a hospital. We're not going to buy an over-the-counter test. If I find you're back doing drugs and stuff, we're bringing you home. You're not going to school anymore. We'll cut all that out until you're right."

A week or two later, I went to OU and took him to a testing place, and everything came back negative. No drugs. That's when I told him, "Sometimes you act like you're perfect, and other times I don't understand what's going on with you." He's said, "Yeah, I don't either sometimes, Dad."[71]

Around that same time my wife, Heather, and I were looking to buy an RV. We wanted to start going camping, take the kids with us, do some more family stuff like that. We found one, and I asked Cody to help me pick it up. We drove out there together, and he and I had a great time. We played music and were singing, which we never did. It was a great moment for me.

The happiness didn't last long. The week before Cody died, my wife got a call from him in jail. He said he'd been arrested for public intoxication, and they found drugs in the cruiser when they arrived at the station. He was telling us he needed help. They were not his, so they must have been the guy he was out with. He was distraught. I was beside myself. Then he called back an hour later to say that everything was okay and he was released. The guy he was with finally admitted the drugs were his.

Heather said she was going to see him and asked if I wanted to go. I said, "Hell no." I was so mad at him; I thought he might be doing drugs again. My wife got an over-the-counter kit, tested him, and Cody was clean. That was a total relief to me. I felt bad thinking that way about him.

Something Happened to Cody

May 29th we're sitting on our friend's deck on a really nice day. Cody called. I answer Heather's phone, "Hey, Cody, what's going on?" Not much, he said. I kind of pushed him off because I know when the kids call they only want to talk to their mom. So he's talking to Heather, just usual chit-chat. He and his grandpa were out on the boat fishing.

All of a sudden, Heather is saying, "Cody, Cody, Cody." She said, "Something happened to Cody. Something happened to him." I'm confused not fully under-standing what was going on. She said, "He all of a sudden quit talking. I think something happened."

---

71   Dr. Mike Brooks, "Is football causing CTE?" *APA Center*, October 16, 2017, accessed September 12, 2018 https://www.apacenter.com/is-football-causing-cte/

So I grabbed the phone. I'm listening, and I can hear Heather's dad tell someone that Cody is young and a good swimmer. I think Cody has probably gone in the water to rescue somebody. Then I hear her dad say, "Yeah, he just fell over, and he never came back up."

I'm on this phone, and after a few minutes, I could hear her dad talking to somebody, describing Cody.[72] That's when I knew: "Cody died. Cody's dead." Of course, her dad doesn't know that Cody's phone's there, because he actually jumped in the water after him. I couldn't listen anymore because I knew my son was gone. I hung up the phone.

We were trying to call Cody's girlfriend, who was there at the lake. We lost all communication. Nobody would answer, and nobody would call us, so we knew what happened. We got on the road. We couldn't drive, so a friend drove us. It's a three-hour trip.

Finally, we get ahold of his girlfriend. She had been asleep in the cabin. We told her we thought something happened to Cody, and she said, "Yeah, there's a helicopter and stuff." She hung up the phone to find out what was going on.

By this time we've called our daughter to let her know. We got ahold of somebody who said they were taking Cody to Miami Valley Hospital. We stopped there and went to the emergency room. But Cody wasn't there. The staff there made a call and said, "Yeah, he's at the coroner's, and you can't go over there."

So we ended up going home and waiting. It was crazy, unbelievable and surreal! I wouldn't wish that on anybody!

The events of that day are still the hardest to talk about and even think about.

This is what happened, from Heather's dad's point of view: Cody was standing up in the boat, had his phone crocked in his ear, on his shoulder. He had a cast out on the fishing pole; the line was in the water; he was talking to his mother on the phone. All of a sudden, Cody's arms go straight out in front of him, he kind

---

72   "University mourns geography student who drowned on Sunday," *College of Arts & Sciences Forum,* Ohio University, accessed September 16, 2018 https://www.ohio-forum.com/2016/06/university-mourns-geography-student-drowned-sunday/

of shook, everything dropped, and Cody went straight over the boat into the water. He said he didn't fight. He said there wasn't a single bubble that came up.

He said he was gone. He said, "He went over into the water, and that was it."

Cody's grandpa jumped in after him and, of course, couldn't find him. It's kind of muddy water. He said Cody didn't fight. Cody's grandpa was convinced Cody had a seizure, which would later be confirmed by the medical examiners. A key piece of their evidence was that Cody bit right through his tongue.

It took the police 40 minutes to find Cody in the water. He was, I guess, stuck on the bottom, but they pulled him up. Heather's dad said he heard the chopper fire up and they said, "We got a pulse, we're taking him." The chopper was getting ready to take off, but 30 seconds later, the engine shut off.

They said, "We lost him."

We were at home with family and, obviously, it was a trying time. We were trying to add everything up in our minds. We'd never seen the movie "Concussion," believe it or not. I didn't know much about it, other than what I'd heard on the TV and radio. I started thinking, well, there is the movie, and Heather's dad said that when they were on that boat that day, Cody was talking to him about brain injuries. He told his grandfather that he felt he had effects from them.

He really did say that.

We later found out that he had also been talking to his girlfriend about feeling like he was having effects of CTE.

Then I start adding up all this zany behavior. I went online and did research. My reaction: Wow. A lot of Cody's stuff is what they see in people with CTE. So I called the coroner. "Are you guys going to check his brain for anything?" They said no. I told them to hold off, and I called Cincinnati Children's Hospital for advice. I end up getting a call back within an hour from North Shore in Chicago, which had done numerous brain examinations. They asked me a lot of questions about Cody and said they would like to examine his brain.

Four months later, we got the results back. They said Cody had three areas of distinct brain damage, and that he suffered from Stage I-II CTE.[73]

At that point, we didn't know what to do, honestly. I wanted to get the word out because I wanted people to realize what had happened. I'm not a social media guy, but my daughter got me on Cody's account, and I posted something. I don't remember exactly what I said, but it was something like, "Look, it's come to light that he had CTE and I think it was caused by youth football. Maybe you guys will think about this when you have young kids. Think about what could happen."

Cody was athletic out of the womb. He started walking when he was nine months old. Heather, my wife, and I would be in the living room while the kids were napping. We'd hear a big thump on the floor, and all of a sudden here comes little Cody, smiling, walking down the hall. "How did get out of your crib?"

I hid in his room one day when Heather put him down for his nap. We knew he was jumping out of his crib, and I'm thinking he's going to get hurt. So I sit there, and I watch him get up, and he actually reached over the crib and grabbed hold of one of the bars, and flipped out. He flipped over the edge and landed on his feet and walked down the hall. It was the most amazing thing.

At a very young age, we played Whiffle ball with him, and he just loved it. He loved anything to do with any kind of ball. He'd go to bed and have all of his balls with him: soccer ball, baseball, football.

I started playing baseball with him and before he was in kindergarten. He was throwing overhand and catching. I had already gotten him his own little aluminum bat. I could pitch to him overhand, and he could hit. He could catch. He could throw.

Things progress to the next year when he was finally able to play on a rec team. He played in Miamisburg on a Tee-ball team and in West Carrollton on a

---

73   Jordan Bowen, "Seizure, CTE contributes to former Miamisburg football player's drowning death," January 12, 2017, updated January 22, 2017, accessed January 20, 2019 https://www.google.com/amp/s/www.wdtn.com/amp/news/seizure-cte-contributes-to-former-miamisburg-football-players-drowning-death/1003267490

coach-pitch team at the same time. He was the youngest kid on the coach pitch team by two grades and he, lo and behold, made the All-Star team and the whole nine yards. He was an excellent baseball player. He wanted to practice all of the time. He loved it.

In first grade, Cody started hanging around some kids in our neighborhood and a few of their older brothers. There was a guy I knew from high school, and his son was Cody's age. The summer after first grade, the dad came to me and asked if Cody played football. I said no. (He was playing soccer along with baseball.) The dad said, "Well, he should play football." I asked why. "Because he is incredible. He can run, he can throw. He's amazing."

Heather and I discussed it. We actually did talk to a doctor because I never played, and Heather was pretty nervous about it. The doctor said, "Most of the time in football, injuries happen after they start going through puberty. The younger kids don't run fast or hit hard enough to really cause any damage with all the equipment. I don't see any reason shouldn't play."

So we let him play.

In Cody's first game ever, he scored one or two touchdowns. From that time forward, baseball was a distant second sport for him. Football just charged him up so much. I can't tell you how excited he was to play football after that.

As a matter of fact, in his first season, Cody was the only kid on his team to score a touchdown. He had 18 of them. He was the only person the coaches gave the ball to, and a lot of parents were upset. Of course, he also played on defense because he was the fastest kid on the team. So he played the entire game, non-stop. Parents, coaches, kids – they couldn't believe what they were seeing.

In my mind, football was about exercise. For both our kids – our daughter, Heidi, played soccer through high school. I said, "You guys just need to continue just to do stuff, just keep active."

We had a pull-up bar hanging in a door frame, and I told Cody that every time he walked by the door, he should do ten pull-ups to make him a better, stronger football player. I don't know how many he did, but every time he walked through the hallway he would jump up there and do ten pull-ups. We did the same thing with sit-ups and push-ups. When he got to maybe nine years old, he kept a log of how many he did, and he'd do 100 of each almost every day.

He was motivated to be a better football player. He loved to hit, and he loved tackling. I would say more than anything he loved running the ball, and he would lower the boom on kids. Even back on his Pee Wee Vikings teams when he was going to get tackled, he would take it to them. It wasn't easy to tackle him.

At that time, we had no concerns about him playing football. But here's where things get a little weird.

A friend that I went to school with at West Carrollton, his son played on Cody's third-grade team. He came up to me one day and said, "You might not believe what I'm about to tell you because Cody's in such good shape, and he's such a good athlete. But it's not good for a kid to play as many plays as he does. I played football and baseball in college, and I'm telling you if a kid plays as much as he does, it could cause some injury."

I didn't know what to say, because I was never in this situation. I just told Cody, "If you ever want to take a break, make sure you tell the coach. He said he would, but he never feels like he needs a break! That conversation now haunts me!

In Miamisburg, the youth football teams practice every day except Saturday and Sunday. So the kids would practice two hours in the evening, Monday through Thursdays, and sometimes on Fridays too. They'd play their games on Saturday, and Sunday was a rest day. Leading up to the season, we practiced six, eight weeks before the first game. They did a lot of hitting and a lot of running and a lot of drills. These are kids; I'm talking little kids.

The Bones Dying

Cody started complaining of his knee hurting. Our fifth-grade team was scrimmaging a sixth-grade team, and, of course, the sixth-grade kids were really trying to put it to the younger kids. Cody came over to me during the game and said,

"My knee is hurting me." He pointed to his kneecap. You know, dumb dad, I said, "Well, that doesn't seem like it's a ligament or anything. That might be growing pains or something, Cody. I don't know." I told him, "If you need to sit out, sit out," and he did. The next week was their first game of the season. He started the game then sat out for a couple of plays, and he got up. He's on the sideline all itching to run. He tells the coach, "I feel better," and they put him back in for a few plays, but then he was out the rest of the game. He said his knee hurts too much.

That night we went out to dinner, and we're walking to the table, and he falls. He just falls on the ground like his leg just went out from under him. His mother and I look at each other, like, "Holy crap, this isn't good."

So we end up taking him to an orthopedic doctor, and they say he has a condition called osteochondritis dissecans. He had it in both knees. In an X-ray, if you looked at the top of his femur, where the bones underneath the kneecap, it looked like a bite had been taken out of both of them. The doctor said, "That's the bones dying. That's dead bone tissue."

It was bad. The doctor said Cody would have to stop playing football. The condition, he said, had something to do with continuously hitting the same spot over and over again.

We got a second opinion from a pediatrician who said to let him play, which we didn't think sounded right, so we looked for a third opinion. Then we found a doctor at Cincinnati Children's Hospital who had written a paper on the condition. This doctor examined him, and she said, "This is bad. You guys need to get this taken care of right away, or he could be in the wheelchair by the time he's 40 years old." Both knees need to be operated on at the same time.

She drilled right through the cartilage in his knees, got the blood blow going, and the surgery was considered a success. On both legs, Cody was in a cast from his crotch down to his toes. He was in a wheelchair. He had to do schoolwork at home.

When he finally got everything off, the physical therapist said, "Okay, I don't know if they told you this or not, but when you have both legs operated on at the same time, it's like a computer being reset. The brain doesn't remember how to use the legs." He said, "He will have to relearn to walk," and he did, using a walker commonly needed by elderly people.

Fast forward, and now we're between sixth and seventh grade. Of course, football season's coming back around. This is Cody's first year of junior high. So Cody and I talked, and I said, "Cody, I don't think it's a good idea for you to play football." Of course, he wanted to play. I said, "Look, man, you just had operations on both of your knees. You don't even know if you can run, especially carrying a football and stuff." I said, "Let's just wait another year, okay?" He was like, "Okay, Dad."

About a week goes by, and Cody mentions something about football practice. I asked him what that was about, and he said he signed up. I went to his mother and asked her what was going on. Heather said, "Well, he came to me. He said he really wants to play. They're not going to start him anyways; he won't play."

You know how dads are. I said, "Whatever."

At that point, I went to any practice I could. I knew the coach personally from work. I wanted to go there and make my case. I told him about Cody's injuries and said, "I don't care if you play him at all." He goes, "We'll see what happens." The boys at that age chose what position they wanted to try out for, and Cody ended up choosing quarterback. That's how he went from a running back to a quarterback. From that day forward, he was considered a quarterback. He won the starting job, and I think they went undefeated in this first year of junior high football. Cody had a great season, and he could still run. He ran for a lot of touchdowns.

In eighth-grade football, Cody hurt his foot early in the season. He told the coaches about it, and they said he should go to the doctor. We were going to do that, but he said, "Nah, I don't want to go to the doctor. I think I'll be okay." He played an entire season as a running quarterback on the bad foot, and he had a great year.

When it was all over, Cody was going to play basketball. He went to go to try-outs, but came back and said, "My foot bothers me too much." We took him to the doctor; they did an X-ray, and, sure enough, he played the entire football season with a broken foot. "I figured it was something like that" was Cody's response. So he walked around the next two months with a cast on his foot.

Between eighth grade and ninth grade, one of the high school coaches came up to me and said, "Hey, do you mind if Cody comes up and starts working out with varsity over the summer? Varsity kids in the weight room and stuff." I said, "Dude, he's never worked out with a weight in his life. I've never had him do weights.

"I don't want him getting hurt." The coach assured me, "Oh, I'll be up there. I'll be taking care of him."

Cody started going up there, and, of course, he ended up hurting his back. We found out about it on vacation when he was walking funny. He told us something "popped" when he was doing deadlifts. I said, "They have you doing deadlifts?" He probably weighed no more than 155 pounds. "Was the coach there?" "No," he said.

We had him checked out by a surgeon, who said Cody had a herniated disc. Cody was worried about not being able to play. The doctor said, "He doesn't have any alignment issues. His spine is perfectly straight. He's got a strong back. A lot of people have herniated discs, even at young ages.

The doctor said to Cody, "You can do whatever you want to do as long as you can handle the pain because you are going to hurt." Cody said, "Okay, I want to play."

Usually, a good ninth-grader would go into junior varsity, and Cody went through all of the practices. He was doing fine, loving it, enjoying his teammates. And then the coach comes up and says that he wants Cody to be the starting quarterback – on varsity!

I said, "Coach, I see all of these practices. He's not the best quarterback out there. This other kid is better than Cody." The coach responded, "We think Cody's the best, the better athlete. We think he should start." I told him I'd talk to Cody.

When I told Cody about what the coach said, he didn't want to be up on the varsity. He said he wanted to play with his buddies on JV. So I went to the coach and said, "Look, I don't think he's ready, and he doesn't think he's ready," and the coach says, "Well, we think he's ready, and he's going to be the starter."

So Cody started as a varsity quarterback in ninth grade, weighing 160 pounds at most. We had a really bad team in Division I, which is the biggest division in Ohio. And Cody just got pounded the entire year. I mean, crushed.

Well, that varsity coach didn't make it past his first year. The old coach came back for Cody's 10th-grade season and said he's going to be a running back. So Cody played running back that year, and they made it through the season. Nothing extraordinary happened, or so I thought!

Cody's junior year rolled around, and his team was now without a quarterback, so they put him back in that position. He was the quarterback from his junior year all through his senior year. Junior year, he had just an outstanding season. He threw for 1,000 yards, ran for 1,000 yards, and was selected All-Ohio first-team. He was recruited by some Division I schools and a lot of others calling.

Still, there was something strange about Cody's junior year. After the first scrimmage, I see him working on his foot. I asked him what was going on. He said they were treating him for turf toe, but he knew that was the wrong diagnosis. He admitted that he knew he'd broken his foot again. He said, "I'm just going to let them tape my foot up for turf toe every game, and I'll just run on it."

And he did. He never went to the doctor, played the whole season and, no joke, when football season was over, he said, "All right, I need to go to the doctor." We went to the doctor, and he said, "Yep, he's got a broken foot." They put him in another walking cast. So he played two years of his football career with a broken foot.

All this time in high school, he had back pain for every game he played. I would pick him up after practice, and he'd be the one kid who'd come off the field and jump in the tub of ice for his back. His senior year started okay, but he ended up having a lineman roll on his ankle, and he missed a few games. It was just a lousy season for everybody.

Brain Injury

Cody did have a documented brain injury in high school, and Heather and I remember the game vividly. It was against our crosstown rivals his sophomore year. Cody ran the ball around the left end, and he hit a kid square, knocking the crap out of this kid, who flew three yards back. The kid didn't get up, but Cody popped right up.

The next three plays, Cody took the handoff and got drilled. He went back to the bench and sat down. Cody never sat on the bench. He always stood on the sideline, bouncing from foot to foot. I told Heather, "I think he's got a concussion."

It wasn't long after that the trainer waved us down to the fence. He said, "Hey, Cody's got a concussion. We're taking him in. He's probably done for the game." We said, "Yeah, we understand. That's fine."

After halftime, the team came out, and Cody marched right out on the field. He was playing again. We're confused, and we go down to ask the trainer what's going on. He said, "The doctor cleared him. He said it was just mild; he's okay."

After the game, we talked to Cody and one of his buddies. And his buddy said, "Yeah, after that hit, when we were going back to the huddle, Cody was walking to the other team's bench. I had to grab him and say, "Over here Cody. We're this way." He wasn't even supposed to take the next hand-off, but he just kept taking them.

Cody said he didn't remember the game. He didn't remember that game the rest of his life. Nothing before that play, nothing after that play, the entire game was lost to him.[74]

That makes me recall another conversation I had with Cody and his friends after an eighth-grade game. I walked down the field afterward, and the boys were talking. I hear them saying something about "seeing stars." I asked Cody if he'd seen stars in games before, and he said three or four times. One of the other kids said, "Yeah, I've seen them too."

I said, "Guys! That sounds like you may have had a concussion or something. If that ever, ever happens to you again, you need to let your coaches know. They need to know if you have a concussion."

---

74   Orna Feldman, "Football and the brain: Lifestyle impacts health," Harvard Medical School, accessed September 12, 2018 http://neuro.hms.harvard.edu/harvard-mahoney-neuroscience-institute/brain-newsletter/and-brain-series/football-and-brain

Used and Abused

Honestly, after Cody's great junior year, I could see some changes in his drive for football. I could see he just didn't have it as much. He went to some combines and did well. Watching the other kids, to me he was a standout. He just looked phenomenal.

After another combine one day, I told him there would be another the next day. He's said, "You know, Dad, I don't want to do it." So I kind of knew that he didn't have the drive like he used to, and I felt like he was in pain a lot. I felt like he didn't want to play, but didn't want to tell people. He got plenty of calls from colleges, but I don't think he wanted to talk to them much. And so he didn't play football after high school – at least, for a while.

Cody went to Columbus State College for a year and did well in his classes, including making the Dean's List. He moved in with some buddies, and his sister was going to Ohio State, which is right next door. But after his first year at Columbus, he came home and said he wanted to play football again. I told him he needed to be checked by a doctor first.

After looking at Cody's MRIs, the doctor said, "You don't need to be playing football anymore. No more contact sports the rest of your life. You should be done." Cody said, "Well, I did it in high school. Nothing's changed so that I can do it now." The doctor said, "I'll tell you what. You can do it, but I will bet that you don't last three practices because college is different than high school."

Sure enough, after his third practice, Cody called and said, "I can't do it. My back hurts too much. I'm done."

When Cody got back home, we had a surgeon examine him. He discovered a previously undiagnosed broken disc. The doctor said, "It looks like these other doctors missed it because it's hard to see. But I can see it clearly. I would say that he played his entire varsity career with it because the bones are so rounded where they've been rubbing up against each other. I can tell you that injury is years old.

"Yeah," the doctor said, "he should never play anything again."

That was really hard for Cody. He never really talked about it with me, but his entire personality at school, and his persona and everything about him, was based around his athleticism and his football. And now it was just gone, with a click of a switch.

Towards the end of Cody's life, he was at Ohio University getting a degree in Urban Planning & Development. He had a new girlfriend. We felt he was doing well. I thought he was doing better than I had seen him do in the previous three years.

Cody was pretty lost after high school for a couple of years. As a child, he was super loving, funny, and goofy. He wasn't a prima donna kid or anything like that. He just loved playing sports. Other than that, he was just a goofball like every other kid. He'd do silly stuff, like let his sister and her friends dress him up like a girl. He didn't care. He was hilarious. He loved watching movies, having sleepovers and all that stuff.

When he got into high school, I saw changes in him. He was quieter. Honestly, at the time I thought, "Well, it's a lot of pressure on him, and he's just trying to keep it cool. Maybe that's what it is." I felt like it really just kept progressing and getting worse.

Even when he had his best years of football, and he'd be happy as can be about his accomplishments, Cody would come home from practice and go to bed almost immediately.

He wouldn't go to sleep; he'd just laid in bed. I thought he was just tired and needed rest. I believe now he probably suffered from depression for a long time.

There were other signs that I looked back on later.

One day, I was working on Cody's car in the garage, and he was helping me. There was a bolt that needed to be put on, and it was kind of in an awkward place. So I asked Cody to do it. Well, he physically couldn't do it. And I remember thinking, "That is really strange to me." I ended up doing it, but I remember telling his mom, "He couldn't even put that bolt on there." In my mind, I'm thinking, "His fine motor skills seem off to me." That always stuck with me.

Honestly, when Cody died, it just burned me. Burned me, consumed me. There's so much guilt, so much stuff that goes through your mind, and it still does. It just never goes away. Every day I just feel guilty as hell about this stuff.

My daughter, God bless her, she's always looking for stuff on brain injuries. She found Kimberly Archie on Facebook and reached out to her on behalf of our family. I had been in contact with local lawyers, but they did not seem to be the proper fit for my son's case. I called and spoke to Kimberly, I told her I didn't want there to be bad memories of my son, and I wanted people to look at him fondly. For this reason, I was really hesitant about pursuing a lawsuit as most people are. Upon reflection, and knowing all that Cody went through, I would later declare "Yeah, we just got to do something." That's how it came to be as far as the lawsuit and everything surrounding it.

I ran into one of Cody's coaches from his Pee Wee teams, and he was beside himself. I had to talk him down. He said, "I quit coaching after this. I don't have anything to do with it anymore. I just feel so bad." I had to tell him, "There's nothing you guys did wrong. I don't blame any coach."

What did I see over the years? First, a kid who's a great athlete is kind of used and abused. Everybody wants him on their team. They want them to produce, so they put them in positions to produce.

These are the things you think about after the fact. Who's going to get the most repetitive hits to the head? The kid who's the best player, who gets all of the playing time. My kid ran the ball all the time; he played on defense all the time. At the time we had no idea helmets weren't made or tested for kids, or that with each hit the helmet made the impact cause even greater harm.

At Cody's practices, when the coaches had a young kid who they wanted to test at linebacker, guess what they'd do? They'd give the ball to my son and say, "Go out there and see what this kid is made of." I watched it for years and years and years, not knowing exactly what I was seeing.

People Are Totally Oblivious

I think about what happened to my son's knees and how it relates to brain damage and later CTE. The doctor told us the bones in his knees were dying because he had a deep bruise that never healed. This was because every time it would start to heal, he'd get another knee bruise. Think about that on your brain in the helmet. If you get hit in the same place, you get a spot on your brain. It starts to heal, but it gets hit again and again, and it's never going to heal.

Hearing the negative stuff from critics has been hard. We had to talk our daughter down a little bit. Finally, I said, "Look, you've just got to get off social media and stop listening to that stuff." It's really disturbing that there's brain injury and CTE data out there, and that people will still think, "What's the big deal?" That's totally bizarre.

Personally, I'm a conservative-leaning person. I don't like government involvement, but when it comes to the elderly and our children, I think the government has to be involved. That's what the laws are for, to protect those people who can't protect themselves. I think that's what our major problem is. The rest of us, we can make our own decisions. People make a decision every day to join the armed forces knowing what can happen. We don't put 6 to 10-year-old kids in the armed forces, right?

It's just crazy to realize that people are just totally oblivious to this when it comes to their kids. I could have watched my kid play flag football or Whiffle ball and been excited. I don't care what it was. I loved watching both of our kids play sports. I loved just seeing them run. They both ran so beautifully. It seemed so effortless.

These people don't understand that they would get as much enjoyment watching their kid play flag football as they would tackle football. If kids want to play tackle football when they hit legal age, college or professional, to me, that's different.

I loved football. My son, in my mind, died for football. I don't want to see football go away. Not the NFL. College, maybe. But youth football, I couldn't care less if anybody plays tackle football as a child. They're not getting anything from it. It's not helping them in any way, and people just can't fathom that fact. They think if a kid's playing football when they're in second grade, somehow it's going to make them a better player when they're 18. It's insane.

I didn't play sports. I didn't play football. I wasn't in the football culture, but I later got ingrained into the football culture because of Cody. When you're the star quarterback's family, they want you involved in gridiron meetings and all this stuff.

And now we have all these high school coaches, trainers, medical people who dealt with our son specifically through the years. It has been no secret in our area about Cody having CTE. It's been in the papers and on the news. Everybody knows about the lawsuit.

And yet never – never has one of those people reached out and talked to us about brain trauma or CTE. I've always found that interesting because to me; it speaks volumes about what people really think about it. They're afraid of it, and when it comes down to it, the topic of brain damage because Cody had brain damage before he had CTE.[75]

There was one person who spoke to us about CTE. He's a guy who is prominent in football in our community. His kids played with Cody. And after the news about the lawsuit came out, we ran into him. He said, "Hey. I just saw about Cody with CTE. I never knew that.

"That's a shame," he added. "I really hate to hear that."

And he kept talking.

"You know what," he said, "I played football my whole life, all the way through college, and I wouldn't change a thing."

---

75   "Blows not concussion cause brain disease, according to new research," *University of Oxford*, January 18, 2018, accessed September 2, 2018 http://www.ox.ac.uk/news/2018-01-18-blows-not-concussion-cause-brain-disease-according-new-research

That was the gist of the conversation. And I just looked at him, like that's the most bizarre thing to tell somebody. You know, "Hey, I just saw your kid died of CTE. You know, I played ball, and I wouldn't change nothing."

I was just flabbergasted. I was completely speechless. But again, it speaks volumes about people-their thoughts on a sport that induces brain trauma.

Just because you weren't damaged doesn't mean other people weren't. That guy got lucky, or rather, perhaps it hasn't manifested yet.

Questions Pop Warner - Youth Tackle parents should consider about tackle football:

- Do you want to play Russian roulette with your child's brain?

- Do you want to take the chance your kid escapes brain trauma when you now know there's proof they may not?

- Is playing the Game worth the risk, are you willing to pay the ultimate price?"

Kimberly Archie, Jo Cornell, Debra Pyka,
Mary Seau - Easter 2018

Kimberly Archie, Jo Cornell, Debra Pyka, James Ransom
Mary Seau CTE Foundation luncheon 2018

Fern Matin, Kimberly Archie, Mary Seau, Jo Cornell
Sacramento CTE Awareness Day 2018

Debra Pyka, Solomon Brannan, Larry Mallory, Congressman
Kind - Brain Injury Awareness Day in Capitol Hill 2018

Kim Jenkins, Marcia Jenkins, DC Chief Medical
Examiner, Kimberly Archie, Debra Pyka - meeting

Kimberly Archie, Congresswoman Joyce Beatty
Brain Injury Day in Capitol Hill 2016

Co-founders, Faces of CTE, Kimberly Archie, Debra Pyka

Kimberly Archie, Mike Haynes, Dr. Herb Appenzeller Dr. Steve Devick, Dr. T.J. Rosandich, awards dinner 11/11/11

Kimberly Archie, Roger Goodell, NFLCommissioner, Canton Ohio, Hall of Fame event 2013

Former President Obama addressing attendees of the White House Concussion Summit in 2014

Calvin Snowden, Mike King, Larry Mallory, Solomon Brannan - Faces of CTE awards dinner 2018

Kim Jenkins, Marcia Jenkins, Kimberly Archie, Deb Ploetz, Debra Pyka, Nicole Pyka, Meg Dudley, Susie Dudley, Karen Bryant - Boston CTE families 2016

COLLEGE
ATHLETES

CHAPTER 6

Zack Langston

August 21, 1987 – February 24, 2014

Zack Langston was the rare mix of the star football player in high school who had a heart for defending the underdog. If a kid was being bullied or was an outsider who needed a friend, Zack was there for him. And at 6-foot-3, he could intimidate anyone he wanted to. His size served him well on the football field, and Zack decided to play in college at Division II Pittsburg State in Kansas. But a neck injury threatened not only his football readiness but his long-term health, and Zack drifted out of the game and into a deep depression. A college degree, fatherhood, a loving girlfriend, and even a tryout with the U.S. Olympic bobsled team couldn't keep him on a straight path. His self-esteem battered and his relationships in tatters, Zack committed suicide at the age of 26. He was diagnosed with chronic traumatic encephalopathy (CTE) so severe that it was compared to the damage suffered by NFL Hall of Famer Junior Seau.[76]

Adrift
By Nicki Langston

As early as I can remember, from the time he could walk, my son Zack was drawn to every ball he saw. Baseballs, basketballs, tennis balls, footballs, anything more or less round that involved active play.

Early on Zack was a fierce competitor for a little kid. In every sport, in pee wee leagues, on the school playground, or in the backyard with his brothers, he put everything he had into it, and he played to win.

The sports at which he excelled were those that required strength, speed and co-ordination. He was born with those physical gifts, and maybe sports that didn't demand massive strength and speed didn't challenge him enough or provide an outlet for his boundless energy.

Zack began playing soccer at 6 years old and was very good at it, just as he was with basketball and baseball. He continued basketball and baseball into his sophomore year of high school, but realized at the age of 10 that if he wanted to play football he would have to choose between it and soccer because they were both fall sports. To my disappointment, he was happy to pick football.

I was against my sons playing football initially because it was so much rougher than other sports. I feared injuries such as broken necks or backs and was afraid

---

76   Patrick Hruby, "How football pulled the trigger: Zack Langston's family reflects on his tragically short life," *Vice Sports*, December 17, 2015, accessed September 18, 2018 https://www.google.com/amp/s/sports.vice.com/amp/en_ca/article/53xz4n/how-football-pulled-the-trigger-zack-langstons-family-reflects-on-his-tragically-short-life

that he could become paralyzed or worse. But football was part of our family tradition. My husband Marc had been a successful college player and loved the sport. I was the only one to have those concerns, and I finally gave in and consented to football for both of my younger sons.

Zack was proud and excited to wear the pads and helmet for a team called the Warriors. His reputation for being an exceptionally hard hitter began his first year, and he took tremendous pride in that ability. I didn't come from a football background, so I had a hard time rationalizing this concept of hitting the other players with so much force. Each time Zack hit a player and that boy appeared to be hurt, I would feel horrible. There were many times I asked Zack not to hit the boys quite so hard because I was concerned he could seriously injure them. Zack just laughed. "Mom, you're supposed to hit as hard as you can; it's what the coaches want us to do!"

I learned to tell myself that this was the way the game is supposed to be played and to keep my concerns to myself. Zack was always a gentle, kind, big-hearted kid when it came to animals or anyone less fortunate than himself, so I found it hard to believe that he was emotionally capable of hurting anyone on the football field and being "OK" with it. But this was football, and he lived for the competitive battle.

Zack was well-liked and respected in high school, but being popular didn't seem to be a big concern to him. He loved making big plays in all of his sports, yet never seemed to want the attention that came along with it. He had a reputation for defending kids he thought were being bullied and was known to make friends with people he thought needed a friend. Zack was pretty quiet at school and never enjoyed taking part in small talk, yet he had an extremely goofy, loud, even obnoxious side that he seemed to share only with close friends and family. He'd walk into the house and let out a huge, happy yell, just to let everyone know he was home. He had a laid-back happiness about him and often was humming and singing around the house.

Zack's personality rubbed off on his younger sister, Emma. She picked up on many of his habits at a very young age and continues those behaviors to this day. Emma will walk in the door and squeal in a very high-pitched, happy scream, as though to say, "I'm here everyone, let's have some fun," just as Zack used to do.

Marc was a successful high school player, yet didn't have the size or speed to move on to a larger college, so he played at a small school in Baldwin, Kansas. When Zack grew to be 6 feet 3½ and had the speed and agility coveted by Division I college football coaches, Marc was thrilled. Scholarship offers began coming in for Zack. As a family, we discussed the opportunities and decided Division II would be the best fit for him.

After hearing stories of players being expected to continue play while injured at the larger colleges, we thought that Zack would be much safer at a smaller school, and Zack believed he'd get more playing time. Our family are fans of Pittsburg State in Kansas, a school known for having a winning record, great fan base, beautiful stadium and good coaching staff. Pitt State was only a two-hour drive from our home in Overland Park, Kansas. Our decision was made; with lots of coaxing from Pitt coaches, we felt that Zack was going to be a huge part of their football program and, indeed, he was.

Zack enjoyed college and made the most of all the social opportunities in a town where the college football players had celebrity status. He rented a house with some teammates and became popular around campus. He was strikingly handsome and drew lots of female attention. When he walked into a room, his presence was noticed. Friends and teammates dubbed him "Leonidas," after the ancient Spartan king.

Zack was a great contributor to his team until he suffered a ruptured vertebra in his neck his junior year. He began seeing doctors and physical therapists, making every effort to heal his injury and return to football. It would seem he was healed after sitting out several games, and he'd return to play, only to have it act up again.

Doctors warned that he could lose the use of his arm if he kept aggravating it. This concern continued into his senior year, and it was decided that he'd receive a medical waiver in order to allow him to spend the rest of his senior year healing. He could then return as a fifth-year senior to play a final year.

One of his friends at Pitt was Danae. Their friendship grew into a romance, and Danae became pregnant after Zack's graduation from Pitt State. The day their son Drake was born was one of the happiest of Zack's life. He was in awe of the tiny baby and loved being a father, not shying away from dirty diapers or crying.

Zack and Danae struggled in their relationship. Danae noticed changes in Zack. He grew moodier and less attentive to her, and some new behavior was out of character for him. He forgot the simplest things. It confused her, and she wondered what happened to the sensitive, giant teddy bear of a man Zack had been at school.

I started to notice changes in Zack in his freshman year at Pitt State, before his neck injury. One beautiful fall afternoon, with all the pomp and ceremony of a Pitt State home game, Zack took an especially hard hit and was carried off the field. Marc and I rushed to the locker room where Zack was being hooked up to an IV. "Dehydration" the trainer said. "He's OK."

But he wasn't OK. Marc went back to his seat in the stands and I stayed in the room with Zack. As he lay on the cot he began to cry. I had never seen him like that and didn't understand the emotion. Did something hurt? Was he *that* disappointed at being taken out of the game?

"I don't know what's wrong," he sobbed, staring up at the ceiling. I went back to my seat and told Marc about Zack's behavior. Neither of us had seen him show that kind of vulnerability. He was a "work through the pain" kid, always pushing himself to the limit. He knew that being knocked down was part of the game, and he usually took it in stride, got back up and kept going.

When his fifth year started and he began football training again, the old injury flared up. He saw more doctors and the news was bad: If he continued to play football, he was risking paralysis. Marc and I expected our super-competitive son to be devastated by that news, but surprisingly, he was not. He seemed disappointed, but taking it in stride.

Someone I Didn't Know

Zack began having episodes of depression. He was home one weekend and I found him sitting in my room, waiting for me. He wanted to talk about feelings he didn't understand. It seemed his life was going well, but he felt hopeless and overwhelmed by sadness. He knew he was depressed and couldn't find a reason for it. He asked me if his dad or I were depressed at his age. Neither of us were. I listened to him and tried to understand why he would feel this way, but I was at a loss.

Zack finished school at Pitt State and was excited to graduate. We sent out announcements, and friends and family members drove to Pittsburg to attend. As Marc, Emma and I were on our way to the event, Marc got a call. It was Zack, and he was upset, saying he was not going to graduate and didn't know why. He told us his name was not on the list of graduates.

He was calling from his cell phone and driving his truck. As he talked he became more upset and irrational, and we were concerned for his safety. Marc tried to reason with him that it must be an oversight and could be fixed. But he wouldn't hear it, insisting any phone call would be pointless. As he drove around aimlessly he became more and more angry. He yelled into the phone that he was stupid and that he always screwed things up, and he pounded his phone on the dashboard of his truck.

We were finally able to convince him to meet us at a restaurant where everyone had gathered to celebrate, though Zach insisted that there be no mention of graduation. We hurriedly phoned the guests to brief them as best we could. He arrived at the restaurant and walked in as if everything was fine. He was smiling and calm, warmly greeting our guests. Marc and I were startled at the transformation and thoroughly confused.

Looking back now I know why he behaved so irrationally, why he was surprised to find that he was not going to graduate. His brain was damaged by the effects of chronic traumatic encephalopathy (CTE). He even said it: "I'm always screwing things up." But none of us knew why.[77]

The next day Zack contacted the administration office at Pitt State and found out that he was one class short to graduate. Zack blamed the administrators. They advised him to pick up the class he needed whenever he could and they would award his degree when he completed it.

He took the class he needed and graduated from Pitt State that summer. I think we were trying to put the bad graduation experience behind us and get back on some normal track, so we decided to take a family vacation to Florida. It was possibly the last family vacation with the boys – Zack and his younger brother Ben.

As it turned out, Marc had a business conflict and couldn't go, and Emma didn't go, so it was just me and the two boys. Zack was out of sorts from the time we left for Key West. By the time we arrived he was being loud, throwing our luggage around and making an angry scene in front of other hotel guests. He sulked in the room and reluctantly went out with Ben and me. Once again, his behavior was totally out of character. This new Zack was someone I didn't know.

---

77 "What is CTE and why athletes need to know about it," WebMD, https://www.webmd.com/brain/what-is-chronic-traumatic-encephalopathy-cte

When we returned from Florida, Zack was living at home again, full-time for the first time in five years. He was angry a lot about insignificant things. He punched holes in his bedroom wall when he got mad, and later we learned he'd done that at a house he shared with teammates. We tried to rationalize his behavior by telling ourselves that he was under a lot of pressure to find a job. With a baby on the way, his relationship with Danae seemed to deteriorate.

Zack landed a job and rented an apartment with a childhood friend, but didn't spend much time there. After Drake was born, he and Danae shared care of the baby while they tried to work out their issues and find a life together. Zack wanted to marry her, but their relationship grew more volatile by the day, and in hindsight I realize it was because of Zack's erratic behavior.

When Zack took care of the baby he stayed at our house. It was a better place for Drake than his apartment, and we were there to help him. As time went on he didn't stay at his apartment much, and he all but moved back into his old room, which now included a crib for Drake. He was still dealing with frequent bouts of depression and anger, and I was more comfortable having him at home, especially with Drake in the picture now. But we still had no clue what was wrong with him and attributed his increasingly strange behavior to the pressures of trying to get started in life.

His mind was everywhere; he was going to join the Marines; he was going to invest in real estate. He was indecisive and without direction. One day he would make up his mind about his job, or buying a car, or even little things like making plans with friends, only to change his mind the next day. He was extremely forgetful about commitments he made, or conversations we had.

He left his first job as an inside sales rep because he hated sitting behind a desk all day, and took a job with an up-and-coming company that involved working from home. He decided he couldn't handle the seclusion of that and said that he had trouble concentrating. His last job was an outside sales position.

His self-esteem was now gone, and he continually thought people were talking about how stupid he was. He continued to trust and confide in me, and about this time he confessed to having used the drug Adderall in college to help him study for tests. He continued to take Adderall because he was having trouble concentrating on his job and just remembering things in day-to-day life.

He tried out for the U.S. Olympic development bobsled team and was assigned to the national bobsled squad. Being from Kansas, we didn't know much about the sport, but learned that it requires athletes with great strength, speed and jumping ability. It was right up Zack's alley. He was excited about the prospect of being part of a team again, and the news seemed to lift his spirits a little.

We were conflicted about supporting such a venture. It seemed like a detour from the life he should be pursuing, now with a family to support. But I think we were desperate to find something that would put him right again. He was a born athlete who couldn't play football anymore. Bobsled was something he excelled at, even with a ruptured vertebra.

Zack spent six months in 2013 training with the U.S. team. When it came time to test for positions that would represent America at the 2014 Winter Olympics in Sochi, Japan, Zack didn't make the cut. He was extremely disappointed and decided to quit.

While Zack was training with the bobsled team, he met a young woman, Morgan, in our hometown. They hit it off right away, and when Zack left the team and returned home, they began seeing each other.

In hindsight, Morgan came into his life, and ours, at a critical time. She is a kind, compassionate, nurturing person, and there was never a time that Zack needed understanding more. After quitting the team he seemed to be in a downward spiral, his behavior becoming stranger every day, and his character morphing into someone we barely recognized. He was trying to shoulder his responsibilities and got another office job, but hated it.

We'd run out of excuses to explain Zack's behavior. He continued to confide in me, but his thoughts were becoming increasingly alarming. During one conversation, he told me that he had no memories at all of his childhood. He agonized over his situation with Danae. He told me that he was having thoughts of suicide, but didn't know why. I suggested he see a psychiatrist and he didn't resist. He knew there was something terribly wrong and was desperate to fix it.

Zack saw a psychiatrist who prescribed an anti-depressant, but it didn't help. Morgan called Marc one night and told him that Zack had bought a gun.[78] He told her about his suicidal thoughts, and Morgan was afraid of what he was going to do. Marc was able to reason with Zack, and Zack turned the gun over to him. We were all becoming frantic.

Morgan, who is a nurse, convinced Zack to check into a psychiatric facility, and Zack went without hesitation. In less than a week they declared him ready to go home and said that with good family support he would be fine. He was not fine. Marc, Morgan and I made ourselves available to him 24 hours a day, encouraging him to talk, and checking up on him regularly. Marc even drove by

---

78   "Benzodiazepines and risk of Alzheimer's disease," *The BMJ*, September 9, 2014, accessed September 20, 2018 https://www.bmj.com/content/349/bmj.g5312/rr/775731

his workplace to make sure his car was in the parking lot. Worrying about Zack consumed all of our lives.

Disturbing Plan

Zack and Morgan had been dating almost a year and they were good together. They laughed, had fun and were growing increasingly close. He was very happy when he was with her. I guess it was because Morgan understood that Zack was sick. She could see the real person inside and she stuck with him. She was his rock.

One time they went someplace together, and he left without her. We assumed he had an anxiety attack of some sort. He had never been a heavy drinker, but began to consume hard liquor, even carrying a bottle in his truck and drinking while he drove. He was health conscious his whole life, careful about the food he ate and working out every day, but he completely lost interest and neglected himself.

Morgan stayed and poured herself into finding a way to help him. Zack told me that he loved her, and maybe that's why he confided so freely in her, even his horribly disturbing plan. He told Morgan and me that he thought playing football and taking so many hits to the head had somehow damaged his brain, giving him uncontrollable dark irrational thoughts, destroying his ability to concentrate, and his memory. He told her that he thought about shooting himself in the heart so his brain could be examined.

Several weeks after the first occurrence Zack bought another gun. By now he was even less reasonable and refused to hand it over to Marc when confronted. Marc threatened to call the police, and Zack finally gave it to him. By this time, Marc was tracking Zack's location by monitoring the movements of his cell phone with a GPS program he installed without Zack's knowledge.

A few weeks later, Marc was able to see by the GPS location of Zack's phone that he was at the gun shop again. He called him immediately, but there was no answer. Marc frantically called Morgan at work, thinking Zack might answer her call. He did, but after first denying he'd bought another gun, he admitted he had.

Marc called Zack and pleaded with him to come home to talk, and he agreed. But, apparently, as Zack was turning the corner onto our street, his phone emitted a signal that, for the first time, alerted Zack that his phone was being tracked. He immediately threw it out the window into bushes, where it was later found. He turned his truck around and left, never meeting with Marc.

Marc was terrified, not knowing how Zack would react to finding out he had been monitored. Now there was no way to find him, so Marc got in his car and went in search. He called me at work to tell me that Zack had a gun and had ditched his phone. I remember a sick feeling coming over me. We hung up and I stayed by the phone, not returning to my class of preschoolers. An ominous foreboding gripped me.

A few minutes later, Marc called back to say he found Zack's truck in the parking lot of a bank not far from our home. But there was no sign of Zack. The bank is across the street from the apartment complex where Danae and Drake, who was now 2, lived. Marc called again to tell me there were several police cars in the complex parking lot and many officers in the stairwell leading to Danae's second-floor apartment. My head was spinning. I felt dizzy and sick as Marc hung up again.

The last time Marc called was to tell me that Zack was dead.[79] He had shot himself in the heart, just as he said he would do, on the stairs outside the door of Danae's apartment.

It was February, and a bone-chilling winter storm blew in the day of the funeral, bringing the coldest weather of the year. Our church was packed with friends and family, all stunned at what happened. Zack had everything going for him. He was 26 years old, a college graduate with a good job, a young woman who loved him, and a little son who adored him. There was no explanation, no understanding.

Morgan's mother worked with the county coroner's office, and someone had the presence of mind to remember Zack's wish that his brain be examined, so it was

---

79   Zachary Joseph Langston Obituary, *Legacy.com,* accessed November 1, 2018 https://www.legacy.com/obituaries/name/zachary-langston-obituary?pid=169896065

sent for autopsy. We had no idea what we were looking for, just trying to honor our son's fervent wish that we try to explain and understand.

When the results came back they were "normal." There were no findings of injury or disease. We struggled to understand what had happened, what had gone wrong in his life, why he suffered from a life-ending depression. But nothing we could come up with made sense. He had been a bright, happy kid with a loving family. He had lots of friends and every opportunity to pursue passions and interests. I've heard that anger is part of the grieving process, and in our grief we tried to find someone to blame. But no person had ever done anything to Zack to hurt him that badly.

Losing a child is like being adrift in the ocean with the waves pushing you under. You fight to get your head above water, only to get pushed under again. It feels like the harder you fight and the longer you keep your head above water, the longer you're under when the next wave comes. Life as we knew it is gone, and making it from one day to the next is a struggle for all of us. There are times when it seems nothing matters anymore; just that Zack is gone.

It must have been about six months later that I got a call from my sister Debbie. "You have to see this program," she said. "It is just like Zack."

She was referring to a PBS "Frontline" documentary called "League of Denial."[80] Interviewed in the program was a doctor, who spoke about CTE and football. I immediately found the documentary online, and the symptoms and behaviors described were eerily familiar. I looked up the things the program mentioned: CTE, the brain studies, and Dr. Bennet Omalu, who discovered CTE and linked it to football players. It might sound weird, but it gave me hope that maybe there was another explanation for Zack's death besides just being mentally ill.[81]

I contacted the brain bank as soon as I could. They were very interested in talking to me, which gave me even more hope. A representative of the research center

---

80   Michael Kirk, Jim Gilmore, Mike Wiser, "League of Denial," *PBS Frontline*, October 8, 2013, accessed November 1, 2018 https://www.pbs.org/wgbh/frontline/film/league-of-denial/

81   Omalu, B., DeKosky, S.T., Minster, R.L., Kamboh, M.I., Hamilton, R.L., Wecht, C.H., "Chronic traumatic encephalopathy in a National Football League player," *NCBI*, July 2005, accessed January 27, 2019 https://www.ncbi.nlm.nih.gov/pubmed/15987548

called and I told them the whole story, including that Zack's brain had been examined soon after his death by the local coroner and found to be normal. The rep explained that the damage done by CTE would probably not be detected in a routine autopsy. The problem: Did the coroner's office keep Zack's brain tissue? If it did, was it damaged by whatever preservation methods were used?

Relief

When I found that the coroner's office had kept Zack's brain tissue, I was excited. They sent it to the brain bank, where it was determined that the sample was viable for study, and I was once again hopeful.

It seems strange that I should have been so excited about the examination of Zack's brain for a disease I'd never heard of a few months earlier. But I think I was excited at the prospect of getting some relief from the relentless, haunting mystery of why he killed himself.

The study would take seven to eight months, so in the meantime I read everything I could find about CTE. I was surprised to learn that CTE can develop even if there was no history of a brain injury. In trying to make sense of Zack's suicide we recalled repeatedly that he had never been treated for brain injury.

But Zack's brother Ben reminded us of an incident when their opposing college teams played each other. Ben told us that at one of those games, after Zack took a hit, he was disoriented and walking the wrong way on the field. Ben had to guide his brother back to his own huddle. How many times did our son stay on the field and deny pain and injury?

In the spring of 2015, over a year after Zack died, we were notified that his brain was indeed damaged. *It was one of the most severe cases in a college athlete that had been detected.*[82]

---

82   Patrick Hruby, "How football pulled the trigger: Zack Langston's family reflects on his tragically short life," *Vice Sports*, December 17, 2015, accessed September 18, 2018 https://www.google.com/amp/s/sports.vice.com/amp/en_ca/article/53xz4n/how-football-pulled-the-trigger-zack-langstons-family-reflects-on-his-tragically-short-life

The doctor explained to us that Zack's CTE was at a level comparable to football great Junior Seau, who committed suicide in 2012 when he shot himself in the chest. We had trouble comprehending that our 26-year-old son who played Division II college football had this disease at a level anywhere close to that of a 46-year-old man who played in the NFL for more than 20 years and was one of the most notable players of his time.

I couldn't help but ask myself, "Did Zack push himself this hard at the game or did we, his family or coaches push him to play that hard?" I will continue to wonder how and why this disease attacked my son, and I will always feel a tremendous level of guilt, thinking that as his mother and protector, I could have and should have done something to save him from brain damage.

My healing comes from feeling that I am following Zack's wishes to help make the public aware of brain injury, damage and disease, and hopefully to have a hand in preventing it from attacking as many young athletes as possible. The feeling that Zack is my teammate in this venture in many ways keeps him alive in my heart, and at the same time keeps a large portion of sadness and loss at bay.[83]

---

83   Jessica Glenza, "A tragic death and college football's reckoning over brain injuries amid a new class-action lawsuit," *The Guardian*, November 25, 2017, accessed November 1, 2018 https://www.google.com/amp/s/amp.theguardian.com/sport/2017/nov/25/college-football-cte-ncaa-lawsuit-zack-langston

CHAPTER 7

Ryan Hoffman

July 15, 1974 – November 16, 2015

As a young man, Ryan Hoffman was a beach-loving Floridian, laid-back and affable – traits that belied his toughness on the football field. At 6-feet-5, he earned the attention of colleges around the country as an offensive lineman and landed a scholarship to the University of North Carolina, where his Tar Heels teams reached three bowl games. But soon after his college career, Hoffman began showing signs of disorganization and despair. For the next 10 years, he would battle mental illness, scrapes with the law and homelessness. His plight was detailed in two pieces by the New York Times – the second chronicling his death, at the age of 41, when he rode a bicycle into 50-mph traffic. A study of Hoffman's brain discovered he suffered from

Stage II chronic traumatic encephalopathy (CTE). While he was alive, Hoffman told a New York Times reporter in 2015, "I'm confident – well, I'm pretty sure – that football had something to do with it."

Tainted Memories
By Kira Hoffman-Soto

Ryan Christopher Hoffman was born on July 15, 1974, in Marion, Indiana, almost exactly three years after I was born.

Growing up, we lived in various places around the "heartland" of America until moving to Florida in 1986. You wouldn't know it from his 6-foot-5 stature as an adult, but Ryan was once a very thin and sickly child due to numerous health problems caused by his tonsils. Once they were removed, his natural athletic ability started to emerge.

In high school, Ryan excelled in basketball and football. He was also a very good street skateboarder and liked to surf. Always surrounded by friends, he was laid back, affable and shy around girls.

He always had a lot of interests and was busy enjoying life being a teenager in Florida. He starred in a high school play, "Bye Bye Birdie," and enjoyed sculpting and music.

It wasn't long into his high school athletic career that Ryan was being noticed for his skill in football, and he was heavily scouted by NCAA Division I teams. They all came calling – Nebraska, Florida State, North Carolina, and others.

Ryan was so humble about things, but I clearly remember how excited he was for his future. We all were. For my brother, signing his football scholarship papers with North Carolina was one of the biggest achievements of his life. In hindsight, we now know that my brother's agreement may as well have been signed in blood.

Ryan was on the UNC football team for five years. He loved the school and his college town of Chapel Hill. He had a steady girlfriend, was well-liked and highly regarded by his coaches and teammates.

He played left tackle on the offensive line and was a strong contributor to the success of Tar Heels teams that played in the Gator Bowl, Sun Bowl and Carquest Bowl. He consistently showed he was a player with great heart. He graduated from UNC with a bachelor's degree in Communications. (He once told me that if he had it to do over again, he would have majored in Philosophy.)[84]

Losing Everything

Ryan's position as a left tackle was a head-banger. He was always colliding with equally big and strong defensive linemen, head-to-head, and yet there are no school records showing that Ryan was diagnosed with a concussion during college or high school.

Our family had no real way to measure the damage that was being done because so little was known or disclosed about the silent injuries caused by consistent head trauma. It is now known that it isn't necessarily brain injuries that cause CTE, but, rather, sub-concussions and the repetitive jostling of the brain that produce symptoms of the brain damage and later CTE.[85]

As someone who has loved and lost an athlete to CTE, it taints every positive memory of events that I attended over the years. I am stricken by the thought that I was cheering as Ryan was being permanently injured. Cheering. We all were. We just didn't know.

To this day, my mother blames herself for not protecting Ryan by steering him onto a different path. I have to continually remind her that Ryan wouldn't have taken her redirection at that time. Playing football was something he wanted for himself, and he loved UNC. In fact, I think it was this sentiment about the game

---

84   Juliet Macur, "Homeless and mentally ill, a former college lineman dies on the street," *New York Times*, December, 2, 2015, accessed, January 25, 2019 https://www.nytimes.com/2015/12/03/sports/ncaafootball/ryan-hoffman-north-carolina-tar-heel-dead.html

85   "NFL concussion facts," *CNN*, August 26, 2018, accessed January 1, 2019 https://www.cnn.com/2013/08/30/us/nfl-concussions-fast-facts/index.html

that prevented him from attributing his health problems to college football until right before the end.

Perhaps that ultimate admission that football badly damaged him hastened the coming of Ryan's death. After all, how much would it hurt to know that one of your proudest accomplishments was the very thing that stripped you of everything? That's a bitter pill to swallow, and I think the realization drowned something precious inside of him.

Demons Never Rest

Ryan was a strapping young man, and to outward appearances, he was just fine. It took years of baffling changes over a long period of time for us to realize that something was seriously wrong, or that it was linked in any way to his career as a football player.

The changes in Ryan, post-UNC and football, were dramatic and uncharacteristic compared to the Ryan we knew for the first 22 years of his life. We began noticing that something was going seriously wrong as soon as he returned home from college.

He experienced sudden, loud sounds that he described as "gun shots" in his head that woke him from sleep. He complained of rushing thoughts, dizziness and headaches. He had night terrors in which he'd seem trapped between consciousness and unconsciousness. He lost weight and started having sleeping problems and PTSD-like symptoms.

Ryan was once organized, and yet he kept things on the floor of his room in plastic bags rather than in dressers. He explained he had to see everything to remember where items were. He also would lose consciousness for brief periods. He used to attribute it to standing up too quickly, but we now believe these were seizures.

Doctors could find nothing wrong, and he was misdiagnosed repeatedly and given pills. Ryan confided to me that none of them really seemed to relieve the underlying issues, but they made him feel "better" in some way. Sometimes, that was a welcome change; other times, it was not.

Upon reflection, I see now that this was the beginning of Ryan using medications to compensate for his new "normal." His efforts to get help and relief instead put him on a pathway of using medications as a diversion and subterfuge.

This caused many problems for Ryan in his relationships with others. He'd forget to close doors, leaving the house wide open. He lost too many keys, wallets and cell phones to count.

We lost the happy-go-lucky, upbeat person that Ryan used to be. He clearly was struggling and frustrated, and his demons never took a break. They just marched on and eventually dragged all of us into a constant cast of "fixers" of Ryan's inevitable dilemmas. We were weary a lot, but still had hope. There was still time, we thought – that thing we don't have anymore of now.

A few years after college, Ryan married. They had a daughter, and Ryan adopted his wife's son. They had some good years, but the marriage didn't last. He remained friends with his ex-wife, and despite any differences that led to their breakup, I never heard him say a single bad word about the mother of his children.

Ryan remained in close contact with his daughter and son right up to the end of his life. He truly loved his kids and did what he could do to be a good father. But his overwhelming problems took an enormous toll – financially, physically and psychologically. He could not maintain adequate employment, and between jobs he survived by living in various homes with friends and relatives.

Uncharacteristic to who he was before college, Ryan began to have what was to be many brushes with law enforcement. Most encounters were over minor things, such as lifting fried chicken from a grocery, but cumulatively, it was enough to ruin his chances for gainful employment. He survived by working at construction and other labor-intensive jobs.

The common consensus among bosses and co-workers was that Ryan was one of the hardest workers they'd ever met, but he lost many opportunities because of his disability. For instance, he was an accomplished welder, and that got him into a prestigious marine welding program in Jacksonville Florida. But, ultimately, the life issues that plagued him kept him from being allowed to participate at the last minute.

That was just another of many crushing disappointments in Ryan's numerous attempts to better himself. He just couldn't seem to find traction anywhere. His life was chaotic and left no quarter for raising children. I know this was one of his greatest laments – not being there for his kids day-to-day.

Nothing to Help College Players

The financial gains to college football programs are enormous. Athletes who earn a college degree, but inherent brain damage along with it, find their degree is useless. That was true for Ryan.

It took his death and a post-mortem biopsy of his brain to conclusively make that link. It also was a fact that, unlike the case of professional athletes in the NFL, there is *nothing* in place at the college level to help these players in their struggle. As long as we are silent, the dangers will be there.

There needs to be a change in the way college athletes are compensated when they sustain debilitating illnesses due to the sport. Ryan had cognitive tests prior to his death that strongly indicated all the areas of his brain affected by CTE were showing signs of deterioration and dysfunction. Yet he couldn't get any help with disability insurance, and there was nothing in place from the school or the NCAA to contribute to his care.[86]

The assumption was that since school athletes are not paid, they're not owed any further coverage. It's a flawed system that leaves these players adrift to face their damages with no assistance.[87]

The silver lining to this story will be change. The college sports industry needs to step up and take responsibility. There has to be a drive to make the schools provide support for the injured athletes after their playing days. As it stands now, that is not happening.

When someone you love dies unexpectedly, everything changes.

Some people try to put a time limit on their grief, but I don't think it ever truly ends. There are days when this horrible tragedy has made me appreciate things

---

86   "NCAA accused of failing to protect football players from head injuries," *CBS This Morning*, September 7, 2018, accessed January 1, 2019 https://www.cbsnews.com/news/ncaa-wrongful-death-lawsuits-cte-head-injuries/

87   "NCAA footballers with head injuries look to buck settlement trend," *Bloomberg Law*, December 11, 2018, accessed January 1, 2019 https://news.bloomberglaw.com/product-liability-and-toxics-law/ncaa-footballers-with-head-injuries-look-to-buck-settlement-trend

about life more than I ever did before, and there are days when I have prayed to God for the grace just to get out of bed.

I often remember Ryan's laugh. It makes me sad to think of how short in supply laughter was toward the end of his life, but I'm thankful to have my memories of his humor and loud laughter from happier times. Maybe this is my brother's way of letting me know he's happier now, or maybe it's just my subconscious finding ways to self-soothe. I like to believe that it's the former.

The thing that isn't clear about grieving at first is that it is a war between dark and light. People will tell you that there's no right or wrong way to do it, but I'm not so sure. The range of emotions I've battled is uncomfortably broad and exhausting. It has brought me to the depths of despair, and for a while, it consumed me in darkness. I spent some time sorting and untangling the emotional baggage to identify the one overarching feeling that I identify with the most.

Today, I feel that my brother and everyone who loved him was robbed. His "beautiful brain" was just one of many stuffed into a helmet and sent out onto a field to follow plays that jarred him internally with force, over and over again.

Those hits left their mark in grueling headaches, light sensitivity, sleeplessness, impulse control, depression, mood swings, drug dependency and homelessness.

There was no warning that permanent brain damage and early death could be caused by playing a sport, although I am quite sure that the evidence has existed for some time, and it was most likely suppressed by the corporations and individuals benefiting financially.[88]

CTE and other brain damage robbed my brother of everything, and then turned around and robbed his children, family and friends.

Our family unanimously moved to honor Ryan's last wish to donate his brain for study. There, the final piece of the jigsaw puzzle fell into place: Ryan was diagnosed with Stage II CTE widespread. We finally had our definitive conclusion,

---

88   "NFL concussion fast facts," *CNN*, August 30, 2018, accessed January 1, 2018 https://www.cnn.com/2013/08/30/us/nfl-concussions-fast-facts/index.html

but it provided no closure. It was a Pyrrhic victory, and this time, nobody was cheering.

My parents have a hard time knowing what to say and at the same time they have said much in the past about losing Ryan yet feel no sense of greater comfort or peace.

Of any parent, it can be truly said that there are few, if any, things worse than losing a child. The wound festers perfectly fresh and memory provides the salt to coat the wound. The duty of parents is to guide, nurture and protect their children. On that basis, a swirling vortex of guilt and second-guessing is your constant companion.

The importance of telling Ryan's story is that it's a cautionary tale for other parents out there who don't think that it could happen to them, or that it would not take the tragic turn that Ryan's life did.

It's imperative for parents to realize that putting their child into any contact sport can have similar consequences. It's important that people know that brain damage and CTE is a silent destroyer, and not easily detected.

So how does such a beautiful beginning to a story turn so dark? To all those parents aspiring to raise the next star, our family would caution them to be careful what they wish for. CTE has long been with us, but hardly recognized. Not until today, when athletes have become increasingly bigger and stronger, has the prevalence of the disease forced it into the realm of public consciousness.

We cannot undo what was done to Ryan. That he signed up to play a game that ruined his future, thinking that it was going to have the opposite effect. But I can speak out and warn parents to strongly consider his story and hope it will be a pebble dropped into the ocean that causes a ripple that finally reaches many and results in the kind of change that is needed to prevent anyone else from suffering such a loss.

My father asked, "Why has this taken so long, and so little been done?" The answer centers on the immense amounts of revenue and prestige that these gifted athletes can create for both institutions and individuals.

He felt Ryan did not live his short life solely to help others fill stadium seats, or earn a seven-figure salary, or provide rich monetary fodder for avaricious members of the legal profession and distant relatives. No. He was a person, just like any of us, who was not perfect. He deserved a chance to stay on life's road, finding himself and his true purpose.

Shame on all of us who either willingly or unwittingly provided the wrong road map. The hazards of that path are clearly marked now.

CHAPTER 8

Greg Ploetz

February 11, 1949 – May 11, 2015

Greg Ploetz loved football, but there were so many other passions in his life. Though he starred as a defensive tackle on a University of Texas team that won the national championship, Greg was just as comfortable at an easel, creating stunning and imaginative pieces of art. He would share that love with hundreds of students as a high school art teacher – work that made him profoundly happy. Yet dementia began to creep into his life while Greg was still in his 50s, and it would only worsen as time wore on. Cared for lovingly and with unending devotion by his wife, Deb, Greg sunk further into the darkness of a mind truly lost to the damage that had been done playing football years earlier. A dearly loved father and grandfather, Greg died at the age of 66 because of the ravages of dementia. When his brain was examined, he was found to have the most advanced form of chronic traumatic encephalopathy – Stage IV.

Strangled Neurons
By Deb Ploetz

Many people don't want to believe it! How could their favorite sport and American pastime cause this kind of damage? Even my husband didn't want to admit it. After his first diagnosis of dementia, he said, "Why do you think it is from football hits, if it's just now showing up?"

Greg died from Stage IV chronic traumatic encephalopathy (CTE) at the age of 66. Everyone has tau proteins in their brain, and they build up after traumatic brain injuries sustained during football.[89] These proteins strangled Greg's neurons, and that caused dementia.

Greg's body shut down like someone suffering from Alzheimer's. There was no history of Alzheimer's or dementia in Greg's family. His father died at age 57 from a seizure, suspected to have been caused by competitive boxing in his younger years. The Air Force completed an autopsy on his father and his frontal lobes had shrunk. Greg's mother died at the age of 87 and her mind was as sharp as a tack.

Does your loved one have this disease? Hopefully, the information in our story will help if you see any of the behaviors I'm going to write about. I feel you need to know something about how Greg showed signs of the disease. It's clear he had the degenerative brain disease long before he was diagnosed.

Gregory Paul Ploetz was a Renaissance man. He was brilliant, clever, and could do most anything. He was not only a gifted teacher, artist, and public speaker, he could change the oil in his car, or plumb and wire an entire house.

Greg was one of the kindest, most thoughtful, giving, loving men one could know. This disease changed his personality, his behaviors, and outlook. His decline was totally out of his control.

---

89   Associated Press, "NCAA settles CTE lawsuit with family of former Texas player Greg Ploetz," June 15, 20148, accessed January 1, 2019 https://www.google.com/amp/s/amp.si.com/college-football/2018/06/15/ncaa-cte-lawsuit-greg-ploetz

His success as an athlete was evident in his role on the University of Texas 1969 national championship team. He was a formidable defensive tackle and was elected to the Southwest Conference first team twice, as well as being a second-team All-American. Unfortunately, his years in football caused him to suffer from CTE and other brain damage. He died in May 2015 after more than a decade of battling the disease. After the completion of a brain autopsy, a diagnosis of Stage IV CTE was confirmed.

Greg began his life in Buffalo, New York, on February 11, 1949. He was the third child of seven born to a loving Air Force family that lived in many states over the years. He started in youth football in Colorado at the age of 10 and played his last game in college at 22. At 5-feet-10, 205 pounds, Greg's size didn't allow him to pursue a pro career.

After graduating in 1972, Greg continued his studies at Texas in the art department. He completed his master's degree in Fine Arts and went on to teach college and high school levels for 40 years. He also lectured at many art institutes, museums and galleries. His work was included in numerous art exhibits over the years, though his work slowed as our family grew.

Golden Years

It was love for us after our first date in December 1977, and we married five months later. We were both educated in the arts, both athletes, had the same religious and political views, and came from similar economic backgrounds. We were best friends for 37 years.

Most of our journey began after we were married on June 3, 1978. Many people thought we were free spirits and somewhat irresponsible, because we both left our teaching jobs and took off for Europe on what we liked to call our "six-month honeymoon." Greg always wanted to see as much art in the free world as he could. I was lucky to be learning and observing from an art scholar such as him. It's funny how things work out. We were cheated of our "Golden Years," but got to spend them together on the front end.

One of the funniest times in Europe happened in Italy. Greg had a partial plate in his front four teeth. One of the facings of a tooth fell off. We went to a drugstore in Italy to buy some glue and left with something called Tacky TuTu. We laughed for days about it.

We ended up living in London for two months in a one-bedroom flat, and after two months there we flew to Greece. While on the islands, I found out I was pregnant. Unable to get any substantial employment in Europe, we headed home.

Our first child, daughter Erin, was born in 1979, and our son, Beau, arrived in 1983. Greg was a doting and loving father, even though he had a busy schedule of teaching and coaching. We had an "Ozzie and Harriet" life and were very happy. Greg also had a son, Chris Fry, from his first marriage, and we were fortunate to spend time with him during Greg's final two years.

Looking back, I realize that it was in 1998 when Greg started experiencing behavior changes, problems learning new tasks, outbursts, forgetfulness, and language and math issues beginning. At the time, we'd bought some land and built a home in Weatherford, Texas. I noticed he was not his agreeable self. He got very agitated with me and the repair work on our house. We had a long history of buying and selling homes, and because he was so handy we did a lot of the fix-it stuff ourselves.

Greg taught art at Trimble Tech High School in Fort Worth, Texas, beginning in 1994. By 2006, he was complaining about the duties and demands of the job, even though these years seemed to be among his most rewarding. He always got exemplary marks and recommendations. He was totally committed to the students and their progress. He was in the habit of picking up one of his more serious art students every Tuesday night to take him to the weekly lecture at Fort Worth's Modern Art Museum. For two years, he added coaching to his schedule, but found the demands too taxing. He was interested in trying to resurrect his own art career.

Greg thought about retirement because he didn't like the changes in the education climate. As in most schools, technology was taking over. He struggled to learn how to use the computer, input grades, or send emails. He still wanted to use pen and paper for his assignments and grades. Greg was losing cognitive ability and could not learn a new task. He retired for the first time at the end of the school year in 2006.

After a year hiatus, Greg missed the classroom. His impressive resume and art experience got him a coveted art teaching position at Aledo High School in Aledo, Texas, in the fall of 2007.

In the summer of 2008, Greg opted to have a joint fusion to repair damage to an ankle that was twice broken in football games. His strong work ethic kept him from recuperating properly. While hobbling on crutches in the classroom, he fell and broke out the pins holding his ankle together. After a second emergency surgery, he couldn't go back to work for several months and had trouble keeping up. The behavioral and cognitive decline seemed to worsen after the surgeries.

The principal at the high school got wind of his inability to keep up, and I suggested he take a medical leave of absence. She was not sympathetic to this older man and just wanted him off her staff.

Dementia was making it difficult for him to perform his job as he'd done in the past. This was Greg's first workplace encounter in which someone thought he was inadequate in his job. He went into a severe depression from losing the work he loved and his community of people.

Greg was diagnosed, at the age of 60, with early onset dementia in February 2009. The first neurologist thought football could have something to do with it. A second opinion was warranted.

Based on all the data and psychological testing, the second research scientist was unwavering in her Alzheimer's diagnosis. Then a third neurologist who had more experience with head injury and football patients believed the damage was very likely caused by football. Unfortunately, there was no way of knowing until after Greg's death. This doctor said one out of four dementia patients develop Alzheimer's, because the hippocampus, where memory is stored, is finally affected.

Amyloid protein development is suspected of causing tangles in the neurotransmitters in Alzheimer's.[90] Tau protein dispersion from neural damage causes those tangles in CTE. In my opinion, your frontal lobes are damaged first because of the impact in football to the front top of your head. This frontal lobe damage in a person affects problem-solving skills, impulse control, language, etc.

After our experience with so many memory care facilities and observing different patients, I can confidently say that people with different dementias exhibit different behaviors. The brain is so complicated that it's difficult for the experts to make a proper diagnosis.

---

90   "What happens to brain with Alzheimer's disease," National Institute on Aging, *U.S. Department of Health & Human Services,* accessed January 2, 2019 https://www.nia.nih.gov/health/what-happens-brain-alzheimers-disease

For some reading this, you may be looking for answers to try to discern if your loved one's behavior may mean he or she is suffering from brain damage. The experts themselves are struggling to diagnose before death, so I feel like an ordinary person's examples might be the best help you can get.

"Please don't leave my side"

You are the one best equipped to recognize your loved one's changes in behavior. I kept a journal and tracked my husband's changes as best I could. Greg was not able to problem solve as in the past; he became easily agitated; he could not express himself; and all of that left him very frustrated. He could not process what people were saying. He got words mixed up. He forgot how to add and subtract.

Greg always prepared our taxes and balanced the checkbook. One year, he announced, "I do not want to do it anymore." I just thought he was burned out, but now believe he must have felt inadequate and afraid of making a mistake.

I took over those duties. Greg always took care of our technology challenges in the house, such as setting up a new TV, VCR, or programming remotes. Those duties also became mine.

When Greg was still teaching high school, he'd come home and ask me to help him send an email. When I helped him, I'd give him a clear direction such as "push the send button," and one minute later he could not do it. He would say, "Please don't leave my side."

I was doing most of the driving when we went on trips. I don't know if it was because he was nervous driving, or I just took over. We had flip cell phones back then, and while driving to San Antonio to see his family, I'd suggest he call to alert them about when we'd arrive. I would have to tell him the number and then say "push the green button" to make the call go through. He couldn't understand that "green" meant go. He not only got confused using the phone, he didn't want to talk on it either.

During our one-to-one conversations, Greg got confused, and I'd have to hold his head with my hands and ask him to pay attention to me. I thought he was just being obstinate. I thought maybe he had a hearing problem, and I took him for a hearing test. His hearing was excellent. The sad reality was that he could not process what I was saying.

We would go out to dinner with longtime friends and he couldn't keep up with the conversation. He'd look at me to complete his thoughts and sentences. He'd get very frustrated and sometimes would leave the table. He eventually didn't want to socialize with anyone but me and close family.

One of the saddest memories for me was when he needed a phone number. He forgot how to use the phone book. He asked for my help, and when I went to assist, he said, "Please, Deb, just watch me and make sure I look up something correctly." He said he *wanted* to do it by himself.

Greg would misplace his wallet, keys, and cell phone almost every day. He couldn't perform the simplest of task, such as measuring and sawing a board, measuring and cutting his art paper, or even grading papers. He prided himself on being a backyard mechanic. One day he put oil – not gas – in the tank of our tractor. He burned up approximately seven batteries in our cars over a period of 16 months. He either left the keys in the ignition and car on, or he left the door open.

These mishaps brought on more depression and isolation. He cried often and finally agreed to take the anti-depressant Zoloft. It helped him stop crying. He also agreed to take a drug called Strattera that was supposed to help him focus. He only took the drug for three months, even getting his barn/art studio cleaned up, but he stopped taking it because it upset his stomach.

In 2011, we started planning a move to San Antonio. Greg wanted to retire there near his family, and I needed the support.

I thought we were settled in San Antonio, but Greg became more and more agitated and lost. I felt isolated and wanted to live near our daughter, Erin, and soon-to-be-born grandson. Erin felt helpless with us that far away and wanted us near her. In 2013, we bought a small house one mile from Erin in Dallas.

Greg's behavior and agitation became aggressive. He began kicking the bed and stomping on the ground outside because he couldn't express what he wanted. We hadn't been to his doctor for about three years and I called for an appointment. They said they couldn't see him for three months. The nurse practitioner said there was nothing they could do for us and to take him to a psychiatric hospital. I did, and he was released early after I pressured them to let him out. After being on two drugs when entered the hospital, he came out using five medications. It felt like the medical community wanted to shut him down, and the drugs were meant to do just that.

The anti-psychotic drugs made him start hallucinating. He would say there were people in the other room. He'd peer out the windows to see if someone was out-side. He'd sleep in his clothes and shoes. Someone once told me that was a sign of fear because he was ready to escape.

He wouldn't take a shower, using the word "drown" at one point. He lived in fear. He was afraid of everything and everyone.

Greg was never aggressive in his life, except when he was on the football field. I believe most of his behavior – kicking, thrashing, yelling – was because he couldn't communicate his needs or wants. He never hurt me, but would push me if I was trying to get him to do something he didn't want to do. I'd stay calm, hug him, and redirect him.

I believe most people think the behaviors of those who are suffering are intentional. They are not. Greg would go into protective mode when he was approached or forced to do something, especially by large, male caregivers. He was following his instincts, like in football, to protect himself. It is so sad to see how people like Greg are mistreated. Three times, he was strapped to a gurney and taken to a hospital. They treated him like an everyday criminal. Here was this gentle soul in a place you would never have seen him if he had not had this disease.

At our home in Dallas in 2013, I tried to keep him busy. To distract him from anxious behaviors, I bought many puzzles that were meant for young children. We'd work those together for an hour, then move onto something else. He'd go to our garage/studio, passing time by opening and closing boxes. We could have bought stock in the packing tape business because we purchased about a roll almost every day.

Greg woke up at about 4:30 every morning. He'd pace for hours up and down our small hallway with me in tow. He wouldn't let me sleep because he was afraid. I don't think he was afraid of his surroundings, but was fearful of being alive and of what was happening to him. Many dementia patients voice, "I want to go home," and what some experts think is that they're actually feeling, "I want to go back to the way I was before I got sick."

Greg looked to me for answers. One day, peered at me across the kitchen table and said, "Deb, please help me. I don't want to be like this."

I did figure one thing out to help him. I procured a marijuana joint, and he smoked two puffs. It calmed him immediately and he didn't show any fear, paranoia, agitation, and he sat for hours staring at the TV. This was unprecedented, and he even seemed to understand some of the conversation on the TV. He'd even laugh at times. I knew I was on to something.

The next week we were headed to Golden, Colorado where our son, Beau, lives. The first month of that journey was very difficult, but we secured a medical marijuana license and I became his legal caregiver. It allowed me to buy the medical marijuana oil and administer it to him. He wasn't able to make those kind of decisions.

I found a memory care facility in Colorado that would let him live there, with my stipulation that I could come twice a day to give him the oil. He lived there for seven months, but it wasn't without problems. They ended up asking us to leave and said it was because they didn't want marijuana on the premises. I believe the real reason was they wanted to get rid of me. I became a thorn in their side because I called them out on the improper care of my husband, but also for other residents. There was a lot that didn't seem right in this facility.

We went to our daughter's home in Dallas for three weeks and finally found a memory care facility that would take him for respite, until I figured out our next move. It was very nice, cost $6,000 per month and the care was good compared to the other facilities we'd experienced. They were kind enough to work with me on the amounts of drugs they'd give him. They pretty much kept him off the anti -psychotic drugs and introduced heavy doses of Benadryl and Klonopin. That kept him somewhat calm, but he could barely walk because he was so sedated.

Several years earlier, he kept saying the word "Arkansas." I finally figured out he wanted to move to Arkansas. He was doing that for me! He wanted me to get the support and help from my sisters. He was so kind and sweet, even in his condition, to think of me.

We moved to a rented house in North Little Rock in February 2015. Greg told me he wanted to live with me, and, of course, I wanted to be with him. He obviously didn't realize how difficult it was caring for him. The poor man wanted to get better, and he wanted his dignity. Our relationship over the last three years turned from one of husband/wife to patient/caregiver. I was determined to care for him myself as best I could. My sisters came almost every day to help me.

During this entire journey, you would not know Greg was sick by just looking at him physically. He had no other health issues, and people would say to me, "He seems fine." Close to the end, he started losing weight. He was then admitted to hospice, which sent a nurse twice a week to help me bathe him. I hired a very caring young woman, Courtney, to come sit with him four days a week so I could exercise.

Four months before Greg died, our daughter and grandson visited. The week after they were gone, he looked across the room to where our grandson had played, pointed, and said, "Kid?" I asked him if he was asking about our grandson and he said, "Yes." Once, he looked at a picture on the wall of a person snowboarding. He said, "Beau." Our son is a snowboarder.

One month before he died, we were sitting on the couch together. He said, "Deb, you are the love of my life." The best parts of my day were when he would hug me. I told him he was the love of my life, and I thanked him for being with me for 37 years. He would say the word "money." I asked him, "Are you worried about me not having enough money?" He said, "Yes."

Your Child Shouldn't Die This Way

Greg's best friend, Bob Callison, came to visit two weeks before he died. Greg was falling a lot. Bob picked him up off the floor and said, "Buddy, someday you are not going to want to get back up." Bob would cry and wanted Greg to let go because Greg was so sick. Greg was so strong and positive, and wanted to keep living, but as he got worse, his desire to live faded.

Over the five months in Arkansas, our son and daughter came to see him several times, and he recognized them every time. My sisters were amazed how aware he was. My point being, he did not lose his memory like those who suffer from Alzheimer's.

One week before Greg died, he'd finally given up. He stood at the kitchen sink and said, "I want to die." He was gone seven days later. He passed away in a hospice home in Little Rock on May 11, 2015. His family came to tell him goodbye. He died in the middle of the night with myself and his sister, Susie, by his side.

One of the most beautiful things happened. A huge thunderstorm came through and, suddenly, there was a flash from an enormous bolt of lightning. The electricity went off in the facility right at the time he died. It felt symbolic, because Greg loved thunderstorms.

If someone older is having cognitive problems, the medical community immediately diagnoses them as to having early onset Alzheimer's.[91] One expert told me people with Alzheimer's do not complain of headaches. CTE patients do so often. During the late 1990s and early 2000s, Greg complained a lot about having headaches, which was unusual for him. I realize now he already was suffering the decline.

CTE affects the language and executive function of the brain.[92] Not being able to communicate is so frustrating. The bottom line is that these people are losing their minds. This damage kills the brain slowly, and they are suffering with no relief! Why does it progress faster in some than others? There is so much need for research!

Some of these men take their own lives by suicide, some die of accidental drug overdoses, and some die from reckless behavior. We know this disease causes severe personality problems that are not controllable. I believe many men with CTE are pegged as having bipolar disorder and end up in prison for murder, domestic abuse, assaults, etc.

If I could offer comfort to those who have lost loved ones to suicide, and find out later that they had CTE, I can say confidently that I understand why they wanted to end their lives. Life is hard enough to navigate without having this brain disease. It adds an equation that is difficult to overcome. A person's chance of creating a safe and grounded life is diminished by having this disease. It causes such undue stress and noise in their heads. Our daughter explained Greg's effort

---

91   "Ten early signs and symptoms of Alzheimer's," *Alzheimer's Association,* accessed January 3, 2019 https://www.alz.org/alzheimers-dementia/10_signs

92   Montennigro, P.H., Baugh, C.M., Daneshvar, D.H., Mez, J., Budson, A.E., Au, Rhoda, Katz, D., Cantu, R.C., Stern, R.A., "Clinical subtypes of chronic traumatic encephalopathy: Literature review and proposed research diagnostic criteria for traumatic encephalopathy syndrome," *NCBI,* accessed, January 26, 2019 https://www.ncbi.nlm.nih.gov/pmc/articles/PMC4288217/

to talk was similar to a static radio when driving down a country road. Her dad was thinking clearly one second and the next his thought was gone.

People don't want to accept that football causes brain damage and CTE. The following are some of the things I've heard from very educated and loving people. They just don't know the risks or don't want to face them.

Naïve people have said, "I played football and nothing is wrong with me. Not everyone gets it, so hopefully my child won't." One or two concussions don't cause CTE, but can lead to seizures and second-impact syndrome. Football puts you in a more vulnerable position to sustain not only several concussions, but hundreds of sub-concussive hits. It's this silent traumatic brain injury that causes the disease. The younger the age you start and the longer you play contributes to the likelihood you'll have this degenerative brain disease.

"Not everyone gets CTE, so I have no problem with my child playing the sport." Parents say they want their child to be able to make the decision for themselves. What age is it that makes them mature enough to learn the facts and make an intelligent decision? By law, parents must make their child wear a seatbelt because they know an accident can cause death or serious brain damage.

Why can't they see that this silent killer is harmful to their child? You might as well put a helmet on your child's head and tell him to run into a brick wall 20 times a day. The helmet is meant to protect the skull, not the soft brain tissue inside. It's not unlike shaken baby syndrome.

Greg's damage to his tau protein possibly occurred at an early age, and it spread like an invasive cancer until the protein totally smothered his neurotransmitters. Once this damage occurs, it is totally irreversible.

Some football players say they'd still play the sport, even if they knew they were going to die from this disease. CTE not only causes dementia, researchers have begun to study its possible contribution to Parkinson's and ALS. Many older football players are told they have Alzheimer's. It could very well be CTE! There is a difference! It may look similar in some ways, but behaviors and damage in the brain are different. One sportswriter said, "CTE is old news." I am trying to make an impact on the football world so that this is a disease that no one should have to endure because someone else is making a profit!

Many of my friends' grandchildren are playing football, even though their parents saw Greg and told their children how much he suffered! Their response is "You die of something; 66 years is a long life; and having dementia is a pretty easy death because you lose your memory." Greg knew who we were until the very end.

Many people say, "The things you learn from a team sport outweigh the risk of playing football." I say, "Pick another sport."

If I had one piece of advice with anyone taking care of someone with this disease, it would be to consider the use of medical marijuana. The person is going to die of the disease, so why not give them some relief? It was amazing the cognitive function Greg had while on medical marijuana. It seemed to slow the noise in his head, and he could talk more.

I hesitate to tell our story because I don't want to hurt Greg's good name. He was a caring, compassionate man who would want to save lives. My journey caring for my wonderful husband and best friend was very difficult, but it was nothing compared to what Greg was going through. I just kept on loving him and tried to find him some peace.

Some of the saddest times for me came after his death, when naïve people would say things like, "At least Greg didn't suffer like some other people I know." They said dementia is nothing like a stroke or cancer, and he was not in pain. Greg was in terrible mental anguish, and he couldn't put a voice to that. All I can say is that people don't know how much Greg suffered.

I'm asked if I think Greg would have played football if he knew he was going to suffer like this. I say, "Absolutely not." He quit watching football in 2012. He chose to play football and loved it, but had no idea about this disease. He loved his team and the sport, but his true passion was for art.

Being able to tell our story helps me grieve. At the time of his death, I knew Greg was still the same sweet, loving, compassionate person I married. I knew Greg was still inside. He couldn't communicate his needs through language, but he did through touch.

If Greg's suffering can save one person from this horrible disease, then the suffering in his life and death was not in vain. Yes, we are all going to die, but after you've read this, you can choose for your child not to die *this way*. How much worse can it get?

CHAPTER 9

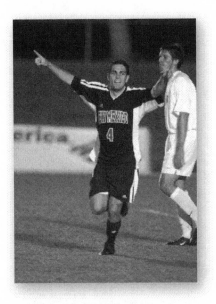

Patrick Grange

November 4, 1982 – April 10, 2012

Patrick Grange owns a unique and sad place in the history of brain trauma and sports. After his shockingly quick death at 29 years old after being diagnosed with ALS only 17 months before, Patrick became the first soccer player to have chronic traumatic encephalopathy (CTE) discovered in his brain by doctors at Boston University. His case garnered national attention when CTE was just beginning to be talked about in the media. Football had been the focus of many reports about CTE, but doctors were also beginning to understand the effect of the constant blows to the brain through "heading" in soccer. Patrick was a star high school player and a member of two Division I college teams, but also suffered numerous head injuries early on his life that may have contributed to his condition. When he died, his parents donated his brain, and it was discovered he had Stage II CTE, the damage was considered as the worst doctors had seen for someone in his 20s.

Empty Chair
By Michele and Mike Grange

Just two weeks after his 28th birthday, our son, Patrick Grange, was diagnosed with ALS – more commonly known as Lou Gehrig's disease. Of the 5,000 people each year who are found to have ALS, very few are in their 20s. The average age is 58.

After a valiant struggle with this horrific, paralyzing illness, Pat passed at the age of 29 on April 12, 2012 – only 17 months following his diagnosis.[93] We lost him much quicker than the three to six years the doctors had predicted.

ALS was the cause of Patrick's death, but as we would find out, the damage to his brain had been done years before.

Concussion Legacy Foundation requested the study of Patrick's brain, and what they discovered became a piece of history in the studies of brain damage in athletes. He was found to have chronic traumatic encephalopathy (CTE), becoming the first soccer player in the United States to be diagnosed with this disease.

Doctors found severe frontal lobe atrophy and 30 instances of the presence of the protein tau. It was concluded that Patrick had stage II CTE, and the doctors said his brain damage was the most advanced they'd seen for someone in his 20s.

---

93 Patrick Grange obituary, *Albuquerque Journal*, accessed January 5, 2019 http://obits.abqjournal.com/obits/show/225014

Doctors and the Media Take Notice

The ESPN program "E:60" produced a short documentary,[94] and Pat's story was included in another documentary – "Head Games, the Global Crisis."[95] *The New York Times*[96] and "Good Morning America"[97] covered Pat's story. *National Geographic* included a piece on head trauma and soccer featuring Patrick as part of its "Explorer" series.[98]

Patrick suffered major concussions in high school and college, being both knocked out and requiring stitches. But what we, his parents, believe to be the primary cause of his brain damage was constant practice doing repeated headers, as well as intense play and collisions from preschool through middle school.

Noteworthy are the many instances Patrick "banged his head" as a youth. Being the youngest of three boys, he was athletically active and showed advanced coordination.

At the age of 1, he hit his head on the edge of a concrete driveway and received stitches. Starting at the age of 3, Pat would spend hours throwing up a soccer ball and heading it into the net.

Through elementary and middle school, Patrick always played his hardest, colliding with other players and performing headers often. In third grade, he was knocked out when he ran into a pole on the playground. And in sixth grade, while playing basketball, he collided with another player whose nose was broken.

It has been discovered that the young brain, especially for children under the age of 14, is extremely fragile and should not be exposed to these types of injuries. We believe that these early instances of multiple, repetitive brain trauma greatly contributed to Pat's brain disease.

94   ESPN "E: 60" Pat Grange (Full Segment HD), *ESPN* https://youtu.be/ibvIrWle_yI

95   Steve James, "Head games: The global concussion crisis" trailer, *YouTube,* accessed January 26, 2019 https://www.youtube.com/watch?v=FnHN-CwyRBQ

96   John Branch, "Brain trauma extends to the soccer field," *New York Times,* February 26, 2014, accessed January 3, 2019 https://www.google.com/amp/s/www.nytimes.com/2014/02/27/sports/soccer/researchers-find-brain-trauma-disease-in-a-soccer-player.amp.html

97   Gillian Mohney, "First soccer player diagnosed with CTE brings up sport's risks," *CBS News,* February 27, 2014, accessed January 5, 2019 https://www.google.com/amp/s/abcnews.go.com/amp/Health/soccer-player-diagnosed-cte-brings-sports-risks/story%3fid=22697477

98   Graham Donohoe, "Football's new brain bombshell as shock research links motor neuron disease to heading the ball," *Scotland Daily Record,* September 24. 2017, accessed January 5, 2019 https://www.google.com/amp/s/www.dailyrecord.co.uk/news/scottish-news/footballs-new-brain-bombshell-shock-11227657.amp

ALS Diagnosis Rocks Friends and Family

When Patrick was diagnosed with ALS, it was a shock. The disease generally occurs when people are in their 50s. Despite his shy demeanor, generating ALS awareness and research became Pat's focus. He was instrumental in making a difference.

Patrick was born and raised in Albuquerque, New Mexico, and he has two older brothers, Casey and Ryan; two sisters-in-law, Melissa and Ali; a niece, Addison; and a nephew, Michael. In addition to Pat's family, his amazing supporter during his illness was his girlfriend, Amanda Aragon.

Patrick was best known for being a standout athlete. He also has been described as quiet, optimistic, kind, non-judgmental, brave, loving, sensitive, humorous, and very handsome. He possessed a brilliant smile and sparkling eyes. Many have said that he had a magnetic personality and everyone enjoyed being around him.

Pat demonstrated extraordinary sports skills and coordination at a very young age. "Ball" was his first word and he rarely was without one. He was an amazing basketball point guard and a Little League All-Star catcher, but his passion was soccer, which he played his entire life.

Patrick grew up playing club soccer, won state championships and traveled around the U.S. for tournaments. He was a member of the Olympic Development Program for three summers.[99] He assisted his high school in qualifying for the state final and was the first soccer player to be inducted into the Albuquerque High Sports Hall of Fame.

In his high school senior year, Pat was chosen as the *Albuquerque Tribune's* Soccer Player of the Year. In college, he played for two NCAA Division I programs – two years for the University of Illinois at Chicago and the final two at the University of New Mexico. Patrick's multiple goals in his senior year earned UNM a place in the Sweet 16.

After college, Pat played for the Albuquerque semi-pro team, Asylum. Additionally, he played on a team in the Premier Indoor Soccer League that made it to the national finals. He also spent three months in England pursuing a pro soccer career.

After returning to the United States, Pat continued to play and be involved in soccer. He served as a coach at the club, high school and Olympic Developmental Program levels. He worked as assistant manager at the International Indoor Soccer Arena in Albuquerque and greatly enjoyed being a soccer instructor for the Lil' Kickers youth program. He also continued to play on multiple adult soccer teams.

Honoring an Athlete

Pat touched many lives, and his impact lives on through various events organized by those who want honor him.

UIC alumni sponsor a golf tournament and an Ales for ALS music festival each year in Pat's name to raise money for ALS. The University of New Mexico hosts a yearly soccer tournament dedicated to Patrick and the Albuquerque PDL team, Sol FC, also has a Pat Grange game annually. Friends and family walk in Pat's honor at the annual Albuquerque ALS Walk each September.

---

99   Stanley Kay, "Deceased soccer player's brain reveals presence of CTE," *Sports Illustrated,* February 26, 2014, accessed January 5, 2019 https://www.google.com/amp/s/amp.si.com/si-wire/2014/02/26/deceased-soc-cer-player-brain-cte

The Albuquerque Public Schools are incorporating into their curriculum the "Team Up/Speak Up" class designed to educate youth on head trauma. And every February 3rd is Pat Grange New Mexico ALS Awareness Day in the state legislature.

We are pleased and proud that all of these events have helped spread brain injury awareness.

The Grange family loves sports and supports athletic activities that establish fitness, character building, leadership and team work. But we strongly encourage head trauma awareness and stress the great importance of resting the brain after a head injury – for a minimum of two weeks, possibly longer, if necessary.

It should be noted that concussions are not necessarily only present when a person loses consciousness. Even seemingly minor hits to the head can cause a person to experience dizziness, "seeing stars," blurred vision, problems with balance or memory, and headaches. Those are all symptoms of head trauma.

We also would like to stress that the damage from multiple small hits can worsen with each subsequent hit, or when those hits come closer together. Subsequent concussions seem to happen more easily and can cause more harm.

Our hope is that coaches of all sports involving young children will eliminate the practice of hard contact play. We are happy that soccer's governing body, FIFA, has changed the rules for heading drills, which may not be included in practices until the age of 11, while heading during games before that age is ruled as a foul. (We support extending this rule to age 14.)[100]

We would like to reiterate that if a child appears to have had mild head trauma, in any activity, the child should be held out of rough play and organized contact sports, and they need to rest their brain for at least two weeks.

The continuing study of CTE and the promotion of brain injury awareness to help reduce the occurrence of this terrible, devastating disease deserves to be a priority for everyone! Because few players will become professionals in their sport, the danger of head trauma is not worth the risk and consequences.

---

100   Darren Rovell, "Proposed heading ban to curtail concussions," *ESPN,* November 9, 2015, accessed January 6, 2019
      http://www.espn.com/soccer/united-states/story/2707094/court-settlement-proposes-ban-for-heading-
      the-ball

Kimberly Archie, NFL Hall of Fame Cornerback, Mike Haynes and Debbie Pyka at Brain Injury Day on Capitol Hill in 2016

Kimberly Archie with the founder of PINKConcussions, Katherine Snedaker

Kimberly Archie, Luisa Seau, Tiaina Seau Sr., & Mary Seau

Group Photo Faces of CTE Annual Awards Dinner 2018

Mary Seau CTE Foundation Annual Gala 2018, Kimberly Archie, Nathan Fletcher, NFL HOF Cornerback Mike Haynes, California Assemblywoman Lorena Gonzalez, and Mary Seau

Larry Mallory, Kimberly Archie - Faces of CTE families first meeting, Boston, October 2018

Kimberly Archie and Solomon Brannan
at the Super Bowl 2019

Debra Pyka, Kimberly Archie, Cyndy Feasel

Mary Seau, Solomon Brannan, Jo Cornell
San Diego 2018

CTE families at the Faces of CTE breakfast 2017

Sean Morey, Mike Haynes, Debra Pyka, Congressman
Pascrell Brain Injury Day on Capitol Hill 2016

Junior Seau and Mary Seau

PROFESSIONAL ATHLETES

CHAPTER 10

Grant Feasel

June 28, 1960 – July 15, 2012

Grant Feasel was a center who played in 117 games in the span of a decade in the NFL. Drafted by a Baltimore franchise that moved to Indianapolis, the bulk of Feasel's career came with the Seattle Seahawks. He grew up in Barstow, California, and attended Abilene Christian in Texas, enjoying a standout college career that put him on NCAA Division II "Team of the Quarter Century" that was announced in 1997. After retiring in 1992, Grant, his wife, Cyndy, and their three children – Sean, Sarah and Spencer – moved back to their hometown of Dallas to start the next chapter of their lives.

The following is an excerpt from Cyndy Feasel's
2016 book, "After the Cheering Stops."[101]

A Life in Anguish
By Cyndy Feasel

I knew the Dallas area pretty well, having grown up there, but I didn't know where Colleyville was. I was clueless because this community of 13,000 sprang up in the shadow of Dallas-Fort Worth International when the airport became a major hub in the 1980s. I soon learned that Colleyville attracted upper middle-class families with median household incomes of well over $100,000.

I had no desire to live in such an upscale area. We had lived in Rockwall and it felt like a broken-in pair of slippers—comfortable and warm. New and fashionable, Colleyville felt like the unknown. When our son Sean heard that we were looking at homes in Colleyville, he got upset. He had lots of friends in his fourth-grade class and loved his school.

Grant had an answer for that objection. He said that he'd heard that Fort Worth Christian School, close to Colleyville, was a great place to send your kids.

The new homes that Grant was looking at were at least double the cost of our home in Rockwall. "Shouldn't we be talking about moving into a more economical neighborhood?" I asked. "What about looking closer to Dallas Christian School, which would put us nearer to the airport like you want?" If Grant was dead-set on living closer to DFW, we could move a bit more west without disrupting the kids' schooling or our membership at Saturn Road Church of Christ.

Grant shook his head. "Nope, not going to work. We'll move into the house we want, and that will be the house we will live in forever."

---

101 Cyndy Feasel, "After the Cheering Stops: An NFL Wife's Story of Concussions, Loss, and the Faith that Saw Her Through," accessed January 25, 2019 https://www.amazon.com/dp/B01F9LQ0YY/ref=dp-kindle-re-direct?_encoding=UTF8&btkr=1

Grant's mind was made up. I couldn't get him to budge. Although something didn't feel right about this move, he was the leader of the family.

At nearly 4,500 square feet, our new home was certainly an upgrade from Rockwall, and it was easy to get caught up in the excitement of "moving on up" into a grander home. I believe the price was $400,000, twice that of our Rockwall home. Fortunately, our old place sold quickly at a good price, but we had to live in a Residence Inn for two months until our new house was finished.

In the coming years, Grant's decision to move us to expensive Colleyville would put us under incredible financial stress, expose the growing divide in our marital relationship, exacerbate Grant's drinking problem, increase his addiction to painkillers, and eventually lead us into a very dark place.

In hindsight, I believe this is the time when chronic traumatic encephalopathy (CTE) began triggering progressive degeneration in Grant's brain tissues.[102] I say that because the Grant Feasel I married—the peaceful, easy-feeling guy—was rapidly changing into a mean-spirited and abusive person I barely recognized. His actions would propel me into years of therapy, suffering from post-traumatic stress disorder (PTSD) because of what happened with Grant in Colleyville.

Our financial woes through the years would become a huge embarrassment.

One time, I drove to Albertson's supermarket. I wrote a check out for my grocery purchase and handed it to the cashier. She punched in some numbers and scanned the check. "Sorry, ma'am. The check's no good."

"Really?" My face turned red. I felt mortified as my groceries were packed up and placed in a shopping cart that was pulled off to the side. I drove home feeling extremely upset.

Grant's explanation? "I didn't know there wasn't any money in the checking account." He had enough cash on hand to allow me to return to Albertson's to pick up the groceries, but what happened bothered me greatly.

---

102 "Chronic traumatic encephalopathy, *Mayo Clinic* accessed January 22, 2019 https://www.mayoclinic.org/ diseases-conditions/chronic-traumatic-encephalopathy/symptoms-causes/syc-20370921

That night, before Grant went into our bedroom to relax with his "Diet Cokes," he handed me an American Express card. "If you're going to use this card, you have to let me know before making any purchases," he said.

This was so unsettling. It wasn't long before I got a phone call from American Express notifying me that this card was in arrears and we were being sent to a collection agency.

I hung up and waited for Grant to come home from work. After describing the phone call, I asked, "How come we're not paying on the card?" Grant wasn't even making the minimum payments.

"I'm working on that," he said. Then he offered an excuse. "They charged me for something they shouldn't have, so we can't use that card anymore."

One day, I happened to get the mail when Grant was out of town. There were two statements in the mail from Citibank Visa. I didn't know that we had *two* different credit cards from Citibank. The identical letters notified us that we were over the $10,000 limit, and since Grant hadn't been making the minimum payments each month, our credit was being cut off. Oh, and we needed to pay off the cards immediately or be sent to collection.

"What's going on here?" I demanded. "No wonder we can't buy furniture."

"Things will get straightened out when I get some money in a few weeks," he said.

Again, I was in the dark about how much Grant was earning or when he'd receive his next commission check. A couple of days later, Grant found me in the kitchen. He was holding a new credit card in his hand. "Here, use this, but only after you've cleared it with me." It was another American Express card.

"Why am I getting another American Express card when we can't pay off the other American Express card or our Visa cards?" I thought it was a fair question.

"I got a solicitation in the mail, so I called in and got the card. It's turned on and ready to use."

This was getting crazy. "Grant, how bad are our finances?" I asked.

Grant refused to answer.

I asked Grant if I could help out with the checkbook, he looked at me and smirked. "No, you'll just mess things up. I know you too well."

"I can get a calculator and do the checkbook," I said cheerfully, doing my best to ignore the barb. I had a checkbook in college, and while I didn't like doing the math or keeping track of the ledger, I managed to not write any bad checks.

"Nah," Grant replied. "You can't imagine how many bills we have and how I have to juggle everything. Forget it. I'll handle things. You'll just mess things up even more."

The condescension was overwhelming. I would find out later that Grant paid a moving company $10,000 to pack us up and move us 50 miles, had given a $15,000 loan to a friend with a gambling problem (that was never paid back, of course), and took out a separate bank loan to pay for the construction of the swimming pool—and stopped making payments to the bank. Eventually, Grant stopped making our mortgage payments and we lost our home to foreclosure. Meanwhile, he continued to pay for family trips to California several times a year, with stops at Disneyland, Sea World, and Knott's Berry Farm – activities we weren't even close to being able to afford.

Years later, I said to my sister, Lori, "Why didn't anyone in the family say something to us when we sold our home and moved to Colleyville?"

Lori replied, "Because we thought Grant was an ex-NFL football player who could afford anything he wanted."

So did I.

"Strange and Surreal"

The move to Colleyville was the start of what I call the "strange and surreal" period of Grant's life. I was becoming more and more flabbergasted by the way he was talking to me. The putdowns were constant, and his belittling manner denigrated me at every turn. We could not have a civil conversation unless the kids were around.

This was so unlike the Grant I knew in the early years of our marriage. I missed the soft side of him, a sweet guy who strummed Eagles' songs on his guitar and felt vulnerable enough to sing to me. Now he was always on my case for just about anything and everything, especially our precarious financial situation.

We got into it one night after the kids were asleep. I'm not sure what precipitated the conversation, but it was probably about how the credit cards weren't working.

"Grant, something isn't right here. I just need you to tell me what it is. Why did you think we needed to move to Colleyville and buy a house this size?" I asked.

Grant leaned back with a smug look. "It's your fault we moved here. You're the one who wanted to move into a big new home like this."

"That's not true! You know it's not."

"You had to have this house. You got what you wanted because nothing else was good enough for you. You wanted a fancy new kitchen and a game room for the kids and all those extra bedrooms."

I was incredulous that Grant was putting the blame on me.

One day, Grant found me in his closet and went ballistic.

"What are you doing in my closet?" he yelled. "I told you not to stick your nose into my business!"

"All you do is drink when you come home from work! You're drunk half the time!"

Something snapped in Grant. He suddenly pressed his big right hand on my chest and shoved me. He was still strong as a mule. I tumbled into a folding chair that he kept in the closet and spilled onto the carpeted floor, which was a sea of dress loafers and Nike sneakers. I was catching my breath when Grant slammed the door, leaving me totally in the dark.

Did this really just happen?

This was the first time Grant was physically abusive with me. As I gathered myself, I knew I was going to get up and walk out of the closet, but I was afraid he would be waiting for me on the other side of the door. I began crying, then picked myself up and cautiously exited the closet. Grant had left. I walked out to the kitchen, saw the kids doing their homework, and never said a word about the ugly incident to them or anyone else.

I didn't speak to Grant for a week. I never even made eye contact with him. He said nothing about it, as if it never happened.

We'd lived in Colleyville for a couple of years when Grant asked me if I would accompany him to a hospital fund-raiser in a fancy hotel ballroom. Grant bought a table for 10 on behalf of Hill-Rom and invited several doctors and key hospital personnel and their spouses to join him. Grant felt it was important that I accompany him since the social gathering could become an important deal-making event for him.

Hospital galas are dressy occasions, so I wore a formal black evening dress. Grant dressed in a tux. A valet took our car in front of a luxury hotel in downtown Fort Worth.

It was a long night with a three-course meal. I noticed early on that a bottle of red wine was stationed in front of Grant, and I wasn't keeping up with him. After refilling glasses of his guests, he'd pour himself a refill. Ten, twenty minutes later, he'd do the same thing. And then another bottle of wine would appear in front of Grant. By the time Larry Gatlin came on, his guests said they'd had enough. Not Grant. He kept right on pouring.

At the end of the evening, we stood up to leave. Grant looked like a California redwood about to topple to the forest floor. When he started walking, it was apparent that he was drunk. This was the first time I'd ever seen him stagger from drinking too much.

I insisted on being behind the wheel, and as I drove our Suburban home, my emotions got the best of me. I was furious and embarrassed.

"What happened tonight? Don't you know how you looked in front of all those people, many of whom are your clients?"

"Shut up," he said. "Just get me home."

This was Grant's first public intoxication. In the coming years, there would be many more incidents of him staggering in public, slurring his words, and falling to the ground and hurting himself.

We continued our pattern of fighting. Even though we were at each other's throats most of the time, the kids never heard us fight. We only raised our voices and pointed our fingers when the kids weren't home or were outside playing, or when we were behind closed doors in our bedroom.

To the outside world, we were all smiles and looked like one big happy family. But that was so far from the truth.

At some point in the 2000s, I stopped staying in touch with my friends. I was wrapped up in my teaching job and caring for my kids, but life was easier when I let relationships fall by the wayside. If we didn't talk to anyone or go anywhere, then they wouldn't know how messed up our family was—or see the pain on my face.[103] Nobody knew the truth about Grant's alcoholism or the abuse he heaped upon me. Not even my parents or two sisters.

Grant didn't cultivate friendships either and stopped calling his family. I felt that we should keep the communication lines open, so I would send e-mails and occasionally pick up the phone to call his mother, Pat, or his sister, Linda, to describe what the kids were up to or what was new in our lives.

Grant was living in some alternate universe. I had begun exercising regularly, and Grant began accusing me of having affairs. At one point he told me that he'd been Googling my name. "I've seen all sorts of pictures of you with different men on the Internet," he said.

"What are you talking about? You Googled my name?"

"Yeah, I have. Wait until your dad finds out what you've been doing."

"This is crazy."

I turned on my heels and went to our home computer and Googled my name. Looking under "Images," there were four or five headshots of me, mostly from the Fort Worth Christian faculty page. Not one photo of me with another man, including Grant. I guess I had never done anything Google-worthy, but that's how delusional Grant was becoming.

I should have excused his warped view of my world as a product of the alcohol, but I couldn't. Grant *wanted* to hurt me with outlandish accusations and spiteful words. That's the way his passive-aggressive personality worked; he didn't yell at me, but he sure cut me into pieces.

What happened was so unbelievable and depressing that I just wanted to stay at the gym and be as far away from him as I could for as long as possible. The longer I ran on the treadmill, the happier I was because the minute I came home, Grant was all over me, ripping me constantly.

Did he ever say these things in front of the kids? Of course not. He made sure he spoke nicely to me when they were in earshot. But if we were in his home office or the bedroom door was shut, he would go on and on about how I was having an affair and had been two-timing him throughout our marriage and had even cheated on him before we got engaged. "And I still married you, to be nice," he said.

This was the time in our marriage that I compare to living in a mental institution, listening to a tape of him calling me a fat b—, asking me if I was seeing someone at the gym, and accusing me of having an affair.

There was no pleasing him in any way, shape, or form. He didn't like me fat, and he didn't like me skinny. He never told me I was beautiful. He never told me I was pretty. The way he treated me was so degrading and terrible. I don't know why I stood for it. I should have told him off and gotten in the car and driven away.

"I'm going to leave you because you don't love me," I said one night in our bedroom.

Grant chuckled. "You're not leaving me. Where would you go? Live with your parents? Really, Cyndy? You can't afford to live anywhere. You're a schoolteacher. You don't make enough to live on your own. The kids would never come live with you. Our kids want to have nice things, and they want to live in a nice house. They don't want to live in some nasty apartment somewhere. They don't want to go with you and live with your parents."

Our marriage was in tatters.

I left Grant in the summer of 2011. His health continued to deteriorate as his liver started shutting down. Twenty years of daily drinking had taken its toll.

He was hospitalized in the spring of 2012, and it was apparent that he did not have long to live. I visited Grant every night in the hospital. Toward the end of June, I asked Grant if I could lie next to him in his hospital bed. He nodded his approval.

I saw his DNR bracelet on his left wrist—Do Not Resuscitate—and shuddered. The years passed by in a flash. Standing before my dad and family and friends, we had given our lives to each other, for better or for worse, for richer or for poorer, in sickness and health, till death do us part.

Till death do us part. I held my breath because we were on the precipice of his death.

As if reading my mind, Grant took my hand and looked in my eyes, which were wet with tears. "I'm sorry for what I've done to you," he said, and he meant every word.

His simple sentence of contrition jolted me. I had never heard him say he was sorry for what he put me through.

"Thank you," I managed. "I'm sorry too. This is not the way we wanted it to be."

Grant exhaled, as if he wanted to get something more off his chest. Then he uttered the most profound sentence I ever heard him speak: "If I'd only known that what I loved the most would end up killing me and taking away everything I loved, I would have never done it," he said.

There wasn't anything I could say or add to what he said, because in a few words, he had said it all. Grant had made amends, and that released me.

We had a moment. I felt lighter than I had felt in years. I planted a light kiss on his cheek, said goodbye, and left the hospital feeling so sad. *He's going to die. He's really going to die!*

I'll never forget my last visit. When I walked into his hospital room, I was greeted by a surprise: Grant's eyes were open and clear, revealing a pure green pigment. Gone was the blackness. Grant's eyes hadn't been that clear in years!

Grant had a pair of plastic tubes inserted into his mouth, so he couldn't speak. I held his hand and cried, knowing that I was close to losing him. Grant tried to say something but couldn't. "You don't to have talk," I whispered. "I'm here to say goodbye."

Grant blinked his comprehension. I left the hospital feeling like we were at peace.

I never saw Grant alive again.[104]

---

104 Grant Earl Feasel obituary, *Legacy.com*, accessed January 7, 2019 https://www.legacy.com/obituaries/name/grant-feasel-obituary?pid=158609369

Grant's brain and spinal cord were sent to the brain bank to be examined. The results: Grant had brain damage including Stage III CTE.

The revelation that Grant had CTE was a game-changer for me. I now had a much better understanding behind the underlying reasons for his outrageous behavior. That didn't—and couldn't—excuse him for the way he belittled and abused me all those years, but this news gave me an explanation and context.

I'm heartbroken that Grant had CTE. I loved him. I loved him in spite of his addictions, and I loved him in spite of his CTE. I'm anguished and sad that our lives came to this and he fell into such a downward spiral after his NFL career ended.

CHAPTER 11

Justin Strzelczyk

August 18, 1968 – September 30, 2004

Justin Strzelczyk played nine seasons for the Pittsburgh Steelers as an offensive line-man. In college at the University of Maine, he appeared in the 1990 East-West Shrine Game, and so impressed Steelers head coach Chuck Knoll that he was selected in the 11th round of the 1990 NFL Draft. Known for picking up the sideline phone to the coaches' box and screaming into it, "Run the damn ball!" Strzelczyk was a key player in the Steelers reaching Super Bowl XXX. His death, at the age of 36, and his portrayal in the movie "Concussion," made him among the first to raise awareness of chronic traumatic encephalopathy (CTE).

Crash and Burn
By Keana McMahon

I heard the garage door open like so many nights before. I'd rolled over to look at the Bose clock next to our bed and in the light green I saw the time – 4:38am –blinding me, taunting me. It was the morning after our eighth wedding anniversary and we did not spend it together. There was no point. We were done with one another. I made sure I was scheduled to work the night of our anniversary, and Justin went out drinking.

The sitter was with the kids when I got home at 10 the night before, and all was quiet. I tried to fall back asleep like so many nights before, but instead laid awake staring at the ceiling. Eventually, I heard his footsteps on the stairs. Then the guest bedroom door slammed shut. I rolled over to pet my dog, Dylan, my only bed companion for months. I couldn't cry. I felt numb. After two years of this nightmare, the tears had dried up, and I knew what must be done, what I had avoided for so long.

The next morning, I got our children, Sabrina and Justin Jr., to school, came home and went upstairs to the guest bedroom. I opened the door and saw him lying there, smelling of sour beer and smoke. I was so angry. I yelled at Justin to wake up and asked where he had been all night. I don't remember his exact words, but he told me to leave him alone, let him sleep. I glared at him and said simply that he needed to go, that this was not working, that we couldn't keep doing this.

So he left. It was an uneventful departure. Justin took a few bags and moved in with his sister in our old home, which we kept as a rental property. No fighting, no tears, just some bags in the truck, and he was gone. The kids were used to him not being there. It worked better this way.

The previous two years had been a nightmare. The fighting got so bad at times that occasionally I'd leave with the kids to go "visit" my parents for a few days or more. Just to escape. I never told my family the real reason, just that I wanted to see them, and that the kids missed their grandparents. The two-hour drive went fast, and my kids loved going. One night, I had to come clean with my family. I had to tell them what had been going on, how had it had become. I never knew who Justin would be from one minute to the next. Sometimes he was a loving husband; 10 minutes later he was screaming at us for things that didn't make sense.

There was one day that brought out the worst in both of us, when we hit a new low. We were invited to a birthday party and everything was going well with us. A couple of months earlier we were fighting constantly, and I was spending more time at work trying to avoid being around him. He left for five days, but he came back and we were trying to work it out. I was looking forward to spending a fun night with friends.

I was rifling through my closet with that dilemma that all women have – had nothing to wear – so I decided to run to the mall while he stayed with the kids. I was gone for a couple hours. When I returned, his truck was gone, as were the kids. I thought nothing of it. Maybe he had taken them to grab something to eat before the sitter got there at 7 o'clock; maybe they just ran a quick errand. I was almost ready to go, had my new outfit on, and was ready to enjoy the evening when I heard him downstairs. I called for him, but got no answer. I went down to see him standing by the front door with a strange look on his face. I asked where the kids were. He said he had dropped them off at the sitter's because he didn't want them to be there, that he was leaving again, this time for good.

He headed upstairs and started to pack his bags. I begged, screamed and cried for him not to leave. I grabbed at his shirt trying to make him stay. I couldn't understand why this was happening. Everything had been going so great. We'd just taken the kids to a local amusement park the week before, had recently visited family in Buffalo and seen Niagara Falls. We were talking about a Disney trip. He seemed on board with it all. I couldn't let him go.

But within minutes my sadness turned to anger, and my anger turned to rage. I saw red. I grabbed his bag, threw it at him, and screamed at him that he couldn't do this – that we should just go to the party. I begged more, but it didn't matter. He didn't care. He walked past me, not taking his bag, and headed for the door, like I wasn't even there. I tried to block him, but he just pushed past me and kept going. When he got to the garage, I slammed the door and locked it. I was sobbing when I heard his truck start. I grabbed the keys to my Suburban and ran out the front door. I jumped into my SUV, then followed him down the driveway. We lived on eight acres in a secluded, very large home. Our driveway was about 80 yards long and is known as a governor's driveway because it splits, then loops to eventually meet again. He went left and I went right. At the merge, I didn't stop. I wasn't going very fast, but enough that when metal hit metal, I felt a jolt. I had run into his truck, on purpose, to make him stay, to get him to notice me, or maybe just because I was pissed.

We got out of our cars. Suddenly, I was scared. I thought maybe I had gone too far, that he was going to come after me. I ran back to the house and locked myself inside. I sat in my laundry room, sobbing, wanting it to just be OK, for him to knock on the door and say he was sorry. That's when I heard the sirens. He had called the police and claimed I was suicidal.

I went outside to plead my case, telling them I was fine, that it was just a fight. I pleaded with Justin to tell them the truth, but he only stared at me, not saying much other than a few things to the officers that I couldn't hear. I heard him say something about calling my mom, and that he would follow us to the hospital and make sure my family knew what was going on. An officer told me he had to take me to a hospital for an evaluation – that when a spouse says another spouse is a threat, it's what they have to do.

I knew I was in a bad situation, so I complied with everything they asked – until I tried to run into the woods. After about 50 feet of running in bare feet, suede pants, and a tank top, while being chased by two officers, I knew it was hopeless, and that I was just making myself look like an insane person. So I stopped running, got into the ambulance and went to the hospital.

Oddly, they didn't take me to the large psychiatric hospital in downtown Pittsburgh. They took me to a now-defunct Sisters of the Divine Providence hospital, which I thought was strange, as it was not known for seeing "mental" patients.

It was a small hospital on the north side of Pittsburgh that Justin was sent to after developing a staph infection. He played a game with staph raging through his body and a 104-degree temperature. They just shot him up with antibiotics and let him play. Later I found out that the Rooney family, owners of the Pittsburgh Steelers, had heavy ties to this small hospital, and that it was possible, out of fear of "media attention," the ambulance driver was told to go there. Looking back, it was all very suspicious, as if Justin had planned this all along.

I used the pay phone to call my parents and tell them what had been going on, how much I had hidden from them, and how bad it had gotten. I was released four hours later. Justin was told to leave the premises, not to return to the house, and to "cool off." That's what the doctor told me. A friend came to get me at 3 a.m. I went home, fell asleep for a few hours, and was at my daughter's preschool for a board meeting by 9 a.m. because there was nothing to do but pull it together for the kids.

While I was sitting in the hospital, submitting to a ridiculously quick psychiatric evaluation, Justin went back to the house, cleaned out his closet, and left. Looking back, I think it was a ploy, a trap, and I fell right into it. He knew enough to know that if he called the police on me, they would have to take me in, and he could escape.

My brother-in-law, who was a cop two hours from Pittsburgh, was on the phone with me while I was at the hospital. He had his suspicions, too. He told me that in his experience, the spouse who calls the cops, pointing the finger at someone else and saying they are crazy, is usually the one who is crazy.

Here is the worst part: A week later, I let him move back in. He was behaving normally again, I thought. Maybe, just maybe, this incident made him realize how much I love him and that we are meant to be together.

I could not have been more wrong. I didn't know what was going on inside his skull, or that his brain was slowly deteriorating. Or that the worst was yet to come.

The following year was full of fighting, crying and more nights that he disappeared, leaving me alone with the kids.[105] There was his weekend trip to Las Vegas that turned into six weeks of us not hearing much from him. We were supposed to go on a trip to Europe together, but he went with his best friend instead. I told him to just go and take Dan. We were nearing the end, and I just didn't have the strength. Then came our eighth wedding anniversary, when he left again, this time for good.

Over the next three years he floated in and out of the kids' lives, attempting to be the best dad he could. He took them every other weekend – at least to start, but eventually would leave them with his sister. Sometimes she'd call me to come get them because he had walked out the door, left them with her, and she had plans that night. I could never count on him. When he would show up, my daughter usually cried and didn't want to go. Our son, being the dutiful child he always was, went with his dad, sometimes looking scared, but other times happy to spend time with him.

Far Away

Near the end, Justin was sliding so far into what I thought was bipolar disorder and alcoholism that it was hard to have a sane conversation with him. He spoke in rapid-fire sentences. He made no sense.

Six weeks before he died, he quit smoking marijuana and drinking. I feel like he was living in such a haze that he couldn't see reality until the fog was lifted and he was clean. Then reality hit him harder than any blow on the football field ever could.

The week leading up to his death was a series of crazy phone conversations, and for the first time I started to fear for the safety of my children. We had friends who lost a son some years before, and it hit Justin and me pretty hard. The mom was one of my first "football wife" friends, we were pregnant with our sons at the same time, and took trips and had family outings together. Their son passed

---

105   "Keana McMahon, ex-wife of late Steelers player Justin Strzelczyk, refuses to watch the NFL because of the aftermath from his head trauma," *TribLive,* January 2, 2016, accessed January 8, 2019 https://youtu.be/J01PbsYPrZw

away at 6 years old in a shocking motorcycle accident, and the anniversary of this little boy's death was just a few days before Justin died.

Justin showed up on the third anniversary of the boy's passing at my doorstep with his crumpled funeral card from three years before stuffed into his pocket. He said to me, "Do you know what today is?" He handed me the funeral card with tears in his eyes. He started to babble about God, his father, the death of this child. I grabbed him by the arms and said, "Look at me, look in my eyes. Are you on drugs? What is going on?" He backed away from me and in a soft, pleading voice said, "No, no, I'm clean Keana, I've been clean for six weeks. I've never seen so clearly before in my life, don't you see that?"

I can't remember what I said to him. I just knew he was worse. He got into his black BMW and drove away. I grew increasingly worried throughout the evening, while trying to focus on the kids. I called some of his friends and begged them to go talk to him. One did. He was a doctor, and he called me to tell me that he believed Justin's behavior was consistent with someone suffering from a manic bipolar episode. He tried to get him to go see a doctor friend of his, but Justin refused. Justin said he would go see him the following weekend, but that weekend never came.

The next day, Justin burst into our pediatrician's office, demanding to see the kids' records. He asked what kinds of medications they were on. He told the doctor that drugs were bad, that the kids shouldn't take them. He was erratic and frightening – so scary that the office staff locked the doors, fearful he was going to come back with a gun. They called me to tell me what happened, fearing for my safety as well. I drove straight to my children's elementary school, explained the situation to the principal, and asked that Justin not be allowed to pick up the kids, and to alert the staff so that they would be aware of the situation. The principal told me to go get legal papers showing I had custody, bring them back the next day, and he would take care of it.

During one of our last conversations, Justin called the house at an ungodly hour to tell me he had seen God. I offered to come sit with him, to talk to him after I took the kids to school, even though I was a little scared of him. Then he got angry with me, telling me not to come. Before he hung up, he said, "I love you."

I didn't know how to react. I had become engaged 17 days before and let go of what we had a long time ago. I had to move on, for my kids and for my sanity. I told him that I loved him, too, but not like that. I don't even know what those words mean, but it's what I said. I should have just said, "I love you, too." That's all I should have said.

After he hung up the phone with me, he called the main switchboard at my fiancée's company and asked for him by name. They had never spoken, other than a few choice words on one occasion when we had to pick up the kids from his place because he was "too busy" to keep them the rest of his weekend. The conversation was brief, but he asked Matt about the Boy Scouts fishing trip he was taking Justin Jr. on in the coming weekend. Matt was confused. He was trying to understand where the call was going, but at the end Justin simply said: "Take care of my kids because I just ... I just can't right now."

The day he died I had just finished having lunch with my daughter, Sabrina, at her elementary school. I did that quite often. I just happened to walk out of the school that fall afternoon, and the sky was a perfect blue with big, white, fluffy clouds. I remember because I had just taken a drink from the water bottle I was carrying, forcing my eyes to look up to the sky.

Then my phone rang, and that was the beginning of our lives without Justin.

It was his best childhood friend, Dan. When I answered the phone, he said "Keana, where is Justin? Where is he? When did you talk to him last?" I told him I had spoken to him the night before and that he was behaving erratically. He stopped me mid-sentence. "Oh God, Keana. He's dead, he's dead!"

There had been a car accident.[106] Justin's uncle was going to identify the body. They were hoping that his truck had been stolen because there was no ID on the driver – that maybe, just maybe, it was someone else.

Just then, my phone went dead, my battery died. I felt so completely helpless. I ran as fast as I could back into the school, into the principal's office, crying, telling

---

106   Alan Schwarz, "Lineman, dead at 36, exposes brain injuries," *New York Times*, June 15, 2007, accessed January 10, 2019 https://www.nytimes.com/2007/06/15/sports/football/15brain.html

them what happened. He calmed me down and started to call the Pennsylvania State Police to ask about accidents that had been reported, anything linked to Justin. They had nothing, no accidents fitting any of his vehicle's descriptions. We didn't know they had nothing because the accident had been in New York.

I calmed down enough to get back home, hoping that it was all a huge mistake, that he was alive. Then my closest friends and some family began arriving at the house. We waited to hear more, and eventually our fears were confirmed. It was him. He was gone.

I chose to leave the kids in school because it would be the last normal day they would have. In five hours, they would be home and their lives would be forever changed. I just wanted a little bit more normal for them, just a few hours more. Matt and I walked to the bus stop at 3:50 p.m. By then, Justin's death was all over the news, and other parents just looked at me. A few spoke, offering help in any way that I needed. Then the bus rolled up. I don't remember my children's little faces as they got off the bus, but I do remember they were surprised to see us because they usually walked down to the house together. Sabrina jumped on Matt's back for a piggy-back ride, and I will never forget what she said: "Matt, I can feel your heart beating through your back!" His heart was beating so hard, for fear of what was about to come.

We walked towards the house. Halfway down the long driveway I sat them down on the warm concrete because I couldn't tell them in the house. I didn't want them to look at the couch the rest of their days and think, "This is where I found out." With the four of us sitting there I simply told them: "Your father was in a very, very bad car accident."

I'm sure I was choking back tears, but I don't recall. I just remember them both looking at me. Sabrina said, "Is he dead?" Justin said, "Is he alive?"

"No, he's not alive," I told them. "I'm sorry."

Justin broke into tears, laying his head on my lap. Sabrina asked whether they would have to go to the school the next day. The reaction of the kids, while similar, should have prepared me for the aftermath. They had their own person-alities and would react very differently to this as they grew up.

The next decade of our lives was riddled with more heartbreak to overcome. It seemed that my strength as a mother was constantly being tested. My mom was diagnosed with ovarian cancer, and three years later she was gone. It was particu-larly hard on my daughter, who had a special relationship with her. My dad died 16 months later.

We moved from the home we shared with Justin, had a wedding, experienced fertility issues, I got pregnant three times and had two babies. The kids had new baby brothers, a new place to live, and a new family. I thought they were doing well. I thought therapy wasn't needed. I went for myself, trying to cope with his death and the question of, "Why did he do this to us?" But I thought the kids would get through it with lots of love, friends and toys.

What Everybody Doesn't See

What the NFL, the fans and the public don't see is what happens next: The struggle to stay afloat, to keep your family from falling apart. The nights you lie awake worried about what is going to happen because your kids just got kicked off of government insurance and the NFL doesn't cover families for more than three years after they retire. The nights you cry because he had no will, no life insurance, no plan for their future, and you have no idea how you're going to make the next mortgage payment. Assets are frozen. You are paying for estate lawyers to help you through the process. New York State, where his accident was, may sue for the damages and clean up – a hefty $800,000 bill for that one. That's just about how much money Justin had when he died. There were other people he hit during the accident in which he was killed, and we had to wait to see if lawsuits rolled in.

Nobody sees that, and very few people care. They care when you're on the field. They want a picture, an autograph, or tickets. When you're gone, they don't care anymore.

Then the hits kept coming. In early 2011, a few months after my dad passed, my daughter Sabrina, who was 13, suffered an emotional breakdown. There was so much she had been hiding from me, and I had no idea. I had failed her as a parent. I didn't see the signs, and I didn't take her to therapy when I should have all those years ago when Justin died. I just thought it would all be fine. Justin died, we mourned at two different funerals in two different states, then laid him to rest next to his father. We moved on. It would pass, I thought.

The next four years were spent in therapy, hospitals and in the courtroom. Through the therapy we had learned that Sabrina took his death a lot harder than she had ever let on. She had been holding so many of her feelings in for the past seven years. With Justin's money tied up in legal trusts for the kids, it was hard to access any money for them, and we always had to go before a judge at Orphan's Court to ask for anything. Usually it was for medical bills, college application fees, or a down payment on a car.

My daughter was in such a bad place, I had to get her into a clinic. There was one outside of Chicago that had a bed available in a few weeks. We set up a court date to ask the judge for money from her account. The car was packed, and we were so sure he would allow money to be spent on this because Sabrina was so mentally distraught. We had been in therapy for 10 months. She wasn't getting better and this was a last resort.

We asked the judge for $30,000 to be sent directly to the clinic for a six-week stay. Sabrina took the stand to tell her story and told the judge she wanted to get better. I took the stand, answering all of his questions about how much I had done to help her. The judge left the courtroom for 10 minutes, and when he returned, he said he felt badly for our situation, but could not approve removing money from her trust for treatment. He said his job was to protect the money, not the child.

Sabrina broke down sobbing in the courtroom. I remember looking around and seeing the stunned faces of not only her attorneys, but of the court clerk and the bailiff.

This is what the fans don't see, what the owners don't see, what the coaches don't see, and it is something so many former NFL athletes families go through in one way or another.

By then we knew that CTE had caused Justin's decline. Dr. Bennet Omalu tested brain slides from the Herkimer County (N.Y) coroner three years after he died.[107] When he told us the results, we were shocked. How could football do this to him? He loved football. It gave us so many good things.

I still got angry at the mess he left behind. My daughter was angry at herself for being afraid of her dad near the end, hiding from him when he would come to get her, staying with me, and crying the whole way to his car. She thought she had "treated him like shit and look at where that got him." I figured she was only 7 at the time and wouldn't remember, but she did.

This was the mess that nobody else saw, the aftermath, my hell as a parent. I was angry at the fans who paid to watch this game that killed their father. I still am. I was mad at the NFL for ignoring so many men. I still am. I was mad at myself for not doing enough, but after 12 years, I think I did just about all I could do. When I reflect on the past, I thank God that the kids were not in Justin's truck that day, that he didn't harm them. They were safe, and I try not to beat myself up too much.

He Comes to Me in Dreams

Years went by and in 2014 a director from Hollywood called me. He wanted to put part of my story in a movie called "Concussion," starring Will Smith.[108] It wasn't an easy decision. I had lunch with the writer/director of the film, Peter Landesman, one afternoon and listened to what he had to say. I was scared to put my family out in the "spotlight" that way. I had to sit down with Sabrina and Justin to make sure it was all right with them. If they said no, it would not have

---

107 Jeanne Marie Laskas, "How one doctor changed football forever," *GQ*, September 15, 2009, accessed January 11, 2019 https://www.google.com/amp/s/www.gq.com/story/nfl-players-brain-dementia-study-memory-concussions/amp

108 "Former Steeler Justin Strzelczyk's wife talks about her involvement in 'Concussion' movie," *Observer-Reporter*, accessed January 11, 2019 http://videos.observer-reporter.com/Former-Steeler-Justin-Strzelczyks-wife-talks-about-her-involvement-in-Concussion-30071035

been done. But they were fine with it. My husband was on board. It would call awareness in such a big way. What more could I ask for?

We gave the props department all of Justin's belongings that we had, even his motorcycle. Most of his things, even his motorcycles, were sold at auction when he died because he had no will.

On Father's Day in 2011, Justin Jr. was curious about where his father's motor-cycles were. He went on Craigslist and typed in "1995 Road King." That was the first year Harley-Davidson made the bike. Justin bought it the year our son was born with the hope to pass it on to him someday.

The first hit he got on Craigslist said "former Pittsburgh Steeler Justin Strelczyk's motorcycle." There were no photos yet, just a phone number. It had only been posted for seven minutes and my son stared at his phone, completely stunned. He showed his stepdad, who quickly was on his phone calling the man who posted the listing. After several phone conversations, a photo of the title, and more photos of the bike, it was real. We bought the bike back.

The man drove it to our home one afternoon. I heard the roar of the bike and looked out the window to see my husband and son standing there, watching him pull it into the garage. I ran downstairs, so excited to see it. I got to the garage door, opened it, and was immediately hit with that smell. I had to shut the door, go back inside and cry. They say smells bring back memories, and this one did. It brought back good memories, bad memories, memories of late-night fights after Justin rolled up on the bike, way too late and way too drunk. It was the same bike we took a Christmas card picture with as we held our first-born son.

You see, Justin always had a way of communicating with us, even after he was gone. It sounds so ridiculous until it happens to you.

He comes to me in dreams. A couple of months into the shooting of the film "Concussion," I was still anxious, worried that I had made a mistake, worried about being out there for many people to scrutinize. Then one night I had a dream. I realize it sounds a bit odd. I'm aware that many of my stories do, but there have been times since Justin's death where he has vividly come to me in a dream and spoken to me. It's usually at a time when my body is just waking up. He always speaks, but I never do. This time I was sitting in an interrogation room that was all white, except for a stainless steel table in front of me. He was standing in front of me in his biker gear. Beside me was the director of the film, Peter, looking over storyboards and sketching with his pencil. Justin said, "It's fine, you're going to be safe with him, it'll be OK." Then he walked out the door, and that was the last time he came to me in a dream.

Reward is not worth the risk

After that I let go of the anxiety. A year later, "Concussion," was released. I thought it portrayed what I went through perfectly, especially the pain I felt after Justin was gone. The movie brought a much-needed awareness to many people, but sadly, I still have friends that have played or are married to players who refuse to watch it because they fear they are looking at their future. And you know what? Many of them are.

I now spend my time fighting the good fight, calling awareness to CTE and the dangers of youth football.[109] It's not easy. Football is so ingrained in our culture. But I have heard from many mothers and fathers who agree with me, who have decided not to let their kids play, who realize that the reward is not worth the risk. If I can change one parent's mind about letting their child play youth football, that's a start.

I've found comfort in others' stories, but the ones that hit me the hardest are the mothers who have lost a child to CTE.[110] Sometimes when I am in a room with them I feel like I am not worthy to be sitting with them, that what they have gone through is so much more than what my family and I endured. I don't know what it is like to lose a child, and I don't pretend to. I just know that together with them and many other women who are living the nightmare I once did, that we can slowly bring about changes.

Protect the children. Fight for the players' rights. Make other parents aware of what can happen. And help others get through some of their darkest days.

Because in the end I never want another NFL wife to have to sit her kids down, look them in the face, and tell them their dad is gone.

And that it was football that killed him.

---

109 Adam Howard, "Ex-wife of player who had CTE: 'Nobody said death was an option,' " *MSNBC*, April 1, 2016, accessed January 11, 2019 https://www.google.com/amp/www.msnbc.com/msnbc/ex-wife-player-who-had-cte-nobody-said-death-was-option/amp

110 Josh Kosman, "Mothers who lost sons to CTE launch awareness campaign," *New York Post*, March 10, 2016, accessed January 11, 2019 https://www.google.com/amp/s/nypost.com/2016/03/10/mothers-who-lost-sons-to-cte-launch-awareness-campaign/amp/

CHAPTER 12

Photo courtesy of Covy Moore

Tyrell Luke Pozzobon

November 9, 1991 – January 9, 2017

There may be no braver endeavor in sports than bull riding. The animals average about 1,500 pounds, and, of course, have sharp horns that can do heavy damage to the human limbs and torso. Eight seconds of riding is required to achieve a score, and in that wild blur, the rider's body and head are violently twisted and shaken with frightening jolts. Of course, the scariest thing is when a rider is bucked off and literally has to fight for his life to escape the hooves and horns of an excited bull. Growing up on a farm in British Columbia, Tyrell Pozzobon dreamed of a professional career in bull riding since he was very young. He achieved that goal, competing at the highest level in the PBR Finals in Las Vegas. But numerous head injuries ultimately affected his mood and outlook, and despite the loving support of his family, he took his own life. An examination of his brain revealed CTE and many areas in which his brain bled.

One More Ride to Save Lives
By Leanne Pozzobon

My wish is to share with you some stories of my son, to describe to you what a beautiful soul he was, and to let you know the medical findings that were discovered as a result of Ty's brain tissue donation.

From the day Ty was born, he was so happy. The only problem he ever caused his dad and me was that he never slept as a baby. All he ever wanted to do was to play. We were soon a family of four, when his sister Amy was born in 1995.

Growing up on a cattle ranch in our hometown of Merritt, British Columbia, in Canada had its advantages. It meant that Ty could ride anything he could catch. He grew up feeding cattle, calving cows, riding the range, and most importantly, he grew up with a loving family that did everything together.

We travelled as a pack to support each other 110 percent in whatever we were doing, and for my family that was the sport of rodeo.

A family bond

Ty had a special bond with his family. Ty and his dad, Luke, had a relationship like no other. Ty looked up to Luke as his mentor from day one because Luke rode bulls professionally in his younger days and worked hard for our kids to travel the rodeo circuit.

Ty was so proud of his little sister Amy and all of her accomplishments in school. He liked to give her a hard time and say that she was so book smart, but needed to have more common sense. That was funny, because we all said that about Ty. Amy also shared a passion for rodeo. They supported each other as they travelled together in Little Britches and high school rodeo. We always laughed because since Amy started rodeo and still, to this day, whenever she rides into the arena, she is never announced as "Amy Pozzobon," but instead as "Ty Pozzobon's little sister." We have so many wonderful memories travelling up and down the road every weekend.

As for myself, Ty and I were so close. His friends and fellow rodeo buddies gave him a hard time about being a mama's boy. He would always respond back that it wasn't his fault his mom loved him so much. They all would laugh and say that when Ty came home from being away for awhile, I would bring out the umbilical cord and put it away when he left. I honestly say with the bond we had, I felt what he felt.

Ty had a huge heart; all his friends were his *best* friends. Sharing some of these stories with you is important to me so you realize what a wonderful life Ty had.

We were very proud of Ty's mentorship he established with children. He always took the time to greet everyone, especially young kids who shared the passion he had. Young riders would email or text videos of their own ride and ask Ty for advice. He never let any one of them down. He answered them all and took the time to share his knowledge and encouraged them to keep riding.

Through this difficult time, I received many messages from parents and kids thanking Ty for the positive impact he had on them. I remember Ty winning a PBR Tour event in Calgary, Alberta, and afterward he gave a young boy the spurs he won. To this day, that boy and his mom contact me regularly to check up on me. Ty would give many kids his gear or trophies just to see the smiles on their faces.

Ty's passion for bull riding started before I can remember. As he grew older, his dad built him a bucking chute with the number 1 on it. He would bring all his friends over and have them ride steers forwards, backwards, doubling, and even saddling the steers. The only safety precaution Luke insisted was that Ty put tennis balls on the ends of the steers' pointy horns. Ty always had to make sure it was all on video, usually by bribing his sister into holding the camera all day. I am sure thankful for those videos now -- so many memories of the fun he had.

Photo courtesy of Covy Moore

Ty's a winner

Ty got on his first bull at the age of 13, and he won everything amateur in our home province of British Columbia, along with the Canadian high school rodeo title. That's when he received a full-ride scholarship to Odessa College in Texas and met his new best friend, Randy Quateiri.

I will never forget the day we drove into Odessa for the first time and read on the neon sign: "Odessa College welcomes bull rider Ty Pozzobon." We were all so surprised. Ty made us go around the block again because he couldn't believe it. He told us the main reason why he was going to Texas was to get connections and meet people so that he could make it the Professional Bull Riders (PBR) circuit. In Ty's high school graduation year, the yearbook asks: What you would like to do in the future? Ty wrote: "I will see you at the PBR finals in Vegas." If we only knew that would come true just a year later.

There was a change

I would like to share with you on what it was like for us after the World Finals in 2016 -- three months before Ty's passing. That is when I first noticed a change in Ty's mental state. He didn't seem to be himself. There was so much to celebrate after the finals were over. He'd just won more than $100,000 and ended up fourth overall. He even won one of the five rounds in the finals.[111]

It was a dream come true. Only a few weeks before, he's won the PBR Canadian title -- another dream achieved. Instead of celebrating with family and friends after the last performance of the World Finals, he joined us for a quick dinner and then went up to his hotel room. He said he didn't feel well and went to bed. As a mom, I knew something was wrong. Ty seemed to be distraught about everything, including his career and future. After the Finals, he went to Texas for a few weeks and arrived back home to Canada in late November 2016.[112]

In Merritt, British Columbia, Ty had a beautiful piece of property where he and his dad were raising bucking stock. Still in the winter of 2016 he didn't seem himself. Ty shared with us that he was not sleeping or eating well. He talked to us all of the time and expressed how confused and worried he was about his future. He kept telling his dad, "What am I going to do if I can't ride bulls anymore?" He was extremely worried about that. His dad and I kept telling him over and over that he was so talented that he would succeed at anything and should have no worries in the world. He was only 25 years old. He'd just finished a successful Ford truck commercial in Canada. He had his bucking bull business and bull riding schools; Ty had lots to look forward to. However, Ty continued to express concerns about his future.

111   "Ty Pozzobon rides Big Cat" YouTube, posted Nov. 3, 2016, accessed March 8, 2019 https://www.youtube.com/watch?v=Qx836PM87rs

112   Covy Moore, "Pozzobon blazes unique path into the world finals" PBR Canada, October 10, 2016, accessed March 8, 2019 https://www.pbrcanada.com/news/features/2016/pozzobon-blazes-a-unique-path-to-the-world-finals/

Overwhelmed and confused

Finally, on December 19, 2016, Ty agreed to go to the doctor, I was hoping the doctor would see how distraught and mentally unhealthy he was, so Ty would undergo medical attention. The doctor only recommended that Ty seek counseling support. Unfortunately, that counseling appointment was made for January 20, 2017, a date that Ty never made.

Christmas came, and Ty didn't look healthy. He always loved Christmas, but it seemed like the holiday could not come and go fast enough for him. He had dark circles under his eyes and lost a lot of weight. As a mother, all I wanted to do was to try to fix everything for him.

Normally when Ty was home, he would love to talk to his supporters. A few days after Christmas 2016, Ty went grocery shopping. Afterward, he came into my workplace looking dazed and confused and he said to me, "Mom, all these people who were talking to me made me feel overwhelmed and confused." I was alarmed and immediately called his doctor. I was told he could *not* see Ty right away.

That weekend, I called a few of his close friends and told them how worried I was about Ty and that if they noticed anything unusual to please let us know. All weekend Ty paced around the kitchen, stressing out about his future. His thought process was all over the map. One minute he was selling all of his bulls, the next he was buying more. He couldn't seem to keep a straight thought, and again he wasn't eating or sleeping well. We talked that weekend as a family and planned on demanding a doctor's appointment on Monday morning. We constantly encouraged him that everything would be OK and we would get medical help.

"I love you guys"

On Monday, January 9, 2017, I woke up and went to work as usual, but I was still worried about my son. I called the doctor as soon as they opened and requested an appointment. I texted Ty, as I did every morning, and I told him that we loved him and we'd get through all of this together. I also told him that the doctor's appointment was booked.

He texted back right away and said, "I love you guys and I am sorry, it's just my head that is doing this and I don't know why." I texted him back and told him everything would be OK. Because of the relationship that we had, we always ended it with "I love you." But that morning I didn't get an "I love you back." I suddenly had a gut feeling that something was wrong. Not once did I imagine that Ty would take his own life.

January 9, 2017, was the day we lost our precious Ty.[113]

It is important to share with you some of the changes we had seen in Ty in the weeks and months leading up to his passing, because it's important to listen to your loved ones and pay attention to the signs indicating mental illness, even when they are hard to recognize.[114]

Brain donation

I trust you understand that the days immediately after his passing was the most difficult time for our family. However, I knew the importance of donating Ty's brain tissue to medical research. We knew as a family that there were definite connections of his recent stress and anxiety to all his injuries, including brain injuries. The decision to donate his brain tissue was very easy.

What was *not* easy was the process behind of the scenes to make it happen. We were running out of time as each day passed. We didn't think we would be successful after our local coroner's office turned us down to assist the coordination of the tissue donation. However, we were successful only because of the massive news coverage that a professional bull rider had taken his own life. A company called Nucleolus Bio contacted us. They asked us if we would donate Ty's brain for research to the University of Washington School of Medicine. The brain tissue donation was successful and occurred simply by a collaboration of our local hospital and a team of specialists.

113   Ted Stovin, "Remembering Ty Pozzobon" PBR Canada, January 9, 2019, accessed March 8, 2019 https://pbrcanada.com/news/features/2019/jan/remembering-ty-pozzobon/

114   Kelsey Bradshaw, "Report: 25-year-old pro bull rider Ty Pozzobon took his own life" mySanAntonio.com, January 12, 2017, accessed March 8, 2019 https://www.sfchronicle.com/rodeo/article/Report-pro-bull-rider-Ty-Pozzobon-death-suicide-10853124.php#photo-12166659

As part of this process, we had to obtain all of Ty's medical records. He had experienced brain injuries since the time he was 18 years old. These are just a few of the doctor's statements between 2012-2016:

> *Patient is riding a lot, a couple of big crashes, fell over backwards and landed on his forehead.*

> *Bull horn hooked through vest, hit head and resulted in concussion, no loss of consciousness.*

> *Concussion two weeks ago, could not see out of his right eye, landed on forehead and had headaches for one week.*

> *Bad dismount, hit head, hit bull on left shoulder, loss of consciousness, right eye was blurry for half hour.*

Ty's serious brain injuries

One of the most significant concussions that Ty suffered was at the 2014 Canadian PBR Finals. It was a bad wreck and he lost consciousness for more than 15 minutes. He was taken by ambulance to the hospital and released later that night.

Because of the sport, doctors and medical professionals all over North America treated Ty after an injury. Therefore, not one medical facility had his full concussion history until the time of his passing. As a family, it is so overwhelming to learn of all his injuries put in one medical report.

In October 2017, we met with the specialists from the University of Washington for hours and listened to them talk about how serious Ty's brain injuries were. They started the conversation saying that Ty was born with a perfectly healthy brain. These were the three significant findings:

1. He had CTE.
2. He had chronic traumatic brain injury, also known as TBI.
3. He had more than 20 visible brain bleeds at the time of his passing.

The majority of the CTE and TBI found in Ty's brain were in his orbital frontal lobe, which is the area just above the eyes. This area in the brain is responsible for decision-making, mood stability, judgment, memory and personality - many of the things Ty was struggling with near the end of his life.

For those who are unfamiliar, there is a significant difference between CTE and TBI, even though they both have to do with damage of the brain from trauma. CTE is a progressive, degenerative disease found in people who have suffered repetitive brain trauma, including hits to the head that did not result in concussions. TBI occurs from larger and higher impact hits to the head, such as the concussion I mentioned that Ty sustained at the 2014 Canadian PBR Finals.[115]

It's important that people recognize the signs of mental illness. Just because one doesn't see it, doesn't mean it's not there. Each hit to the head needs to be dealt with in a serious manner. Recovery time is so important. It is also important for people to understand the difference a CAT scan and an MRI scan. CAT scans will not show everything. After a hit on the head or if there are concussion concerns, it's important to demand an MRI and to see a specialist. A PET scan may also be beneficial.[116]

His legacy

With the tragedy that has happened in the lives of my family, I believe my son will:

1. Continue to make a positive impact by being a role model in the sport of bull riding.

2. Assist in the medical research of CTE, as Ty is the first professional bull rider to be been diagnosed with CTE. He has set the ground work of further research; he created a legacy dedicated to helping others.

---

115 Karin Larsen, "Champion bull rider from B.C. dies at 25" CBC News, January 10, 2017, accessed March 8, 2019 https://www.cbc.ca/news/canada/british-columbia/ty-pozzobon-bull-rider-1.3927470
116 Katy Lucas, "Two years later, we will remember to live like Ty," Florodeo, January 10, 2018, accessed March 8, 2019 https://www.florodeo.com/articles/6075276-two-years-later-we-still-remember-to-live-like-ty

Ty's best friends created the Ty Pozzobon Foundation to assist riders, much like the Rider Relief Fund. The Ty Pozzobon Foundation's stated mission is "To protect and support the health and well-being of rodeo competitors inside and outside the arena."

The more we all learn together about physical and mental injuries, the more we can provide better strategies to protect our loved ones. If Ty's legacy has helped one athlete, one family, then my heart has been comforted. Our family does not believe you should stop doing what you are passionate about, but that you should do it in a smarter way, and listen to both what the medical professionals tell you, and what your body and mind are telling you.

Ty will be forever remembered as an outstanding competitive bull rider as well as a compassionate, loving and generous young man. I am certain he is proud of the efforts we are making to increase mental illness awareness in and out of the bull-riding arena.[117]

This chapter was very difficult for me to do. I can visualize Ty rubbing his hands together, like he always did when he was excited and happy. I believe he is proud of all our efforts that we are making mental illness awareness an important part of our lives.

---

117   Ty Pozzobon Foundation website, accessed March 8, 2019 https://www.typozzobon.com/

During this difficult time, I have relied on my own spiritual beliefs to help me manage the pain I feel every day. Ty has shared this special poem with me. He is with God now and is our precious angel who watches over all of us.

God had a plan for me from the start
He gave me the drive and he gave me the heart
He helped me learn and he helped me win
He kept me honest to the end

The bulls, they take your body and mind
They leave you in a wreck a lot of the time
You try to shake it off and walk away
There will be other bulls on a different day

Our bodies are not made to do what we ask
They twist and turn trying to meet the task
Even though we are broken and sore
We are always looking ahead for more

God has a purpose for each one to do
He guided and helped me in life too
Mine was to ride bulls, he gave me the best
The talent that he gave me did the rest

A broken, sore body will heal in time
A hit on the head will kill a little of your mind
You know that things are not right
The days are busy, it is really hard at night

Every time you hit your head
You're in trouble your mind says
Your mind gives you more pain
Trying to get you to refrain

You don't want people to know the pain you're in
You try to cover it with a laugh and a grin
But there comes a time when your mind
Says no more pain, it is now your time.

My purpose in life was to be a sign
To help people save the pain and their minds
Don't kill yourself a hit at a time
Let's change what we do to our minds

Mom, stand tall look straight ahead
It is the beginning not the end
My part of the story has been seen
It is time for you and your team

If I had died riding a bull, it would have been a tragic accident
It would not have had near the effect in helping people
Understand that we need to change what we are doing
To stop other people from dying for the same reasons and the same way I did

CHAPTER 13

Tiana "Junior" Seau

January 19, 1969 – May 2, 2012

"Buddeee!" Anyone who was around NFL Hall of Fame linebacker Junior Seau for more than a few minutes heard him exclaim his signature word to someone, whether he'd known that person for decades or five minutes. That was Seau, whose bright smile and outgoing demeanor in public exuded the vibe that he never had a care in the world. A kid of modest means growing up in Oceanside, California, north of San Diego, Seau had lived his dream. He earned a football scholarship to the University of Southern California and was drafted into the NFL by the hometown Chargers. With the Bolts, whom he led to a Super Bowl appearance, he would become a legend,

ferociously making tackles and celebrating with a lashing leg kick and fist pump. In the final four years of his career, Seau played for the New England Patriots, though a Super Bowl win would elude him in a loss to the New York Giants. In retirement, Seau spent time with his four kids, surfed, played golf and managed his namesake restaurant. Still, he struggled with depression and headaches while also not revealing his despair. Seau died after shooting himself in the chest in a bedroom of his beachfront home, and a subsequent brain study found that he suffered from chronic traumatic encephalopathy (CTE). He is the most famous athlete to ever be diagnosed with the degenerative brain disease. In the years that followed, Junior's sister Mary started the Mary Seau CTE Foundation to educate the public on the dangers of brain trauma.

THE Face of CTE

By Mary Seau

"Junior, why did you do this?" My dad was so mad and asked his son that question. It's a question we all had: Why? [118]

What I can say is we know a lot more than we did the morning of May 2, 2012, the day my younger brother, Junior, sat on his daughter Sydney's bed and shot himself in his big, spiritual Samoan heart.[119] At the time, we didn't know why. As an entire family, we were just in mourning, you know?

Our mom and dad were at church the morning Junior took his life and another family member drove them to Junior's beachfront home. They didn't know why they were there until they were at top of the hill above Junior's home.

Meanwhile, I drove to work like every other normal workday, although this day would be life changing. A co-worker, Michael, saw me and said, "Come here." I asked if I could put my stuff down first. He said, "No, come over here to my

---

118   Steven Luke, Mari Payton, R. Stickney, "Searching for answers in Junior Seau's death," *NBC San Diego*, May 2, 2012, accessed January 16, 2019 https://www.nbcsandiego.com/news/local/Junior-Seau-Death-Questions-Surrounding--149903235.html

119   Chris Jones, "Your love won't save Junior Seau now," *Esquire*, May 2, 2012, accessed January 16, 2019 www.esquire.com/news-politics/a13912/jr-seau-dead-8546574/

cubicle." I did, and he showed me a live news story on his computer about my brother and said, "Junior is dead."

I placed a hand on a co-worker and asked him to please tell me it wasn't true. I said, "I have to go home," but I just stood there. I was lost and didn't know what to do. I called my kids and asked them to meet me at home. When the kids arrived I told them, "Uncle's dead." We went to Junior's home and all the family was there, crying in a show of love for Junior.

"Why did you take my son?" our mom asked God through her pain. The day Junior died, it was hardest for our mom. She asked God, "Why didn't you take me?" She kept hitting her chest and asked again and again "Why God?"

I told mom not to question God. This is the time that God wanted Junior, and that there had to be a good reason. It was so hard for me in my shock and disbelief because I had to jump between caring for one elderly, frail parent to the other. I was trying to take care of everybody but myself. Under this incredible stress I was back to my second nature, acting like a second mom.

My parents were standing in Junior's garage. That's when I felt the door into his garage open. I was standing against the wall. And in that moment I felt something really cold. There were three steps down from the house and they were bringing Junior out on a gurney, feet first, in a zipped bag.

They brought him down right in front of me, and the first responders unzipped the bag. I have a vivid memory of Junior's body bag. I remember that the bag was way too small for him, so much so that he had a small cut on his forehead from the zipper. I touched his shoulder and I felt an energy. Mom was standing on the other side. I "heard" his voice, Junior's voice say to me, "Shhh, Sis, don't cry. Be strong. Everything will be OK."

He looked so happy. Then, I felt his energy go away. At that moment I was fine. I stopped crying.

Junior's oldest son, Tyler Seau, coordinated the donation and told his grandparents what was going to occur. He explained, "It's the only way to help find out what happened and to help kids."

My parents said, "Yes, yes." Tyler then asked appropriate questions, did his research and chose the National Institute of Health to conduct the brain autopsy and report on the condition of Junior's brain.

Tyler unexpectedly received a call from San Diego Coroner's Office and was told Dr. Bennet Omalu was there to conduct the brain examination. Tyler used colorful language, and asked Omalu "to get the **** out of there." He now admits he should have used a different expression, but he reacted that way because he did not give Omalu approval to conduct his dad's brain autopsy.

When the news came out that my brother was diagnosed with CTE, it was very hard for all of us. How did it happen? When did it happen? Where did it happen?

Later, we found out it was due to the many hits he took to his brain. Some were big hits, and others were small enough to not look like anything that added up to brain damage.

I now know there's no safe way to hit your brain.

The world changed when it was told Junior had CTE.

There was shock, and that shock remains. The loss of a man who was the heart of San Diego was gone.

The Cliff

When I got the call that Junior's SUV went over a beach cliff in Carlsbad in October 2010,[120] I thought, "Something's wrong with Junior's mind."[121] I quickly drove to our parents' house and told them, "We are going to visit Junior," and they were both excited. But once we passed his beachfront home, mom knew something was wrong, and she went crazy as we drove to the hospital emergency room.

Junior's kids were there and my heart went out to them. They were concerned for their dad's health and my parents worried that Junior "never rests." Junior told everyone he had fallen asleep at the wheel.

Our parents believed what Junior said about the accident. When I was able to speak to Junior alone I asked him, "What's wrong with you? You did not fall asleep."

Junior wouldn't look me in the eye.

I told him, "You can tell me anything."

He said, again, "I fell asleep."

I didn't believe Junior fell asleep then and I don't believe that now. I think it was part of his brain injury.

In his life after football, Junior turned to gambling, I believe, to raise money for a "Toys for Tots" drive, and he had child support payments to make. It didn't make sense to gamble. He drank to excess and used prescription medication in what I believe was an effort to drown out the noise in his head. I now think it was Junior's brain injury that caused his disordered thinking and the way he inflicted harm to himself.

---

120 Matthew T. Hall, Debbi Baker, "Junior Seau injured after car plunges off cliff in Carlsbad," *San Diego Union-Tribune,* October 18, 2010, accessed January 26, 2019 https://www.sandiegouniontribune.com/sdut-junior-seau-injured-car-accident-tmz-reports-it-fo-2010oct18-story.html

121 "Junior Seau drives off a cliff," *ABC News,* October 19, 2010, accessed January 16, 2019 https://abcnews.go.com/GMA/video/junior-seau-drives-off-cliff-11915062

When Junior got drafted by the Chargers, I went to one of the games. He got upset with his teammate, Rodney Harrison, and he was yelling at him and pushing him on the sideline. Rodney didn't do anything, I believe out of respect for Junior; he just sat there on the bench. I know Junior wanted his teammates to do well, and his teammates respected his work ethic and accountability.

But when Dad saw that Junior got upset at Harrison he wanted to talk to Junior. After the game, Junior didn't want to see Dad, and then Dad kept calling because he wanted to talk about what happened. But Junior avoided that discussion. I now call what Junior did that day an "outburst." Yes, I know Junior played with great passion and emotion. But I see that outburst as a sign his brain was injured.

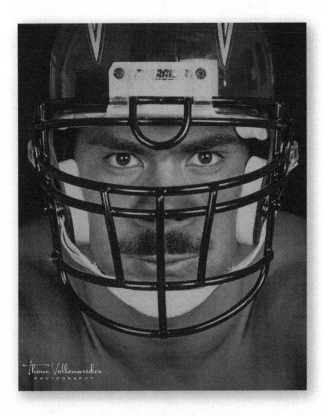

Junior suffered a diagnosed brain injury his first year with the Chargers, and I remember being in his Mt. Soledad home in San Diego and wanted him to rest more. I recall both his eyes were dilated, like a cat's eyes. I asked what was wrong with him, and he didn't want to talk about it. He got upset, left the room and asked me to leave. I believe Junior's dilated eyes told of his injured brain.

Junior's first brain injury was as a youth tackle football player while with Oceanside Pop Warner. Junior played for four years and suffered a brain injury in each of those seasons. He would sit out for two weeks and then return to play. At Oceanside High, he had additional brain injuries, one in basketball and two or three in football.

Football is a violent game of constant collisions. The brain shakes with each hit – twisting, tearing and even bleeding at times. Junior's brain was not sitting perfectly still while being covered by a 4-pound polished helmet. Football helmets are marketed and worn by tykes to those who battle 300-pound men in the NFL, and the sad truth is that every player's brain gets battered with every hit.

Proud to be a Trojan

Junior was so great at football and basketball that colleges were recruiting him for both sports. I came home from work one day, and he said, "Hey Mar, so I got a scholarship offer for basketball and football at USC.[122] Which one should I take?" I said basketball, and he thought it was because I played.

"I just like basketball," I said. "I think you're a great basketball player. You like track; you're always running up and down the court. In football, you're not running as much and you're always taking breaks."

I can honestly say at that time I wanted basketball over football for Junior, and I still feel that way. Junior brought so much energy to his basketball game. The same energy he would bring to the football field.

He said, "Everybody wants me to play football." And he picked football over basketball.

---

122 Matt Potter, "Say it ain't so," *San Diego Reader*, March 6, 1997, accessed January 27, 2019 https://www.google.com/amp/s/www.sandiegoreader.com/news/1997/mar/06/say-it-aint-seau/%3famp&page=al

At the time, I know our dad did not want football for Junior, but Junior made his choice.

After games, when all the USC fans were gone from the Coliseum, I recall Junior being withdrawn quite a bit. This was different for him. I did not feel his energy, and as I think about it now, I believe it was a sign his brain was injured. The same scenes played out again in NFL – Junior with less energy, and to me it was Junior being pulled away. Football was pulling Junior away, but we didn't know it at the time.

He was deteriorating before our eyes.

As I watched Junior through his younger years, I was so proud of him because he was such a nice kid, always smiling. He always made me laugh. And then he went to Oceanside High School, and every time he moved up a grade level, he knew that he had to work extra hard, and he did.

When I won an award at school for Female Athlete of the Year, Junior asked me how I'd accomplished that. I said, "Well, you're already doing that. You've got straight A's; you're nice to everybody; you're nice to the teachers. So all you have to do is do very well in track, football, and basketball, and you'll get Male Athlete of the Year." So he worked extra hard to make sure he was on that level. Junior's self-determination was key to the achievements he would go on to earn.

Junior and I were really close when it came to sports, and he always knew that I was his No. 1 fan. When Junior played his freshman year at Oceanside High, he was the quarterback. He'd say, "OK, Sis, how many throws do you want me to do? Or, when he was in 10th grade, "How many tackles do you want me to make? How many sacks?" That was Junior's way of pushing himself.

On the other side of Junior's joyful personality, he knew that in order to win he had to get mad. He had to be mad to play well. Starting in junior high, every single game, the day before, he would lock himself in his room just to focus. Nobody was to bother him, and nobody did.

I think it was 11th grade. There was a play called in a basketball game and Junior didn't agree with it. He got upset and kicked a chair. We had a talk after the game – he could be intimidating because he was a lot taller than me. I told him, "You better remember what I taught you when you were in elementary school. You thought you were high and mighty; boy, you're not all high and mighty this time. It was God who gave you all of the potential you have. You should be thankful and humble. Take what is given to you and try to turn it into a positive." Through the years, he did make that transition.

The downside – and this is funny – I had to pay him. I paid him a dollar for each sack, and two dollars for each tackle, until he became an 11th grader, and I had to stop because it was getting expensive!

Being Samoan

Junior learned the Samoan tradition of respect, faith and humility, to be all about family and helping others. In Samoan culture it's important to respect other cultures and have respect for other people. From day one, it's about respect for elders, for others, and growth.

The upbringing we received with our Samoan parents, Tianina Seau Sr. and Luisa Mauga Seau, meant we always went to church on Wednesdays, Fridays, Saturdays, and Sundays. Wednesday choir practice, Friday Bible study, and early in the morning on Saturday we'd clean up the hall and the church.

Our minister saw how competitive everybody in our family was when we played volleyball and basketball. We'd even compete to learn Bible verses and then compete in sports. The Seau children, and Junior in particular, showed a lot of faith, care, joy and good sportsmanship whether in the church, the hall, the court, or later on the football field.

When we were growing up we had stray cats who'd come over, I always gave them food and water, and Junior would ask, "Why do you always feed these animals? They're not going to stay here?" And I'd tell him, "So that they won't get hungry when they go back home or wherever they have to go." And he'd say, "You're just wasting your time."

I was trying to show him a lesson in kindness– if you show kindness to animals, you'll to be kind to people, and in turn kind to yourself.

In time, Junior came a long way in what I saw as his soft side, his kind side. Junior would show the world his toughness, competitiveness and his kind heart.

The meaning behind the "Buddeee!" greeting says so much about who Junior was and how he never met a stranger. It also reflects him being Samoan and respecting all people, regardless of who they are, and the status they did or didn't have.

I spoke to Junior about "Buddeee!" and he said he had a hard time remembering people's names and didn't want to disrespect them. In Samoan culture, as a sign of respect, a family friend becomes known as "Auntie" or "Uncle." That's when you *are* part of the Seau family.

Junior first started calling friends "Buddeee!" at Oceanside High School, then more passionately when he was at USC, and finally it became synonymous with Junior being positive, loving and respectful to those he met. It was a sign of acceptance. "We are all in this together." He loved you from the Earth to the sky and back. To this day, especially in San Diego, whether somebody works from a golf cart, at a hotel pool, or drives a limousine, they will all tell you a Junior story with a huge smile on their face.

The Seau family in American Samoa would go out on Saturday in boats to catch fish for Sunday dinners, and for special holidays, weddings and graduations. Here in California, the Oceanside Pier would be a place to fish, gather and tell stories while watching the surfers ride the waves.

As kids, Junior and the rest of us kids would sneak to the beach, without our parents knowing, via a canyon path to the Oceanside Harbor. We did it all summer long, and our parents wondered why we were getting so tanned! As the fifth kid in the family, Junior was the youngest and a follower. He found the beach peaceful, relaxing, and "another part of the world."

After Junior died, hundreds of his friends and fans – his Buddeees! – did a memorial Paddle Out in front of Junior's Oceanside beach home. On their surfboards they placed floral leis in the water to make one unifying circle. It was beautiful!

Where we lived growing up, there were fierce pickup basketball games at Balderrama Park.

Things could get rough, with a lot of trash talk, and that's when an older brother steps up and steps in. That's what happened for Junior with Savi'i, who is 3 ½ years older than Junior. Savi'i was there big-time for his little brother.

There were drugs and death in this neighborhood, but Junior learned respect for all cultures, and in Samoan fashion he did not judge; he prayed and became a bridge in the rough part of town.

Junior balanced street-ball life by being active at the Boys & Girls Clubs of Oceanside. Now, the same place has the Junior Seau Fitness Center and Junior

Seau Teen Center. The two buildings are near the Oceanside Pier where "little" Junior snuck away to on those carefree summer days.

Second Mom

Junior and I had a very close bond. I've always said I was like his "second mom." I was pretty much his guardian. We were such a big family, with four boys and two girls.

When Junior was young, our family didn't have extra funds, and that meant I'd buy his socks, underwear and other necessities from money earned from my part-time job. I acted as a second mom because I loved him and always will.

A funny story I remember is when Junior was dating his girlfriend from Oceanside High, Melissa. They would later have their son, Tyler, together. Junior told me he needed some help. He said he was going out to dinner with Melissa's parents and needed to learn how to use silverware. So I put the silverware around a plate, and I showed him how one fork is for salad and the other is for the main course. And he was so frustrated that he said, "I don't care, I'm eating with my hands!"

Junior came back to me a few days later, and he was so nervous that he asked me to show him again. I set up the silverware again, and told him that when he picked up a glass he had to put out his pinky. He said, "I have to do that too!" I was joking with him, but he ended up being calm and patient, and he learned.

You know what, if you met Junior you would laugh so hard that you'd pee in your pants. When you put Junior and our brother, Savaii, together that laughter was even worse. And you can tell I'm a proud sister-second mom when I say, both of my brothers have big, spiritual Samoan hearts.

There was so much loss for our family. Junior died, and then my brother Antonio died when he was 43 years old of a heart attack. Next to pass away in 2014 was my dad's sister, who had dementia, and I'd provided care for her.

Yet, with all this sadness, I found that didn't really take the time to mourn losing Junior. Then I decided I had to seek counseling. When I finished, that's when my kids asked about their uncle Junior.

My kids said, "We spent time with Uncle Junior, Mom, and he never showed any signs. He was always, like, 'Hey, come over. Hey, let's do this or that.' He was just bubbly, and we never saw any signs." And I'd tell them that's how their uncle was.

I started the Mary Seau CTE Foundation to bring awareness to people about the things Junior could never talk about.[123] Numerous times, I've been called a "bitch" by people with powerful positions in the game of football. My response: I'm proud to be a "bitch" to bring awareness to the world about brain injury.

I want others to know that a brain injury can cause tau protein to go rogue and literally kill brain cells. Once the brain cell is dead, it's dead.

---

123 Tod Leonard, "Six years after Junior Seau's death, sister keeps his wish to raise brain trauma awareness," *San Diego Union-Tribune,* March 30, 2018, accessed January 17, 2019 https://www.sandiegouniontribune.com/sports/sd-sp-junior-seau-cte-death-and-mary-seau-foundation-20180329-story.html

Most football players don't want to acknowledge this because it would damage the game's reputation.[124] But I *know* Junior had concern for the brain health of kids who play the game. He told me so.

Before Junior died, we were talking one day and he told me, "Mary, you need to do some research on kids and brain trauma and brain injury." I didn't know anything about that, and I literally laughed at him. It wasn't until after his death that I realized what he meant.

I blame myself for not acting on his request sooner. If we had worked together on it, maybe I would have understood his concern. I believe there's blame at all levels of football for information that was/is not fully disclosed about brain injury and player's health.

I believe education in schools should include brain health; the government should require the first-ever children's safety standard for helmets; the media should continue its investigation of children's sports and all that impedes children's brain health. That's a sister – and second mom's – point of view.

Thankfully, I listened to Junior and started my foundation.[125] Understandably, it's been therapeutic for me. I've learned about brain injury, brain trauma and the importance of sharing this information with a wider community, so others won't go through what my family, the Seau family, has gone through. To me, football took Junior away from his family, friends, fans and teammates.

The foundation works with other of families of CTE victims.[126] My parents ask for God to bless us in this important work. It's brought them happiness that we're trying to help other people.

124 Cork Gaines, "The 15 most damning quotes from 'League of Denial,' the NFL concussion documentary," *Business Insider*, October 9, 2013, accessed January 17, 2019 www.businessinsider.com/the-most-damning-quotes-from-league-of-denial-the-nfl-concussion-documentary-2013-10

125 Tod Leonard, "At Seau symposium, CTE researcher makes his case against youth tackle football," *San Diego Union-Tribune*, March 31, 2018, accessed January 16, 2019 http://www.sandiegouniontribune.com/sports/sd-sp-cte-symposium-chris-nowinski-junior-seau-20180331-story.html

126 Dan McLellan, "CTE: Mary Seau and Jo Cornell look to save lives by speaking hard truth," *Ironiq Media Network*, September 27, 2018, accessed January 17, 2019 https://www.wblzmedia.com/2018/09/27/cte-mary-seau-and-jo-cornell-look-to-save-lives-by-speaking-hard-truth/

In the years after Junior's death in 2012, other athletes have died with brain damage. The stories in this book are a few, but I believe they represent many more victims.

I believe, along with others – and I don't mean *any* disrespect to others who were lost to CTE[127]– that with Junior's brain donation, he became the true face of CTE. Something changed when we found out he had the disease. CTE became well-known, talked about, and forever linked with Junior Seau and the NFL.[128]

Among many others at all levels of football, the brain donations of three youth players who were diagnosed with CTE – Joseph Chernach,[129] Tyler Cornell and Paul Bright Jr.[130] – were directly the result of the Seau family's decision to advance brain science and donate Junior's brain.

Junior's brain donation impacted sports litigation. After the death of all three young men, their mothers went on to seek justice on behalf of their sons' behalf. They took Pop Warner Little Scholars, Inc. to court for their wrongdoing, including negligence fraud, fraudulent concealment, negligent misrepresentation, wrongful death, deceptive business practices, and false advertisement.

There is hope that we'll see a continued decrease in the number of kids playing Pop Warner, but I don't see the NFL being hurt by it. NFL players make a lot of money, and football exists because of gambling. It's all about gambling. As long as these big businesses can make money, it will never go away.

These days, college recruiting includes coaches venturing to Tonga, Tahiti and American Samoa. As long as there's poverty there and these young men want to help their family escape it, of course they're going to work hard to get to the NFL.

---

127 Tom Krasovic, "From Junior's death, advances in brain science, attitudes," *San Diego Union-Tribune*, May 2, 2017, accessed January 17, 2019 https://www.sandiegouniontribune.com/sports/chargers/sd-sp-chargers-seau-some-good-came-from-tragic-death-20170502-story.html

128 Jason M. Breslow, "Junior Seau suffered chronic brain damage, NIH study finds," *PBS Frontline,* January 10, 2013, accessed January 17, 2019 https://www.pbs.org/wgbh/frontline/article/junior-seau-suffered-chronic-brain-damage-nih-study-finds/

129 *Pyka v. Pop Warner Little Scholars, Inc.*, et.al. http://footballandbraindamage.com/wp-content/uploads/2015/02/Complaint-Chernach-v.-Pop-Warner-Signed.pdf

130 Michael McCann, Austin Murphy," New lawsuit points finger at Pop Warner for mismanagement of head injuries," Sports Illustrated, September 1, 2016, accessed January 27, 2019 https://www.si.com/nfl/2016/09/01/pop-warner-youth-football-lawsuit-concussions-cte

Want to be like Junior?

When my son, Ian, was 6 years old, Junior asked him if he was playing Pop Warner football, and Ian said he was. Junior asked him if he wanted to be like his uncle, and Ian said, "No, I don't want to play football. I want to play basketball." Junior asked why. "Because I don't like to get hit all of the time," Ian said. Junior said, "Good."

Later, Junior told me that he thought football was "a killer game for kids."

Years later, Ian was playing football at the University of Nevada in Reno, and he called to say he was going to pursue a playing career in the NFL.[131] He tried to settle my fears by saying that if anything happened to him with brain injuries, he'd quit.

"You can't promise me that," I said, "because if you have a concussion you won't know any better. The damage is done. You're going to continue playing football like everybody else because they don't know better."

He was silent.

"So don't tell me that if anything happens you're going to quit," I said.

"That's no story any mother wants to hear, the truth is clear, we know Lou Gehrig is ALS, Tommy John is pitcher's elbow, and Junior Seau is CTE."

---

131 Chase Goodbread, "Rams sign nephew of Junior Seau," *CFB 24/7*, May 3, 2016, updated May 5, 2016, accessed, January 26, 2019 https://www.google.com/amp/s/amp.nfl.com/news/story/0ap3000000659737/article/ian-seau-nephew-of-junior-seau-signs-with-los-angeles-rams%3fnetworkId=4595&site=.news&zone=story&zoneUrl=url%253Dstory&zoneKeys=s1%253Dstory&env&pageKeyValues=prtnr%253Dcollege-football%3bevent%253Ddraft&p.ct=CFB%2b24/7&p.adsm=false&p.tcm=%2523ffffff&p.bgc-1m=%2523000000&sr=amp

CHAPTER 14

Our Biggest Play

By Solomon E. Brannan, Jr.

I have played some type of contact or collision sport for 50 years, from 1949 to 1999. I played football, basketball, baseball and ran track. Basketball and baseball started when I was 6 years old, and my football career began at the ripe age of 7. In junior high, I was a starting running back. As you can see, from a very young age I fell in love with sports, and with team sports in particular.

I went on to play at the highest level as a professional football player for the Kansas City Chiefs, New York Jets, Cincinnati Bengals and Detroit Lions.[132] I believe my extensive experience as a player in the game makes my perspective carry a little more weight than the average person, so here it is: For me, the bottom line on the exposure to brain damage in sports is that we need to take a stand for our youth because it is the right thing to do. I may have won an AFL championship in 1967 and went on to play in what is considered the first Super Bowl with the Kansas City Chiefs, but this is the biggest play I'll ever make.

The reason I feel so strongly about taking a stand is because youth players can't make the right decisions themselves, so we should help them do so. Our mission should be to make youth sports reasonably safe. As adults, we should take the lead on enhancing brain health education by working together.

We need to provide parents with useful information, because it will prevent serious problems their children will develop later in life. Families need to come together to help

---

132 Solomon Brennan, "NFL players Super Bowl party," http://officialproplayers.wixsite.com/nfl-super-bowl-atl/solomon-brannan

get as much brain health and injury information as possible so parents become fully informed. The sharing of personal stories and educational material in this book, along with unbiased scientific studies, will have a worldwide impact. Sports is a reflection of society's values, and what happens in sports will spill out into other aspects of our lives.

It's time to stop kicking the can down the road, making excuses, and claiming we don't know that sustaining thousands of hits as a child is harmful to a growing brain and joints.

We shouldn't be more protective of a smart phone than we are of children and their vulnerable, developing brains. A sport, no matter how popular, is not more important than the long-term health and wellness of children. Children are our future.

This is why many former NFL players joined the NFL brain injury lawsuit[133] — not just for our own benefit of medical monitoring or compensation, but to protect children and the future of the game we helped build. Many of us old-timers began to play in the league when it wasn't America's most popular sport and didn't have the TV ratings that you see today. We played for the love of the game.

Getting Educated on Brain Trauma

I met Kimberly Archie in March 2012 in Marco Island, Florida, at a National Football League Players Association convention. Isiah Robertson, the Dallas chapter president at the time, and I introduced her to all the chapter presidents, and I've stayed in touch with Kim since then. She's made several trips to Atlanta to speak on behalf of CTE and brain injury. She has had meetings with various NFLPA chapters and other groups in which she provided information to families on CTE and brain injuries. She has met with families who have lost loved ones and connected them with advocates.

I learned very early that Kimberly loves her family and has a passion for all youth who have suffered brain injuries. She has been on the front lines fighting for CTE and brain injury awareness, while becoming known as the "Mother of Youth Sport Safety". I know how hard she fights to make sure all families have the right education and information and, if sought, proper legal information.

---

133 Associated Press, "Additional former players join concussion lawsuit against NFL," March 31, 2012, updated, July 27, 2012 https://www.google.com/amp/s/amp.nfl.com/news/story/09000d5d827fb3db/article/additional-former-players-join-concussion-lawsuit-against-nfl%3fnetworkId=4595&site=.news&zone=story&zoneUrl=url%253Dstory&zoneKeys=s1%253Dstory&env&pageKeyValues&sr=amp

Even before Kimberly lost her son, Paul Bright Jr., to brain damage and CTE in 2014, she went to bat for families.[134] She made them aware of how to fight and win. In Kimberly's battle for children's rights, she meets with doctors, advocacy groups, and sports manufacturing companies to help with safety advancements related to brain damage and CTE.

Yes, I believe brain damage is much more common than families realize, and this makes it a very real problem in sports. For those who think they or their teammates played and now are fine, they need to realize that brain injuries aren't the same for everyone, and without an autopsy, you can't really compare being "okay" to another player who offered a brain donation.

We need to address the problems and look at the best ways to improve player safety and prevent brain damage as much as possible. Kimberly makes it clear she works as hard for cheerleaders, soccer players, and all youth sport athletes as she does for football players. This brain damage problem exists for females, just as it does for males.

Meeting the Families

In April 2017, I had the opportunity to go to Washington D.C., to meet with families at Brain Injury Day. It was a chance to interact with them and their advocates. I was able to hear some of the stories and share information about CTE and brain injuries. To see and experience the hurt of family members who have lost a loved one to brain damage was a real eye-opener for me.

I spoke with family members who were very impassioned and really wanted to share their loved one's personal struggle. The result of this encounter affected me and made me so compassionate for their cause that I want to work even harder to help educate and spread information to all families with kids in sports.

On Brain Injury Day in 2018, I joined family members and CTE and brain injury groups in speaking to Congressional leaders. We had an information fair on Capitol Hill to display and disperse our educational material. It was a long, interesting day in the trenches, and I admire the families who are channeling their pain to make a difference.

---

134 Jane McManus, "Talking with a mother that sued Pop Warner," *ESPN W*, September 8, 2016, accessed January 27, 2019 http://www.espn.com/espnw/voices/article/17493946/talking-kimberly-archie-mother-sued-pop-warner-football

I believe former players have played a critical part in helping to get the information out. We have been speaking out more, while taking part in studies and tests to help make the world more aware of CTE and brain injuries. I believe we can and should do even more.

We need to urge former players to invest in educational programs and stay involved in the university studies.

Where Do We Go From Here?

Youth players look up to former players as role models. The reason education is so important is because most of our youth can't make informed decisions about their safety. This is why we must educate ourselves and make the best decision for our youth as a society, just as we do for things such as vaccines, seat belts, car seats and what age we're able to drink or drive.

Most youth involved in sports do so because their parents sign them up, but a lot of parents aren't aware of the dangers of contact sports, or they erroneously believe that if they played and haven't been diagnosed with brain damage, then taking all these hits from a young age is reasonably safe for their kids. They think it won't happen to their family.

Parents need to be on the front line of safety, not on the sidelines. There are several things we need to check on: Is the organization I am putting my kid in testing and teaching coaches on safety? Have the coaches been certified? Have coaches passed background checks?

I believe former athletes can also play an important role by reaching out to organizations, schools and advocacy groups, speaking to the coaches and athletes, letting the families know the danger of taking hits, as well as the pros and cons of contact sports.

If we want to save football we need to demand that helmets and playing surfaces are redesigned to correct known design defects that increase athletes' risks of injury. Helmets need to be lighter, have custom liners, so as to not trap heat, and be covered with a soft shell so that they're not used as a weapon.

Manufacturers need to stop selling helmets to youth players when they know the helmets are not designed for them. Children before puberty will never have the physical readiness to sustain repetitive hits. Limiting the hours of hits isn't enough to protect kids from brain damage, so they shouldn't be pushed into playing collision sports before high school.

When kids do play tackle football in high school, there needs to be a standard for helmets for their age, along with programs to count and limit hits, just as U.S. Soccer agreed to about headers in the lawsuit settlement in 2015. Baseball has had a limit on pitches for years. We know that in the workplace, doing the same motion over and over can cause cumulative trauma to joints. Sports aren't any different when it comes to repetitive hits.

Children should play youth sports before high school that do not put them at the same risk as collision sports such as tackle football, rugby, boxing, martial arts and wrestling.[135] We should introduce kids to games that are age-appropriate, such as swimming, baseball, basketball and golf. Youth sports should be fun, and not all about winning or spending thousands a year on equipment, uniforms and travel teams.

If parents want their children to play football, have them play flag. It's fun, and they can learn the basic fundamentals of the game. Many former players and the NFL are already promoting flag football for kids before high school, and some, such as quarterback Drew Brees, have their own flag leagues.

There is a big difference between pros athletes and kids. The pros are aware of the danger and are paid a huge amount of money to play. As someone who played all levels, I am committed to working with CTE and brain injury advocacy groups to help make a difference for youth safety, and to promote brain health education to as many people as I can. I am donating my brain for research and urge other former football players and athletes of all levels to do the same.

I have heard former players say they would do it the same, all over again, and that football was the way to success. I contend that it isn't the only way to success. If I dedicated

---

135 A. Powlowski, "'Concussion' doctor says kids shouldn't play these sports until they're 18," *Today*, September 5, 2017, updated August 24, 2018, accessed January 26, 2019 https://www.today.com/health/concussion-doctor-warns-against-contact-sports-kids-t115938

as many hours as I did to being a football player to any other sport or job, I would have been just as successful. Knowing what I know, I would have done things differently.

Sport Health & Safety Administration

Outside of what each sport needs to do to protect child athletes from maltreatment, we need to have independent oversight of sports governing bodies such as the NCAA, Pop Warner, United States Olympic Committee, and USA Football. Currently, Title IX and the Ted Stevens Act provide a loose and light framework of legal recourse in sports, but there is little oversight, regulation or protection for athletes at all levels.

We need to do better. We need a civil rights movement in sports to protect children from exploitation of their name, image and likeness, as well as preventing child maltreatment, from hazing to sex abuse to abusive brain trauma.

The families of Faces of CTE, as well as those impacted by heat illness, heart conditions, paralysis and sickle cell, have come together to lobby lawmakers to introduce federal legislation. The Sport Health & Safety Administration Act would create a federal agency bearing the same name. It would mirror the Occupational Safety & Health Administration, and the board would be comprised of child abuse experts, former athletes and attorneys who don't have conflicts of interest in the sports industry. It would fall under the Consumer Product Safety Commission, and by adding $1 to each professional sports ticket sold by U.S. leagues, it could be fully funded to create policy, oversee and enforce policies.

From the sex abuse scandals of Penn State, USA Gymnastics and USA Swimming, to hazing and bullying, to the brain damage crisis in football, it's easy to see how we need such an agency. The most important way for parents, former players, coaches and other stakeholders in sports to get involved is by lobbying to introduce the Sport Health & Safety Administration Act on the federal level. People who want to do more can contact us at www.facesofCTE.com for ways to help. We can be proactive and all work together to urge lawmakers to get involved and support legislation that will take the fox out of the henhouse once and for all.

BRAIN INJURY SYMPTOMS

We often hear in the media or from some researchers a list of so-called Chronic Traumatic Encephalopathy symptoms and their associations to CTE pathology stages. However, all of these symptoms are actually brain injury or brain damage symptoms. It's dangerous to mislead the public that these symptoms are specific to CTE as a disease or to the stages of CTE when, in fact, these symptoms are experienced by brain injury survivors who do not have CTE or other neurodegenerative diseases.

Each person who has been found to have CTE has also had other brain damage and suffered from brain dysfunction for years before it developed to the beginnings of Chronic Traumatic Encephalopathy. Because of decades of fraud and concealment, the public has been kept in the dark and science has been held back. In spite of this fraud we know what causes CTE and that those who have been found to have it suffered with brain trauma and dysfunction for years before their untimely deaths. They also suffered with various brain injury symptoms. To help others recognize these symptoms, here is a list compiled by the families who shared their stories in this book. For our loved ones not knowing they had brain damage further complicated the injury and made symptoms and life worse.

Frequent headaches or migraines, sleep disturbances, hormone imbalance, sensitive to light or sound or smell, anxiety, nausea, sexual dysfunction, pituitary & or thyroid issues, balance problems, vision changes, unilateral hearing deficits, depression, mood swings and personality changes.

Slurred speech, suicidal ideation, substance abuse, head pressure, loss of impulse control, fatigue, short and long-term memory loss, autonomic system failure (uncontrollable heart rate, lying down to standing and or sitting to standing) hand-eye issues (vision repeated), gait changes, dementia, trouble managing emotions, outbursts, reckless and erratic behavior, difficulty organizing, lack of follow through, attention deficit, Obsessive-Compulsive Disorder, sleep apnea and difficulty with relationships.

This list is not intended to be medical advice or all inclusive, but a sample of symptoms experienced by our loved ones.

QUESTIONS TO ASK YOUR CHILD'S COACH OR SPORT PROGRAM

1. Do they have a child maltreatment prevention program?

   Ask for a copy. Here is an example of what the plan should entail www.facesofCTE.com/childmaltreatment.

2. Who oversees or is the contact person for parents and child athletes for the child maltreatment prevention program?

3. Does your coach or program have a catastrophic emergency plan? Did they rehearse it?

   Ask for a copy and make sure it was rehearsed each year/season. For an example of this plan go to www.nationalcheersafety.com/ emergencyplan.

4. Have coaches and all volunteers or adults in contact with child athletes had a national back ground check? Have coaches been checked each year to insure they are not on the banned coaches list?

5. Are coaches CPR/first aid certified? Ask for verification of current certification.

6. Does the program have access to an Automated External Defibrillator (AED)?

7. Do they track injuries and provide data for researchers? If so, who or what organizations do they share data with?

8. What type of certification and training have coaches and volunteers received?

9. Do they require heart screenings as a part of the pre-participation physical?

    Go to www.nationalcheersafety.com/physical for more information on proper pre-participation physicals including forms for your child's doctor.

10. What is their brain injury prevention program and protocol after injury?

Go to www.facesofCTE.com/braininjury for more information and minimum requirements for programs involving child athletes.

HOW TO PLEDGE YOUR BRAIN

Whether you have suffered a single brain injury, repetitive hits, exposure to bomb blasts in the military, or never had a brain injury at all, scientists are seeking your brain for research. The brain is our operating system for all our systems and can impact our health in a number of ways making it an important organ to understand in the advancement of improving health and wellness.

If you have had a brain injury researchers can study your clinical symptoms as well as autopsy your brain post-mortem. For those who have not had exposure to brain trauma, you can help serve as a part of the control group, which plays a critical role in research as well. While studies without control groups still have great value, studies with control groups are also needed to learn everything we can about the brain and the differences in outcomes between those with exposure to brain trauma and those who have not.

You may go to our website at www.facesofCTE.com/brainpledge to take the pledge.

For more information you may call us at 800-891-5490 or email info@facesofCTE.com with your questions.

For women who would like more information specific to female brain injury or donation go to http://www.pinkconcussions.com/take-the-pledge/ or email katherine@pinkconcussions.org.

HOW TO DONATE A LOVED ONE'S BRAIN

The decision to donate an organ to science is never an easy one to make. We understand the brain can be an even more difficult choice, so we respect those who do, and those who decide it is not right for their loved one. We also realize for religious or other personal beliefs this option is not viable, and we respect that as well.

First of all, if a loved one has selected a brain donation program prior to their death and consent forms are signed, reach out to that brain bank for assistance with the next steps. You'll want to do this immediately(within 48 hours of their death) to connect the brain donation program with the medical examiner handling the autopsy. It is important to preserve the brain as soon as possible and following the protocol established by the brain bank.

If your loved one did not sign up for a brain bank program before their death, and you would like to have their brain examined for further information and understanding, you can call us at 800-891-5490, or go to our website at www.facesofCTE.com/braindonation, or email braindonation@facesofCTE.com with your name, contact number, loved one's name and their date and time of death.

Debbie Pyka, LPN, and Jo Cornell are the Brain Acquisition Coordinators, they can be reached at braindonation@facesofCTE.com

Marcia Jenkins, RN, is the Family Relations Coordinator, for help with grief or support, she can be reached at marcia@facesofCTE.com

Only the next of kin can make arrangements to donate a loved one's brain to our program.

2018 TACKLE FOOTBALL
Catastrophic Injury Snapshot

In addition to countless concussions and subconcussive blows to the head incurred by tackle football players, the following depicts catastrophic* injuries sustained at all levels during the 2018 football season. Dozens of cases of temporary paralysis and non-contact illness and death are also excluded.

74
total catastrophic injuries caused
directly by football collisions

4 **Youth Football** catastrophic injuries	**54** **H.S. Football** catastrophic injuries	**13** **College Football** catastrophic injuries	**3** **NFL** catastrophic injuries

15 catastrophic **brain injuries** (major brain trauma)	**27** catastrophic **cervical spine & neck injuries**	**13** catastrophic **orthopedic injuries** (non-cervical)	**19** catastrophic **internal organ injuries** (spleen, kidney, or pancreas)

resulting in...

23 helicopter **airlifts**	**10** **paralyzations** (long-term)	**1** amputation	**2** **deaths** (additional autopsies pending)

*catastrophic defined as death, life-threatening injury/emergency, or life-altering injury requiring extensive medical treatment
Data Source: **Kent Johnson** (@37919KJ)
Infographic: **Chris Martland** (@FootballDamage)

THE DANGERS OF TACKLE FOOTBALL
Is playing really worth the risk?

Why is tackle football significantly more dangerous than other sports?

1 Tackle football players are **GUARANTEED** to incur **frequent and repetitive blows to the head.**

2 As a result of frequent head blows, players are exposed to high risk of **concussion and permanent brain damage.**

3 High-speed / high-impact collisions are common (and often occur between players of significantly different body weight).

4 Each year, **dozens of catastrophic* injuries** result **directly from football collisions.**

Main Point

Tackle football players are exposed to high risk of
catastrophic injuries, concussion, AND permanent brain damage.
This combination of risk factors makes it unique and significantly more dangerous than other sports.

Concussions
(of which some players will experience long-term symptoms)

Catastrophic Injuries
(such as major brain trauma and life-altering internal organ, orthopedic, and cervical spine / neck injuries)

Permanent Brain Damage
(such as CTE and cognitive, behavioral, and mood impairment)

football causes brain damage

Infographic: **Chris Martland** (@FootballDamage)
*catastrophic defined as death, life-threatening injury/emergency, or life-altering injury requiring extensive medical treatment

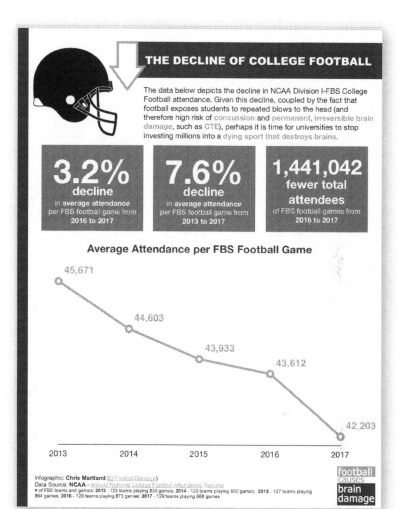

THE DECLINE OF COLLEGE FOOTBALL

The data below depicts the decline in NCAA Division I-FBS College Football attendance. Given this decline, coupled by the fact that football exposes students to repeated blows to the head (and therefore high risk of concussion and permanent, irreversible brain damage, such as CTE), perhaps it is time for universities to stop investing millions into a dying sport that destroys brains.

3.2% decline
in average attendance per FBS football game from 2016 to 2017

7.6% decline
in average attendance per FBS football game from 2013 to 2017

1,441,042 fewer total attendees
of FBS football games from 2016 to 2017

Average Attendance per FBS Football Game

- 2013: 45,671
- 2014: 44,603
- 2015: 43,933
- 2016: 43,612
- 2017: 42,203

Infographic: **Chris Martland** (@FootballDamage)
Data Source: **NCAA** - Annual National College Football Attendance Reports
# of FBS teams and games: **2013** - 123 teams playing 835 games; **2014** - 125 teams playing 850 games; **2015** - 127 teams playing 864 games; **2016** - 128 teams playing 873 games; **2017** - 129 teams playing 868 games

football causes brain damage

ABOUT THE
AUTHORS

Kimberly Archie resides in Los Angeles, California, where she works as a retained legal consultant at Girardi Keese, the law firm made famous in the blockbuster movie, "Erin Brockovich." She is the co-founder of the National Cheer Safety Foundation, Faces of CTE, and a leading expert on the prevention of child athlete maltreatment, a go-to expert often quoted in national and international media such as People magazine, CNN, Al Jazeera and the New York Times. Her legal work has been used to settle more than 50 sports injury lawsuits since 2008, including the NFL brain injury case, and Mehr v. U.S. Soccer, a settlement that removed headers for children ages 10 and under. In 2014, she teamed up State Assemblywoman Lorena Gonzales-Fletcher to pass a law in California to make high school cheerleading an official Title IX sport. Governor Jerry Brown signed the bill into law in 2015, making sports history.

Solomon Brannan is a former defensive back who played three seasons in the American Football League (AFL) with the Kansas City Chiefs and New York Jets. He played college football at Morris Brown College and attended Tompkins High School in Savannah, Georgia. He was a member of the Kansas City Chiefs team that won the 1966 AFL championship. He currently lives in Atlanta, Georgia, with his college sweetheart and wife of more than 50 years, Jean. He is an active member of his church, St. Anthony's of Padua, has been a long-standing member and local officer with the NFL Players Association, and serves on the advisory board of Child Athlete Advocates. He was the inaugural recipient of the Save Your Brain advocacy award for his lifetime commitment to the health and safety of athletes, from kids to the pros.

Tiffani Bright lives in Thousand Oaks, California, with her partner of nine years. She is the web designer for Faces of CTE and the National Cheer Safety Foundation. After sustaining injuries in high school cheerleading, she helped launch child athlete advocacy programs with her mother. She has donated more than two thousand hours to various organizations advocating for her brother, Paul Bright, cheerleaders, and other child athletes.

Jo Cornell has a master's degree in Public Administration and after losing her only child, Tyler, she helped launch Child Athlete Advocates. She is a co-plaintiff in federal litigation against Pop Warner for her son Tyler's death. Jo was a civil litigation paralegal for 27 years with extensive experience in wrongful death cases. She now is focused on the most important case of her career, Tyler's righteous cause for justice. She calls Rancho Bernardo, California her home.

Cyndy Feasel, co-founder of Faces of CTE, is the author of "After the Cheering Stops," the tragic story of her journey into chaos and darkness resulting from the concussions that her husband – NFL center Grant Feasel – suffered during 10 seasons of pro football. Today she is an advocate for CTE awareness and head trauma injuries in sports and educates parents and athletes about the potential damage that head injuries can cause. Cyndy makes her home in Dallas, Texas, where she is an art teacher in the public schools. You can follow her on Facebook at Cyndy Feasel.

Michael Grange lives in Albuquerque, New Mexico, with his wife, Michele. They founded the Patrick Grange Memorial Foundation in 2013 to honor their son, Patrick, who died at the age of 29 from ALS, also known as Lou Gehrig's disease. Patrick was later found to have Stage II CTE and was the very first soccer player diagnosed with the disease. The doctors labeled his case "head trauma-induced ALS." In an effort to promote awareness, Michael and Michele are responsible for prompting New Mexico lawmakers to declare February 3 as an annual statewide ALS Day. As retired teachers, the Granges are proponents for educating youth and their parents on the importance of brain protection and safety. They have two sons, Casey and Ryan, and two grandchildren, Addison and Michael (who are involved in a variety of sports – but play wisely).

Darren Hamblin lives in Miamisburg, Ohio, with his wife of more than 30 years, Heather. He is the proud father of Heidi and Cody. His first grandchild, Zophia, was born in 2017. Darren is the first to sue youth helmet manufacturers for known design defects, fraud and selling a youth helmet never made or tested for kids that increase the risk of brain damage.

Kira Hoffman-Soto has spent 25 years of her professional life fighting for justice inside and outside of a courtroom. She now is taking on CTE and sharing the story of her brother's struggle with the disease that spanned more than two decades. It is her sincere wish to help others who suffer due to this insidious disease and to one day see advances in medicine toward prevention, treatment and a cure for those suffering because "nobody who exits a playing field should leave behind anything more than their best effort."

Kimberly Jenkins is a work force analyst for a major insurance company. She has been a major supporter of her sons and the community as a volunteer helping in all areas of athletics. She is active on social media to help those struggling with head injuries and their loved ones.

Marcia Jenkins, RN, has 30 years in the field of nursing and lives with her husband in a suburb of Indianapolis, Indiana. Much of her career has been devoted to caring for those experiencing the loss of a loved one. Her passion has been supporting families who have lost their children, as well as adults. She also serves on the Hospital Ethic Committee and community awareness projects, and is a member of the Resolve Through Sharing national program that provides education on grief and loss. This educational opportunity is presented to doctors, nurses, chaplains and social workers. She is a co-author of a caregiver handbook "Companioning at the Time of Perinatal Loss," intended for support staff as they care for families. She serves as the family relationship coordinator for Child Athlete Advocate's Brain Donation Program, providing support for families and facilitating a peer support group. She currently is a hospice nurse and bereavement coordinator for a local hospice organization and serves as a parish nurse for her community church.

Nicki Langston is a caregiver. She is a former stay-at-home mother of four who transitioned into the role of early childhood education teacher once her children were grown. She lost her 26-year-old son, Zack, to CTE after he spent most of his life playing football. Nicki has taken on the role of CTE advocate in order to spread awareness of the disease. She lives in the greater Kansas City area with her husband.

Keana McMahon is the former wife of Justin Strzelczyk, who was an offensive lineman for the Pittsburgh Steelers from 1990-1998. Keana is an advocate for education and awareness of brain trauma and CTE, which caused her husband's death. Keana's story with Justin was portrayed in the 2015 movie "Concussion." Keana is a mother of four and a businesswoman. She grew up in Altoona, Pennsylvania, and went to Altoona High School. She and her husband, Matt, live in Pittsburgh, Pennsylvania, with their two beautiful boys and are owners of the Eleventh Hour Brewery.

Deb Ploetz was married to Greg Ploetz for 37 years and has two children, Erin and Beau, and two grand-children, Luke and Britt. After Greg died in 2015 following a long battle with dementia, he was found to have Stage IV CTE and extensive brain damage. Greg was a formidable defensive tackle for the University of Texas and played on the 1969 national championship team. Deb took on the NCAA in the landmark lawsuit, Ploetz v. NCAA, on behalf of her husband. It was the first football CTE case in legal history to go to trial. The case settled during the first week of trial, forever cementing Greg's legacy as a leader in the fight for justice for football families. Deb attended Mount St. Mary's High School and the University of Arkansas, and she resides in Dallas, Texas, where she continues to advocate for athletes and raise awareness about brain trauma.

Leanne Pozzobon lives in Merritt, BC Canada with her husband of 29 years Luke and their daughter Amy. In 2017 she lost her son, Ty Pozzobon to suicide, Ty was a professional bull rider and had suffered multiple concussions throughout his career. Leanne and her family had Ty's brain tissue donated for research. Ty was found to be the first ever bull rider to be diagnosed with CTE and Traumatic Brain Injury. Since then, the Pozzobon family and Ty's close friends have founded the Ty Pozzobon Foundation. The Foundation has been put in place to protect and support the mental health and well-being of rodeo athletes inside and outside of the arena. It's important for Leanne to let others know not to stop doing what you are passionate about but do it in a smarter way and to listen to both what medical professionals tell you and what your body and mind are telling you.

Debra Pyka is a co-founder of Faces of CTE and Save Your Brain, along with working with Child Athlete Advocates to help secure brain donations of athletes in collaboration with the Mayo Clinic and Mt. Sinai. She lives in Hixton, Wisconsin, and is married with five children – Tyler, Joseph, Seth, Nicole and stepdaughter Samantha – and six grandchildren – Braylee, Jordi, Collins, Layla, Dexter and Henry.

Mary Seau is the founder of the Mary Seau Chronic Traumatic Encephalopathy (CTE) Foundation, launched in February 2015 on behalf of her younger brother, former NFL Hall of Fame linebacker Tiaina "Junior" Seau Jr. As a co-founder of Faces of CTE, she has partnered with prominent researchers in the Early CTE Research Program, and over the past four years her foundation has helped provide an understanding on how CTE can impair and destroy the brain. She believes that research, education and prevention is the answer. Her foundation is actively working with research institutions and other organizations to develop imaging techniques to correlate pathological changes and abnormalities so that high-tech imaging tools can be used to screen the presence of early CTE.

RULING

UNITED STATES DISTRICT COURT
CENTRAL DISTRICT OF CALIFORNIA

CIVIL MINUTES - GENERAL

Case No.	16-CV-6603 PSG (PLAx)	Date	October 20, 2017
Title	Kimberly Archie, *et al* V. Pop Warner Little Scholars, Inc. *et al*		

Present: The Honorable   Philip S. Gutierrez, United States District Judge

Wendy Hernandez	Not Reported
Deputy Clerk	Court Reporter
Attorneys Present for Plaintiff(s):	Attorneys Present for Defendant(s):
Not Present	Not Present

Proceedings (In Chambers):   **The Court GRANTS IN PART and DENIES IN PART Defendant PWLS's Motion to Dismiss, and GRANTS Defendant NOCSAE's Motion to Dismiss**

Before the Court are Defendants Pop Warner Little Scholars and National Operating Committee on Standards Athletic Equipment's motions to dismiss Kimberly Archie, *et al*'s Second Amended Complaint. Dkts. # 82, 85. The Court finds the matter appropriate for decision without oral argument. *See* Fed. R. Civ. P. 78(b); L.R. 7-15. Having considered the moving, opposing, and reply papers, the Court GRANTS In Part and DENIES In Part Defendant Pop Warner Little Scholars' motion to dismiss, and GRANTS Defendant National Operating Committee on Standards Athletic Equipment's motion to dismiss.

I.   Background

The background of the case was laid out in detail in the Court's May 12, 2017 Order, and will only be summarized here. *See* Dkt. # 72. Plaintiffs Kimberly Archie (as a survivor of decedent Paul Bright), Jo Cornell (as a survivor of decedent Tyler Cornell), Debra McCrae (on behalf of Richard Caldwell), and Shannon Barnes (guardian ad litem for Chase, Drew, and Cade Barnes) (collectively, "Plaintiffs") bring this putative class action on behalf of their children who at various times between 1996 and 2015 played youth tackle football. *See* Dkt. # 76, *Second Amended Complaint* ("*SAC*"). Plaintiffs assert that Defendants Pop Warner Little Scholars, Inc. ("PWLS") and the National Operating Committee on Standards for Athletic Equipment ("NOCSAE") failed to provide for the safety and health of child participants in the Pop Warner youth football program. *See id.* As a result of Defendants' actions, representations, and omissions, Plaintiffs allege their children suffered various head injuries while playing football which, in the years after they stopped playing, led to troubling behavioral issues, depression, and even untimely death from Chronic Traumatic Encephalopathy ("CTE"). *See generally id.*

UNITED STATES DISTRICT COURT
CENTRAL DISTRICT OF CALIFORNIA

CIVIL MINUTES - GENERAL

Case No.	16-CV-6603 PSG (PLAx)	Date	October 20, 2017
Title	Kimberly Archie, *et al* V. Pop Warner Little Scholars, Inc. *et al*		

Plaintiffs bring the following seven causes of action against both Defendants: (1) negligence; (2) fraud; (3) fraudulent concealment; (4) negligent misrepresentation; (5) wrongful death; (6) violation of California's Unfair Competition Law ("UCL"), Cal. Bus. & Prof. Code §§ 17200 *et seq.*; and (7) violation of California's False Advertising Law ("FAL"), Cal. Bus. & Prof. Code §§ 17500 *et seq. See id.*

In response to Plaintiffs' first amended complaint, PWLS and NOCSAE each filed a motion to dismiss. Dkts. # 50, 53. On May 12, 2017, the Court granted both motions without prejudice. Dkt. # 72. Defendants now file motions to dismiss Plaintiffs' Second Amended Complaint. Dkts. # 82 (*"PW Mot."*), 85 (*"NOCSAE Mot."*). The Court will consider each motion in turn.

II.   Legal Standard

A.   Rule 12(b)(1)

A plaintiff must "have 'standing' to challenge the action sought to be adjudicated in the lawsuit." *Valley Forge Christian College v. Americans United for Separation of Church and State, Inc.*, 454 U.S. 464, 471 (1982) (citation omitted). The "irreducible constitutional minimum" of Article III standing has three elements: (1) the plaintiff must have suffered an injury; (2) that is causally related to the defendant's challenged actions; and (3) it must be "likely" that the injury will be "redressed by a favorable decision." *Lujan v. Defenders of Wildlife*, 504 U.S. 555, 560 (1992) (internal quotation marks and citations omitted); *Townley v. Miller*, 722 F.3d 1128, 1133 (9th Cir. 2013). The plaintiff, as the party invoking federal jurisdiction, has the burden of establishing these elements. *See Lujan*, 504 U.S. at 561. Article III standing bears on the court's subject matter jurisdiction, and is therefore subject to challenge under Federal Rule of Civil Procedure 12(b)(1). *See Maya v. Centex Corp.*, 658 F.3d 1060, 1067 (9th Cir. 2011).

B.   Rule 12(b)(2)

Pursuant to Federal Rule of Civil Procedure 12(b)(2), a party may seek dismissal of an action for lack of personal jurisdiction. Fed. R. Civ. P. 12(b). Once a party seeks dismissal under Rule 12(b)(2), the plaintiff has the burden of demonstrating that personal jurisdiction exists. *Menken v. Emm*, 503 F.3d 1050, 1056 (9th Cir. 2007); *Browne v. McCain*, 612 F. Supp. 2d 1118, 1122 (C.D. Cal. 2009). When a court rules on a motion to dismiss for lack of personal jurisdiction, the plaintiff "need make only a prima facie showing of jurisdictional facts to withstand the motion to dismiss." *Ballard v. Savage*, 65 F.3d 1495, 1498 (9th Cir. 1995). A court may "consider evidence presented in affidavits to assist in the determination." *Doe v.*

UNITED STATES DISTRICT COURT
CENTRAL DISTRICT OF CALIFORNIA

CIVIL MINUTES - GENERAL

Case No.	16-CV-6603 PSG (PLAx)	Date	October 20, 2017
Title	Kimberly Archie, *et al* V. Pop Warner Little Scholars, Inc. *et al*		

Unocal Corp., 248 F.3d 915, 922 (9th Cir. 2001). In the case of "conflicts between the facts in the parties' affidavits," such conflicts "must be resolved in [the plaintiff's] favor." *AT&T v. Compagnie Bruxelles Lambert*, 94 F.3d 586, 588 (9th Cir. 1996) (citation omitted). However, "the plaintiff cannot simply rest on the bare allegations of its complaint." *Schwarzenegger v. Fred Martin Motor Co.*, 374 F.3d 797, 800 (9th Cir. 2004) (citation and internal quotation marks omitted). A jurisdictional attack may be facial or factual. *Safe Air for Everyone v. Meyer*, 373 F.3d 1035, 1038 (9th Cir. 2004). In reviewing a facial attack, the court must accept the allegations of the complaint as true. *Id.* In a factual attack, the court may consider evidence outside the pleadings. *Id.* at 1038-39.

There is no applicable federal statute governing personal jurisdiction in this case. Accordingly, the Court applies the law of California, the state in which the district court sits. *Core-Vent Corp. v. Nobel Indus. AB*, 11 F.3d 1482, 1484 (9th Cir. 1993). "California's long-arm jurisdictional statute is coextensive with federal due process requirements, so that the jurisdictional analysis under state law and federal due process [is] the same." *Urban Textile, Inc. v. A&E Stores, Inc.*, No. CV 14-1554 CAS (ASx), 2014 WL 3955173, at *1 (C.D. Cal. Aug. 11, 2014); *see also* Cal. Civ. Proc. Code § 410.10 ("A court of this state may exercise jurisdiction on any basis not inconsistent with the Constitution of this state or of the United States."); *Roth v. Garcia Marquez*, 942 F.2d 617, 620 (9th Cir. 1991).

C. 12(b)(6)

To survive a motion to dismiss under Rule 12(b)(6), a complaint must "contain sufficient factual matter, accepted as true, to 'state a claim to relief that is plausible on its face.'" *Ashcroft v. Iqbal*, 556 U.S. 662, 678 (2009) (quoting *Bell Atl. Corp. v. Twombly*, 550 U.S. 544, 570 (2007)). In assessing the adequacy of the complaint, the court must accept all pleaded facts as true and construe them in the light most favorable to the plaintiff. *See Turner v. City and Cty. of San Francisco*, 788 F.3d 1206, 1210 (9th Cir. 2015); *Cousins v. Lockyer*, 568 F.3d 1063, 1067 (9th Cir. 2009). The court then determines whether the complaint "allows the court to draw the reasonable inference that the defendant is liable for the misconduct alleged." *Iqbal*, 556 U.S. at 678.

III.   Discussion

A.   PWLS's Motion to Dismiss

PWLS argues that the SAC should be dismissed for (1) lack of personal jurisdiction over PWLS; (2) untimeliness of Plaintiffs' claims; (3) lack of standing; and (4) failure to state a claim under Rule 12(b)(6). *PW Mot.* 3.

UNITED STATES DISTRICT COURT
CENTRAL DISTRICT OF CALIFORNIA

CIVIL MINUTES - GENERAL

Case No.	16-CV-6603 PSG (PLAx)	Date	October 20, 2017
Title	Kimberly Archie, *et al* V. Pop Warner Little Scholars, Inc. *et al*		

    i.   *Personal Jurisdiction*

        a.   *General Jurisdiction*

In its May 12 Order, the Court determined it had no general jurisdiction over PWLS in California. PWLS is a Pennsylvania corporation with its principal place of business in Langhorne, Pennsylvania. *Butler Decl.* ¶ 3. PWLS has no office, mailing address, employees or subsidiaries in California, maintains no bank accounts or agent for service of process in California, and neither pays taxes nor is registered to do business in California. *Id.* Plaintiffs' opposition does not address the general jurisdiction issue, but rather skips over it to specific jurisdiction. *See Plaintiffs' Opposition* ("*PWLS Opp.*") 3. The Court will therefore treat PWLS's general jurisdiction argument as conceded by Plaintiffs.

        b.   *Specific Jurisdiction*

Specific jurisdiction "depends on an affiliation between the forum and the underlying controversy, principally, an activity or an occurrence that takes place in the forum State and is therefore subject to the State's regulation." *Ranza v. Nike, Inc.*, 793 F.3d 1059, 1068 (9th Cir. 2015) (quoting *Goodyear Dunlop Tire Operations, S.A. v. Brown*, 564 U.S. 915, 919 (2011)). The Ninth Circuit uses a three-part test to determine whether specific jurisdiction exists:

> (1) The non-resident defendant must purposefully direct his activities or consummate some transaction with the forum or resident thereof; or perform some act by which he purposefully avails himself of the privilege of conducting activities in the forum, thereby invoking the benefits and protections of its laws;
> (2) the claim must be one which arises out of or relates to the defendant's forum related activities; and
> (3) the exercise of jurisdiction must comport with fair play and substantial justice, i.e. it must be reasonable.

Picot v. Weston, 780 F.3d 1206, 1211 (9th Cir. 2015) (quoting *Schwarzenegger v. Fred Martin Motor Co.*, 374 F.3d 797, 802 (9th Cir. 2004)). Here, the Court labels these three prongs of specific jurisdiction (1) "minimum contacts," which has its own three sub-elements, (2) "arising out of forum activities," and (3) "reasonableness." Plaintiffs bear the burden of proof for the first two prongs, but if both are established, the "defendant must come forward with a 'compelling case' that the exercise of jurisdiction would not be reasonable." *Boschetto v. Hansing*, 539 F.3d 1011, 1016 (9th Cir. 2008). Specific jurisdiction is lacking if any of the

UNITED STATES DISTRICT COURT
CENTRAL DISTRICT OF CALIFORNIA

CIVIL MINUTES - GENERAL

Case No.	16-CV-6603 PSG (PLAx)	Date	October 20, 2017
Title	Kimberly Archie, *et al* V. Pop Warner Little Scholars, Inc. *et al*		

prongs are not established. *Pebble Beach*, 453 F.3d at 1155 (quoting *Omeluk v. Langsten Slip & Batbyggeri A/S*, 52 F.3d 267, 270 (9th Cir. 1995)).

1.   Minimum Contacts

The minimum contacts prong of the specific jurisdiction analysis embodies two distinct concepts: purposeful availment and purposeful direction. *See Wash. Shoe Co. v. A-Z Sporting Goods Inc.*, 704 F.3d 668, 672 (9th Cir. 2012). Purposeful availment is most often used in contract suits, and purposeful direction is most often used in tort suits. *Schwarzenneger*, 374 F.3d at 802. Because Plaintiffs' claims arise in tort, the Court applies the purposeful direction analysis. *See id.* at 803; *see also Adidas Am., Inc. v. Cougar Sport, Inc.*, 169 F. Supp. 3d 1079, 1087 (D. Or. 2016).

Ninth Circuit courts use a three-part test (the "effects test") from the Supreme Court's opinion in *Calder v. Jones*, 465 U.S. 783 (1984), to evaluate minimum contacts in the purposeful direction context. *Panavision Int'l v. Toeppen*, 141 F.3d 1316, 1321 (9th Cir. 1998). The three elements of this minimum contacts test are: "(1) committed an intentional act, (2) expressly aimed at the forum state, (3) causing harm that the defendant knows is likely to be suffered in the forum state." *Picot*, 780 F.3d at 1214 (quoting *Dole Food Co., Inc. v. Watts*, 303 F.3d 1104, 1111 (9th Cir. 2002)). The Supreme Court has held that due process permits the exercise of personal jurisdiction over a defendant who "purposefully direct[s]" his activities at residents of a forum, even in the "absence of physical contacts" with the forum. *Burger King Corp. v. Rudzewicz*, 471 U.S. 462, 476 (1985).

a.   Intentional Act

Under the first element of the *Calder* test, Plaintiffs must demonstrate that PWLS committed an "intentional act." Under the test, an "intentional act" is an "external manifestation of the actor's intent to perform an actual, physical act in the real world." *Wash. Shoe*, 704 F.3d at 674. Plaintiffs allege that PWLS "operates and controls several Pop Warner leagues throughout California," and "plays an active role in creating Pop Warner leagues throughout the state of California." *See SAC* ¶ 64. They allege that PWLS collects a fee of $25 per California league (*Id.* ¶ 67), sells and requires participants to wear PWLS patches (*Id.* ¶ 82), provides helmets (*Id.* ¶ 83), schedules games (*Id.* ¶ 84), and sets deadlines for registration (*Id.* ¶ 85). These acts are sufficient to meet the "intentional act" prong within the meaning of the *Calder* test.

b.   Expressly Aimed

UNITED STATES DISTRICT COURT
CENTRAL DISTRICT OF CALIFORNIA

CIVIL MINUTES - GENERAL

Case No.	16-CV-6603 PSG (PLAx)	Date	October 20, 2017
Title	Kimberly Archie, *et al* V. Pop Warner Little Scholars, Inc. *et al*		

Under the second element of the *Calder* test, Plaintiffs must demonstrate that Pop Warner "expressly aimed" its actions at the forum state. The Ninth Circuit has "emphasized that 'something more' than mere foreseeability [is required] in order to justify the assertion of personal jurisdiction . . . and that 'something more' means conduct expressly aimed at the forum." *Brayton Purcell LLP v. Recordon & Recordon*, 606 F.3d 1124, 1129 (9th Cir. 2010) (first alteration in original) (citations omitted).

Moreover, cases from this Circuit hold that "express aiming" encompasses wrongful conduct that targets a known forum resident. *Bancroft & Masters*, 223 F.3d at 1087; *Automattic Inc. v. Steiner*, 82 F. Supp. 3d 1011, 1023 (N.D. Cal. 2015) ("The express aiming requirement is satisfied 'when the defendant is alleged to have engaged in wrongful conduct targeted at a plaintiff whom the defendant knows to be a resident of the forum state.'"); *Attilio Giusti Leombruni S.p.A. v. Lsil & Co.*, No. CV-15-002128-BRO-EX, 2015 WL 12743878, at *8 (C.D. Cal. May 29, 2015) (same); *Disney Enterprises, Inc. v. Fun Vacation Network*, LLC, No. LACV-15-08062-JAK-PJWX, 2016 WL 7444860, at *4 (C.D. Cal. May 16, 2016) (same).

Plaintiffs argue that PWLS expressly aimed its activities at California when it entered into contracts with California conferences, ensuring California leagues abide by its official rules; when it charges $25 for league registration; and when it mandates that leagues purchase its rule book. *SAC* ¶¶ 66, 71. Further, PWLS requires California players to wear a Pop Warner patch, sold by PWLS. *Id.* ¶ 82. PWLS's website offers a "National League Finder" to help consumers find their local leagues. *Id.* ¶ 81. It also facilitates local California leagues' recruitment of coaches, and provides all necessary forms for California leagues and players (i.e., insurance forms, background check forms, manuals, and calendars). *Id.* "Not all material placed on the Internet is, solely by virtue of its universal accessibility, expressly aimed at every state in which it is accessed." *Mavrix Photo, Inc. v. Brand Techs., Inc.*, 647 F.3d 1218, 1231 (9th Cir. 2011). Courts in the Ninth Circuit "typically examine the 'level of interactivity and commercial nature of the exchange of information that occurs on the website to determine if sufficient contacts exist to warrant the exercise of jurisdiction.'" *Craigslist, Inc. v. Kerbel*, No. C 11-3309 EMC, 2012 WL 3166798, at *4 (N.D. Cal. Aug. 2, 2012) (quoting *Cybersell v. Cybersell*, 130 F.3d 414, 416 (9th Cir. 1997)).

Defendant's website, www.popwarner.com, is interactive in nature in that it helps California leagues and players comply with PWLS's rules, regulations, and calendar, as well as helping people locate leagues and coaches; it is also commercial in that it allows Californians to purchase required rule books and patches. These acts are sufficiently directed at California to pass the second prong of the *Calder* test.

       c.   *Foreseeable Harm*

UNITED STATES DISTRICT COURT
CENTRAL DISTRICT OF CALIFORNIA

CIVIL MINUTES - GENERAL

Case No.	16-CV-6603 PSG (PLAx)	Date	October 20, 2017
Title	Kimberly Archie, *et al* V. Pop Warner Little Scholars, Inc. *et al*		

Under the third element of the *Calder* test, Plaintiff must demonstrate that Defendant's "conduct caused harm that it knew was likely to be suffered in the forum." *Brayton Purcell*, 606 F.3d at 1129 (quotation marks omitted). "This element is satisfied when a defendant's intentional act has 'foreseeable effects' in the forum." *Id.* This element may be established even if "the bulk of the harm" occurs outside the forum. *Yahoo! Inc. v. La Ligue Contre Le Racisme Et L'Antisemitisme*, 433 F.3d 1199, 1207 (9th Cir. 2006).

The same facts discussed above are sufficient to make a showing that PWLS knew any harm suffered by Plaintiffs would be suffered in the forum state: PWLS has approximately 14,000 to 32,000 football participants in California, to whom Defendant sold patches and distributed rule books. *SAC* ¶ 65. PWLS knew Plaintiffs were located in California; they must have also known that any harm suffered would have been felt, at least in part, in California. *See Brayton*, 606 F.3d at 1131 (finding that the harm in the forum state was foreseeable because the plaintiff was known to reside in the forum state).

Accordingly, all three elements of the minimum contacts test are satisfied.

2. Arising Out of Forum Activities

The second prong of the specific jurisdiction analysis "is that the claim asserted in the litigation arises out of the defendant's forum related activities." *Panavision Intern., L.P. v. Toeppen*, 141 F.3d 1316, 1322 (9th Cir. 1998). The Ninth Circuit applies a "but-for" test under which the Court must determine whether the plaintiff would not have suffered injury "but for" the defendant's forum-related conduct. *Id.*; *Shute v. Carnival Cruise Lines*, 897 F.2d 377, 385 (9th Cir. 1990), *rev'd on other grounds*, 499 U.S. 585 (1991) ("The 'but for' test should not be narrowly applied; rather, the requirement is merely designed to confirm that there is some nexus between the cause of action and defendant's contact with the forum."). Generally, the resolution of this prong relies heavily on the court's resolution of the minimum contacts prong. *Dole Food Co., Inc.*, 303 F.3d 1104, 1114 (9th Cir. 2002).

Plaintiffs allege, generally, that PWLS's message of "safety first" misled parents into signing their children up for tackle football and relying on the equipment and coaches, which led to brain injury, disease, and death. *See generally SAC*. As many of the communications, messages, rules, and regulations upon which the parents are alleged to have relied came from PWLS's website, this element is satisfied.

The Court concludes that Plaintiffs have alleged facts sufficient to establish that PWLS has minimum contacts in California and there is some nexus between them and Plaintiffs' claims. Defendants do not raise an argument as to the remaining prong. *See PW Mot* 5-6.

UNITED STATES DISTRICT COURT
CENTRAL DISTRICT OF CALIFORNIA

CIVIL MINUTES - GENERAL

Case No.	16-CV-6603 PSG (PLAx)	Date	October 20, 2017
Title	Kimberly Archie, *et al* V. Pop Warner Little Scholars, Inc. *et al*		

Therefore, the Court concludes that Plaintiffs have established personal jurisdiction over Defendant PLWS.

    ii.   *Timeliness of Claims*

        a. *McCrae's Claims*

PWLS asserts that Plaintiff McCrae's claims are time-barred because the SAC alleges only that her son, Richard Caldwell, suffered multiple concussions while playing youth football between 1996 and 2003, and "sometime after" he stopped playing football, "Richard displayed bouts of erratic behavior and was diagnosed with depression." *SAC* ¶ 3; *PW Mot.* 7. Many years later, Caldwell was injured in a car accident rendering him wheelchair-bound. *SAC* ¶ 3. PWLS argues that any injuries that give rise to McCrae's claims occurred no later than 2003, and are thus barred by the relevant statutes of limitations. *PW Mot.* 6.

A federal court sitting in diversity jurisdiction must generally apply the law of the forum state regarding whether an action is barred by the statute of limitations. *Hendrix v. Novartis Pharmaceutical Corp.*, 975 F. Supp. 2d 1100, 1105 (C.D. Cal. 2013) (citing *Guaranty Trust Co. v. York*, 326 U.S. 99, 109–10, (1945)). Under California law, negligence actions are subject to a two-year limitation period, Cal. Code Civ. P. § 335.1; fraud, fraudulent concealment, and negligent misrepresentation actions are subject to a three-year limitations period, Cal. Code Civ. P. § 380(d); claims under the FAL are subject to a three-year limitations period, Cal. Code Civ. P. § 338(a); and claims under the UCL are subject to a four-year limitations period, Cal. Bus. & Prof. Code § 17208.

Accordingly, because Richard Caldwell suffered injuries no later than 2003 and McCrae did not file suit until January 9, 2017,[1] the Court agrees that all of McCrae's claims in this action are barred by the relevant statutes of limitations.

In response, Plaintiffs raise the delayed discovery rule, which provides that a cause of action accrues when "the plaintiff discovers, or has reason to discover, that he has been wrongfully injured." *Hendrix*, 975 F. Supp. 2d at 1105. In order for the rule to apply, "the plaintiff must specifically plead facts which show (1) the time and manner of discovery and (2) the inability to have made earlier discovery despite reasonable diligence." *Yumul v. Smart Balance, Inc.*, 733 F. Supp. 2d 1117, 1130-31 (C.D. Cal. 2010) (quoting *Saliter v. Pierce Bros. Mortuaries*, 81 Cal. App. 3d 292, 296 (1978)) (other citations omitted). Plaintiffs argue that McCrae "did not become aware that Richard's participation in youth tackle football caused him

---

[1] Although this suit was filed on September 1, 2016, McCrae was only added as a Plaintiff in the FAC, filed on January 9, 2017.

UNITED STATES DISTRICT COURT
CENTRAL DISTRICT OF CALIFORNIA

CIVIL MINUTES - GENERAL

Case No.	16-CV-6603 PSG (PLAx)	Date	October 20, 2017
Title	Kimberly Archie, *et al* V. Pop Warner Little Scholars, Inc. *et al*		

to develop chronic traumatic brain injuries until the issue was widely publicized in December 2015. . . [she] could not have become aware before December 2015 because Defendants actively concealed this information from the public." *SAC* ¶ 3.

This argument falls short of meeting the discovery rule's requirement of pleading specific facts that show how and when the discovery happened and why Plaintiffs were unable to make the discovery earlier "despite reasonable diligence." *Yumul*, 733 F. Supp. 2d at 1130-31. As in the first amended complaint, Plaintiffs still allege no facts about how McCrae's discovery of Caldwell's brain injury occurred and what reasonable diligence McCrae engaged in to discover it—the SAC is lacking even in a threshold assertion that brain injury *did* occur, and that it was eventually discovered. Despite Caldwell's "bouts of erratic behavior," Plaintiffs allege no diligence in attempting to illuminate the cause of that behavior. Rather, McCrae states that "discovery" occurred when she saw the movie *Concussion*; but she offers no facts to connect the dots between seeing that film and discovering an actual brain injury in her son. *SAC* ¶ 3; *PWLS Opp.* 13. Plaintiffs state only that the delayed discovery rule applies, but offer no factual allegations to support its application.

Accordingly, because Richard Caldwell's alleged injuries occurred more than 13 years prior to filing suit and McCrae has failed to plead facts that support the application of the delayed discovery rule, the Court GRANTS Defendant's motion to dismiss McCrae's claims as barred by the applicable statute of limitations. McCrae's claims are therefore dismissed from this action with prejudice.

       b.   *Cornell's Claims*

PWLS argues that Plaintiff Cornell's claims for negligence and wrongful death are also time-barred by the applicable two-year statute of limitations pursuant to Cal. Code Civ. P. § 335.1 (imposing a two-year limitations period for causes of action arising from "injury to, or for the death of an individual caused by the wrongful act or neglect of another."). *PW Mot.* 8; *NOCSAE Mot.* 17.

Tyler Cornell committed suicide on April 3, 2014, more than two years before Cornell filed suit on September 1, 2016. *SAC* ¶ 2. The SAC alleges that Plaintiff Cornell (Tyler's mother) "did not, and could not, discover that Tyler suffered from Chronic Traumatic Encephalopathy until January 16, 2015 when a posthumous test revealed his diagnosis." *Id.* ¶ 218. As explained above, in order to invoke the delayed discovery rule, Plaintiffs "must specifically plead facts which show (1) the time and manner of discovery and (2) the inability to have made earlier discovery despite reasonable diligence." *Yumul*, 733 F. Supp. 2d at 1130-31. In other words, "a potential plaintiff who suspects that an injury has been wrongfully caused

UNITED STATES DISTRICT COURT
CENTRAL DISTRICT OF CALIFORNIA

CIVIL MINUTES - GENERAL

Case No.	16-CV-6603 PSG (PLAx)	Date	October 20, 2017
Title	Kimberly Archie, *et al* V. Pop Warner Little Scholars, Inc. *et al*		

must conduct a reasonable investigation of all potential causes of that injury," and that "despite diligent investigation of the circumstances of the injury, he or she could not have reasonably discovered facts supporting the cause of action within the applicable statute of limitations period." *Fox v. Ethicon Endo-Surgery, Inc.* 35 Cal. 4th 797, 808–809 (2005).

Unlike McCrae, Cornell has added facts to the SAC to support the application of the delayed discovery rule. After her son's death, Cornell sent his brain to Boston University to be examined. *SAC* ¶ 2. The results were made available to her on January 16, 2015, when she learned that Tyler suffered from CTE. *Id.* She could not have learned of the diagnosis any earlier than receiving the results of a posthumous brain examination, because she had no reason to suspect that Tyler suffered from brain disease prior to his death and CTE can only be diagnosed posthumously. *Id.* As soon as he died, she sent his brain off for study—an act of diligence in ascertaining the cause of his suicide. *Id.* She filed her claim on September 1, 2016, within two years of the date she received the CTE diagnosis. Cornell alleges the time and manner of discovery, as well as her diligence in procuring a diagnosis. *Id.*

The Court concludes that the application of the delayed discovery rule is properly alleged, and therefore Cornell's claims are not time-barred.

> c.   *Archie's Claims*

PWLS also alleges that Plaintiff Archie's claims are time-barred. *PWLS Mot.* 7. Archie's son, Paul Bright, died on September 1, 2014. *SAC* ¶ 1. As with Cornell, Archie (Bright's mother) did not discover her son's CTE until it was diagnosed post-mortem on April 9, 2015, by Boston University. *Id.* She, too, filed suit within two years of that discovery. As with Plaintiff Cornell, the Court determines that Archie has alleged sufficient facts as to her diligence in sending her son's brain for study to determine whether he had a brain injury or disease, as well as the time and manner of the discovery on April 9, 2015 that he suffered from CTE. *Id.* Accordingly, Archie's claims are not time-barred.

In conclusion, the Court **GRANTS** Defendant's motion to dismiss for untimeliness as to Plaintiff McCrae, with prejudice; and **DENIES** its motion to dismiss for untimeliness as to Plaintiffs Cornell and Archie.

> iii.   *Article III Standing*

A court does not have subject matter jurisdiction over a case if the plaintiff does not have standing to sue. U.S. Const. art. III, § 2. To satisfy Article III's standing requirements, plaintiff must have (1) suffered an injury in fact, (2) that is traceable to the defendant's acts, and (3) that

UNITED STATES DISTRICT COURT
CENTRAL DISTRICT OF CALIFORNIA

CIVIL MINUTES - GENERAL

Case No.	16-CV-6603 PSG (PLAx)	Date	October 20, 2017
Title	Kimberly Archie, *et al* V. Pop Warner Little Scholars, Inc. *et al*		

can be redressed by a favorable judicial decision. *Chapman v. Pier 1 Imports, Inc.*, 631 F.3d 939, 946 (9th Cir. 2011). PWLS contends that this threshold requirement is not met because (1) Plaintiff Barnes (on behalf of Chase, Drew and Cade Barnes) lacks standing because her children have not suffered an "injury in fact," and (2) Plaintiffs Archie (on behalf of Paul Bright, Jr.), Cornell (on behalf of Tyler Cornell), and McCrae (on behalf of Richard Caldwell) lack standing because they have not shown an injury that is traceable to the allegedly wrongful conduct of PWLS or that can be redressed by judicial decision. *PW Mot.* 9. The Court addresses each argument in turn.

a. Barnes's Standing

To satisfy the injury-in-fact requirement, a plaintiff must show that he has "suffered an 'injury in fact' that is (a) concrete and particularized and (b) actual or imminent, not conjectural or hypothetical." *Friends of the Earth, Inc. v. Laidlaw Env. Servs., Inc.*, 528 U.S. 167, 180–81 (2000). The injury alleged by the plaintiff must be "concrete in both a qualitative and temporal sense." *Whitmore v. Arkansas*, 495 U.S. 149, 155 (1990).

Here, the SAC alleges that the Barnes children played Pop Warner football in the Midvalley Pop Warner Conference, Albany association in Oregon as follows: Chase Barnes from 2009 through 2012 and again in 2015, Drew Barnes from 2010 through 2015, and Cade Barnes in 2014. *SAC* ¶ 4. Plaintiffs have amended their complaint to assert that Chase, Drew, and Cade Barnes "have suffered repeated head trauma resulting in micro-concussions and sub-concussive hits to the head," and as a result have been placed at increased risk of chronic injury, including CTE, that is "substantially certain and impending." *Id.*

Instructive on this point is *Mehr v. Féderation Internationale de Football Ass'n*,, a case in which seven young soccer players brought suit against various soccer organizations. *Mehr*, 115 F. Supp. 3d 1035, 1055 (N.D. Cal. 2015). There, each of the seven plaintiffs alleged that, as a result of the actions and inaction of all defendants, he or she was "at increased risk of latent brain injuries caused by repeated head impacts or the accumulation of concussive and/or subconcussive hits in [his/her] soccer career and therefore is in need of medical monitoring." *Id.* at 1054. The Court granted defendants' motion to dismiss on standing grounds, holding that "the alleged 'risk' of latent brain injuries is speculative and nebulous, rather than being 'certainly impending' such that it constitutes a real and immediate injury-in-fact." *Id.* at 1057–58.

The assertions of injury here are analogous; although Plaintiffs have amended their Complaint to include actual injuries suffered by the Barnes children while paying football, as in *Mehr*, the increased risk of a potential future injury is insufficient to meet the injury-in-fact

UNITED STATES DISTRICT COURT
CENTRAL DISTRICT OF CALIFORNIA

CIVIL MINUTES - GENERAL

Case No.	16-CV-6603 PSG (PLAx)	Date	October 20, 2017
Title	Kimberly Archie, *et al* V. Pop Warner Little Scholars, Inc. *et al*		

requirement of Article III standing. *Whitmore*, 495 U.S. at 157–58 ("[a]llegations of possible
future injury" are not sufficient); *Lujan*, 504 U.S. 555, 564 n.2 (alleged injury too speculative for
Article III purposes where "the plaintiff alleges only an injury at some indefinite future time.").
As repeatedly emphasized by the Supreme Court, the "threatened injury must be *certainly
impending* to constitute injury in fact." *Clapper v. Amnesty Int'l USA*, 568 U.S. 398, 409 (2013);
Whitmore, 495 U.S. at 158; *Lujan*, 504 U.S. 555, 564 n.2 ("Although 'imminence' is concededly
a somewhat elastic concept, it cannot be stretched beyond its purpose, which is to ensure that the
alleged injury is not too speculative for Article III purposes—that the injury is 'certainly
impending.'").

Courts have held that future injury is enough to confer standing where, for instance,
"plaintiffs are not relying on speculative future harm, but on their *present* injuries" (emphasis in
original), *Carlough v. Anchem Products*, 834 F.Supp. 1437, 1454-55 (E.D. Penn. 1993) (finding
standing where plaintiffs had not yet developed asbestos-related disease because exposure to
asbestos necessarily "causes immediate 'bodily injury' ..." even if disease is not manifested until
much later.). Here, on the other hand, Plaintiffs have alleged neither that head trauma sustained
playing football will necessarily result in later brain disease, nor that the Barnes children have
any present brain injury. They have alleged only that head trauma occurred years ago while
playing youth football; they have not alleged that those incidents led to actual brain injury that in
turn could lead to disease or CTE. Similarly, although Plaintiffs use the terms "substantially
certain and impending," they have alleged no facts to establish that chronic brain injury, disease,
or CTE is "certainly impending." Plaintiffs state that CTE can result from "the cumulative toll
of hundreds of traumatic impacts to the brain," and "brain damage can occur . . . from traumatic
forces." *SAC* ¶¶ 38, 48. Nowhere do Plaintiffs claim, however, that all players of youth tackle
football who sustained hits to the head will necessarily develop brain injury, disease, or CTE. In
opposition, Plaintiffs state, for the first time, that "the probability of this occurrence is
undeniable." *See Omalu Decl.* ¶ 24. But they have offered no facts in the SAC that brain injury,
disease, or CTE is an undeniable outcome for the Barnes children.

Accordingly, because Barnes has not alleged that her children Chase, Drew and Cade
have future injury that is "certainly impending," Barnes lacks Article III standing in this action.
The Court need not reach the other two prongs of the standing analysis. PWLS's motion to
dismiss Barnes and her claims on behalf of her three children is therefore **GRANTED**, with
prejudice.

     b. Archie & Cornell's Standing

       i. Injury

UNITED STATES DISTRICT COURT
CENTRAL DISTRICT OF CALIFORNIA

CIVIL MINUTES - GENERAL

Case No.	16-CV-6603 PSG (PLAx)	Date	October 20, 2017
Title	Kimberly Archie, *et al* V. Pop Warner Little Scholars, Inc. *et al*		

Next, PWLS argues that Archie and Cornell lack standing because neither has alleged "a particular injury on a particular occasion in youth football." PWLS Mot. 10. Plaintiffs allege that Paul Bright, Jr. played youth football between 1997 and 2004, and Tyler Cornell played youth football between 1997 and 2002. *See SAC* ¶¶ 1–2. PWLS calls it "pure speculation" that Paul Bright and Tyler Cornell were injured playing youth football, and (quite unnecessarily) points out that there is no risk of future injury to them because they are deceased. PW Mot. 10. These two Plaintiffs do allege head injuries sustained while playing Pop Warner football. *See SAC* ¶¶ 1–2. While they have not specified dates and details of each incident of injury, it is not "pure speculation" that they were injured; further, each was later given a posthumous CTE diagnosis. Id. Bright and Cornell sustained multiple head injuries while playing football, and later received an actual CTE diagnosis; the Court is persuaded that an injury-in-fact as to these two Plaintiffs has been sufficiently pleaded.

Having found an injury as to Plaintiffs Archie and Cornell, the Court now turns to the remaining prong in the standing analysis.

ii.   *Traceable to PWLS*

The second prong is that the injury alleged must be fairly traceable to the defendant's acts. PWLS argues that none of the Plaintiffs have pleaded an injury traceable to an act or omission of PWLS. PWLS Mot. 13. The remaining Plaintiffs (Archie and Cornell) have sufficiently pleaded injuries that occurred while playing Pop Warner football as well as latent brain injuries many years later, as noted above. The causal link between repeated head trauma and brain damage, injury, and disease is well established. *SAC* ¶¶ 39-51; *Omalu Dec.* ¶¶ 14, 15, 25. The Court concludes it is plausible that as alleged, Plaintiffs' repeated head injuries sustained playing youth tackle football resulted in brain injury and CTE, and are thus traceable to acts or omissions by PWLS.

iii.   *Redressability*

PWLS argues that Plaintiffs injuries cannot be redressed because the injuries, including the CTE deaths, have already occurred and none of the Plaintiffs continues to play football. PW Mot. 13. Plaintiffs allege economic losses, however, including loss of income and other money damages arising from their injuries. *See SAC* ¶ 163. The Court agrees with Plaintiffs that a favorable decision from the Court would, at least in part, redress their injuries, and accordingly, this element is satisfied.

PWLS also argues that Archie and Cornell lack standing as "survivors" because they failed to execute an affidavit required by Cal. Civ. Proc. § 377.32. *PW Mot.* 15. Plaintiffs

UNITED STATES DISTRICT COURT
CENTRAL DISTRICT OF CALIFORNIA

CIVIL MINUTES - GENERAL

Case No.	16-CV-6603 PSG (PLAx)	Date	October 20, 2017
Title	Kimberly Archie, *et al* V. Pop Warner Little Scholars, Inc. *et al*		

Archie and Cornell are not, however, bringing survival actions under § 377.32. Rather, they are bringing a wrongful death action, and as parents, they have standing to do so ("A cause of action for the death of a person caused by the wrongful act or neglect of another may be asserted by the decedent's . . . parents." *See* Cal. Civ. Proc. Code § 377.60).

Accordingly, Plaintiffs Archie and Cornell, parents of Paul Bright and Tyler Cornell, respectively, have established standing, and Defendant's motion to dismiss on this basis is **DENIED**.

       iv.   *Abstention*

Defendant PWLS argues that the Court should abstain from exercising jurisdiction "because the Court's expertise is not in establishing medical guidelines or equipment standards . . . if the Court were to grant relief, it would re-write rules for thousands of PWLS associations nationwide." PWLS Mot. 16. Plaintiffs are seeking damages under theories of negligence, fraud, and wrongful death; the only injunctive relief they request that implicates the establishment of helmet safety guidelines or equipment standards is requested of Defendant NOCSAE alone. *SAC* 47:20-24. As discussed below, the Court lacks personal jurisdiction over NOCSAE and dismisses it from the action; accordingly, the Court **DENIES** PWLS's motion to dismiss on this basis.

       v.   *Failure to State a Claim*

Defendant PWLS asserts that Plaintiffs have failed to state a claim as to the First, Second, Third, Fourth, Sixth, and Seventh causes of action. *PW Mot.* 18.

       a.   *Negligence Claim*

Plaintiffs' first cause of action is for negligence. *See SAC* 27. To establish a cause of action for negligence, a plaintiff must allege: (1) the defendant owed the plaintiff a duty of due care; (2) the defendant breached that duty; (3) the plaintiff suffered injury; and (4) the breach proximately caused the injury. *Resolution Tr. Corp. v. Rossmoor Corp.,* 34 Cal. App. 4th 93, 101 (1995). Defendants argue that Plaintiff failed to state a claim for negligence because (1) Defendants owed no cognizable duty to Plaintiffs, and (2) PWLS was not the proximate cause of Plaintiffs' injuries.

       i.   *Duty*

UNITED STATES DISTRICT COURT
CENTRAL DISTRICT OF CALIFORNIA

CIVIL MINUTES - GENERAL

Case No.	16-CV-6603 PSG (PLAx)	Date	October 20, 2017
Title	Kimberly Archie, *et al* V. Pop Warner Little Scholars, Inc. *et al*		

A fundamental element of any cause of action for negligence is the existence of a duty of care running from defendant to plaintiff. *Vasilenko v. Grace Family Church*, 248 Cal. App. 4th 146, 152 (2016). In the sports context, California recognizes that there is no duty to prevent risks "inherent in the sport itself." *Knight v. Jewett*, 834 P.2d 696, 708 (Cal. 1992); rather, there is a duty "not to increase the risks to a participant over and above those inherent in the sport." *Id.*; *see also Avila v. Citrus Comty Coll. Dist.*, 131 P.3d 383 (Cal. 2006) (holding school had no duty to player injured by a pitch thrown during tournament it was hosting); *Balthazor v. Little League Baseball, Inc.*, 72 Cal. App. 2d 337, 341 (1998) (holding league had no duty to provide equipment to guard against being hit by errant balls); *Danieley v. Goldmine Ski Associates, Inc.*, 266 Cal. App. 749, 757 (1990) (holding ski operator had no duty to remove trees because natural obstacles are inherent risk of skiing). Thus, in the context of inherent risk in sports, there is no duty to minimize or decrease inherent risk—only a duty not to increase it.

Plaintiffs acknowledge that head injuries are an inherent risk in the sport of tackle football. *SAC* ¶¶ 142, 145. Their burden, then, is to establish that PWLS *increased* the inherent risk of tackle football. In its first amended complaint, Plaintiffs alleged that PWLS "failed to reduce the inherent risk of the sport," which is not the legal standard with which Defendants must comply. Dkt. # 40, *FAC* ¶ 57. Plaintiffs now state that they "do not allege that Pop Warner failed to minimize or reduce the inherent risks of youth tackle football." *PWLS Opp*. 19. In fact, their SAC alleges exactly that: that PWLS should have taken the actions listed above "so as to minimize the long-term risks" inherent in tackle football. *SAC* ¶ 149. PWLS does not have a legal duty to minimize the inherent risks—they have a duty not to increase them. Despite Plaintiffs word choice, they have alleged sufficient facts of an increased risk to survive the pleading stage.

Plaintiffs argue that PWLS failed to create and implement league-wide guidelines (*SAC* ¶ 143), failed to adopt equipment standards (*Id.* ¶ 144), failed to require brain injury history (*Id.* ¶ 149), and failed to approve the best equipment available (*Id.*). The Court agrees with Plaintiff that by failing to institute league-wide guidelines, PWLS increased the risk of head injury to its youth players. As Plaintiffs note, other sporting associations have, for decades, used and implemented standardized concussion management rules. *Id.* ¶ 146. PWLS, by failing to create similar guidelines, allowed each of its leagues to adopt their own coaching standards and play techniques, which could encompass dangerous, outdated "lead with the head" instructions or other similar tactics. Plaintiffs have alleged an abundance of facts to illustrate the increased risk of head trauma football poses to children, and PWLS's failure to respond to that risk with appropriate league-wide safety guidelines, such as a mandated reduction in head-to-head contact, increased it. *See Id.* ¶¶ 42-46. Similarly, allowing a child with a pre-existing brain injury to play tackle football would greatly increase his risk of further brain trauma, and PWLS increased

UNITED STATES DISTRICT COURT
CENTRAL DISTRICT OF CALIFORNIA

CIVIL MINUTES - GENERAL

Case No.	16-CV-6603 PSG (PLAx)	Date	October 20, 2017
Title	Kimberly Archie, *et al* V. Pop Warner Little Scholars, Inc. *et al*		

that risk by failing to find to take a history from each child and disallowing those with prior brain injuries to play. *Id.* ¶¶ 42, 149.

Plaintiffs also argue that PWLS increased the risks associated with tackle football by "providing defective equipment that was not adequately designed or tested to protect minor participants from harm."[2] *SAC* ¶¶ 23-24, 49. If PWLS indeed provided defective helmets knowing they had design defects that would increase the risk of injury if players received contact to the head, they would certainly have increased the risk of the sport and breached their legal duty. Plaintiffs have not alleged any facts, however, supporting that the helmets were inadequately designed or contained defects, nor that PWLS knew of any such defects. However, PWLS "mandated the use of helmets that 'Meet[] NOCSAE Standards' (*Id.* ¶ 135) and "failed to warn the Plaintiffs. . . about the dangers of using improper equipment." *Id.* ¶ 50. Whether or not the helmets were defective, they were not safety-tested for use on children, and thus "not adequately tested to protect minor participants from harm." *Id.* ¶¶ 23-24, 30, 49. Mandating the use of helmets that have not been safety tested for children, and which bore the NOCSAE seal of approval, increased the risks for youth players; the NOCSAE rating standard, even in adults, results in a high likelihood of concussion. *Id.* ¶ 23. In children, then, the probability of concussion would necessarily be even higher. *See Id.* ¶¶ 42-46. Furthermore, the mandatory use of such helmets means that parents and coaches were not allowed to provide a safer alternative for their youth players.

Alternatively, Plaintiffs argue that Defendants assumed a duty under the "voluntary undertaking" doctrine. *SAC* ¶¶ 134, 135. "A volunteer with no initial duty, who undertakes protective services for another, has a duty to exercise due care if his failure of care increases the risk of harm, or if the other person reasonably relies on his undertaking and suffers injury." *Delgado v. Trax Bar and Grill*, 113 Cal. 1159, 1175 (Cal. 2005). PWLS argues that its "safety first" statements do not rise to the level of establishing a voluntary undertaking, noting that "voluntary efforts at minimizing risk do not demonstrate that defendant bore a legal duty to do so." *Nalwa v. Cedar Fair, L.P.*, 55 Cal. 4th 1148, 1163 (2012) (efforts to discourage bumper car drivers from head-on collisions did not create "voluntary undertaking" duty). Likewise, the court in *Mehr* held that implementing a Concussion Management Program and adopting a Concussion Procedure and Protocol did not create an affirmative duty to reduce the risk of concussion inherent in the sport of soccer. *Mehr*, 115 F. Supp. 3d at 1065. Plaintiffs argue that the cases relied on by Defendant, including *Mehr*, are distinguishable because in those cases, the defendants "did nothing to increase the risks inherent in the sport." *PWLS Opp.* 19. Here, they

---

[2] The Court notes that Plaintiffs allege the helmets had "known design defects," (*SAC* ¶ 49), "were not adequately designed" (*Id.* ¶ 60), and were "defective equipment that was not adequately designed." *PWLS Opp.* 20. Plaintiffs seem to be arguing a products liability claim, though they have not included the helmet manufacturer in this action.

UNITED STATES DISTRICT COURT
CENTRAL DISTRICT OF CALIFORNIA

CIVIL MINUTES - GENERAL

Case No.	16-CV-6603 PSG (PLAx)	Date	October 20, 2017
Title	Kimberly Archie, *et al* V. Pop Warner Little Scholars, Inc. *et al*		

contend, PWLS required the use of "dangerous equipment *designed to increase the risk* to minor participants." *Id.* (emphasis added). Putting aside that Plaintiffs have not elsewhere alleged that Pop Warner's equipment was actually designed to increase risks to youth players, the Court has already determined that Plaintiffs have satisfied their burden of pleading that Defendant PWLS increased the inherent risks of youth tackle football; they need not rely on the alternative voluntary undertaking theory.

ii.   Causation

To establish a claim for negligence, Plaintiff must also show that the harm that it suffered was proximately caused by Defendants' actions. *See Tribeca Cos., LLC v. First Am. Title Ins. Co.*, 239 Cal. App. 4th 1088, 1103 (2015). The test of whether an independent intervening act breaks the chain of causation is "foreseeability." *Paskenta Band of Nomlaki Indians v. Crosby*, 122 F. Supp. 3d 982, 996 (E.D. Cal. 2015) (quoting *Schrimser v. Bryson*, 58 Cal. App. 3d 660, 664 (1976)). "An act is not foreseeable and is thus a superseding cause of injury if the independent intervening act is highly unusual or extraordinary, not reasonably likely to happen." *Paskenta*, 122 F. Supp. at 996.

PWLS argues that "[a]ny act of PWLS is too removed from the risk of injury to be a proximate cause, as a matter of law." *PWLS Mot.* 19. As Plaintiffs correctly note, they are not required to *prove* causation at the pleading stage; they need only allege "sufficient factual matter, accepted as true, to 'state a claim to relief that is plausible on its face.'" *Ashcroft v. Iqbal*, 556 U.S. 662, 678 (2009) (quoting *Bell Atl. Corp. v. Twombly*, 550 U.S. 544, 570 (2007)). Plaintiffs have alleged sufficient facts to establish a plausible scenario in which the head trauma suffered while participating in youth tackle football caused severe brain injury. *See SAC* ¶¶ 37-49. Accordingly, PWLS's motion to dismiss the negligence claim (First cause of action) is **DENIED**.

b.   Fraud and Misrepresentation Claims

Under California law, the elements of fraud are "(a) misrepresentation (false representation, concealment, or nondisclosure); (b) knowledge of falsity (or 'scienter'); (c) intent to defraud, i.e., to induce reliance; (d) justifiable reliance; and (e) resulting damage." *Engalla v. Permanente Med. Grp., Inc.*, 15 Cal. 4th 951, 974 (1997). "In diversity cases where the cause of action is fraud, the substantive elements of fraud are determined by state law. These elements, however, must be pleaded in accordance with Fed.R.Civ.P. 9(b)." *Smith v. Allstate Ins. Co.*, 160 F. Supp. 2d 1150, 1152 (S.D. Cal. 2001). "Under Rule 9(b), a party must state with particularity the circumstances constituting fraud or mistake. Rule 9(b) demands that, when averments of fraud are made, the circumstances constituting the alleged fraud be specific enough to give

UNITED STATES DISTRICT COURT
CENTRAL DISTRICT OF CALIFORNIA

CIVIL MINUTES - GENERAL

Case No.	16-CV-6603 PSG (PLAx)	Date	October 20, 2017
Title	Kimberly Archie, *et al* V. Pop Warner Little Scholars, Inc. *et al*		

defendants notice of the *particular* misconduct so that they can defend against the charge." *Gerard v. Wells Fargo Bank, N.A.*, No. CV 14-03935 MMM (SHx), 2015 WL 12791416, at *6 (C.D. Cal. Jan. 22, 2015) (emphasis in original) (internal quotation marks and citations omitted); *see also Vess v. Ciba-Geigy Corp. USA*, 317 F.3d 1097, 1108 (9th Cir. 2003) ("Averments of fraud must be accompanied by the who, what, when, where, and how of the misconduct charged.") (internal quotation marks omitted). The Ninth Circuit has highlighted two requirements for particularity under Rule 9(b). First, fraud allegations must include the "time, place, and specific content of the false representations as well as the identities of the parties to the misrepresentations." *Swartz v. KPMG LLP*, 476 F.3d 756, 764 (9th Cir. 2007) (quoting *Edwards v. Marin Park, Inc.*, 356 F.3d 1058, 1066 (9th Cir. 2004)). Second, the allegation must also include "an explanation as to why the statement or omission complained of was false or misleading." *Johnson v. Wal-Mart Stores, Inc.*, 544 Fed. App'x 696, 698 (9th Cir. 2013). "As a consequence of this second requirement, the plaintiff is precluded from simply pointing to a defendant's statement, noting that the content of the statement conflicts with the current state of affairs, and then concluding that the statement in question was false when made." *Smith*, 160 F. Supp. 2d at 1153.

Here, PWLS argues that the fraud claims fail because head trauma is an inherent risk of tackle football, and at no time did PWLS misrepresent that the sport was "free of risk." *PWLS Mot.* 23. That is not, however, the thrust of Plaintiffs' fraud claims. Rather, they allege that PWLS misrepresented that safety was its top priority, with coaches trained in head injuries, equipment that afforded the best protection, and rules and procedures designed to protect children from injury—all with the knowledge that none of this was true, to boost the number of Pop Warner participants. *See generally SAC.*

Plaintiff has proffered sufficient facts regarding misrepresentation of PWLS's safety protocols, including coaching staff and equipment use, with specific instances of actual statements issued by the organization. For instance, Pop Warner's website states that "[t]he safety of our athletes is *always the top priority* . . . we provide extensive training for all our football . . . coaches," (emphasis in original) *see id.* ¶ 53, while Pop Warner does not in fact ensure that coaches receive any training at all. *Id.* ¶ 54. PWLS argues that because it makes no representation about what measures are taken to ensure or enforce the coaches' training, they have made no misrepresentation. *PWLS Mot.* 24. Similarly, they argue there can be no false or misleading statement in "safety is always the top priority," because there is no objective standard against which to measure this claim. *Id.* The Court finds these arguments unpersuasive. PWLS's "safety-first" message omitted that PWLS equipment was not safety-tested for children (*SAC* ¶ 149), that it had no league-wide safety guidelines (*Id.* ¶ 143), that it did not require brain injury history (*Id.* ¶ 149), and that it did not monitor whether its coaches received any safety training at all. *Id.* ¶ 54. Plaintiffs therefore "reasonably relied on . . . [the]misrepresentations to

UNITED STATES DISTRICT COURT
CENTRAL DISTRICT OF CALIFORNIA

CIVIL MINUTES - GENERAL

Case No.	16-CV-6603 PSG (PLAx)	Date	October 20, 2017

Title	Kimberly Archie, *et al* V. Pop Warner Little Scholars, Inc. *et al*

their detriment when deciding whether to participate and/or enroll their children" in tackle football (*SAC* ¶ 211), and "Pop Warner's false representations regarding the safety of youth tackle football misled parents . . . into enrolling their children in the Pop Warner program." *See Id.* ¶ 51.

The elements of negligent misrepresentation are the same as those for fraud, but Plaintiffs need not prove scienter. *See Charnay v. Cobert*, 145 Cal. App. 4th 170, 184 (2006) ("[I]n a claim for negligent misrepresentation, the plaintiff need not allege the defendant made an intentionally false statement, but simply one as to which he or she lacked any reasonable ground for believing the statement to be true.").

Accordingly, Defendant PWLS's motion to dismiss the Second and Third causes of action (Fraud and Fraudulent Concealment) and Fourth cause of action (Negligent Misrepresentation) is **DENIED**.

      c. *Business & Professions Code Claims*

California Business & Professions Code § 17200 ("UCL") prohibits any "unlawful, unfair, or fraudulent business act or practice." *See* Cal. Bus. & Prof. Code §§ 17200 *et seq.* California's False Advertising Law ("FAL") makes it unlawful for a business "to make or disseminate . . . any statement . . . which is untrue or misleading, and which is known, or which by the exercise of reasonable care should be known, to be untrue or misleading . . ." Cal. Bus. & Prof. Code § 17500; *see also People v. Dollar Rent-A-Car Sys., Inc.*, 211 Cal. App. 3d 119, 128-29 (1989). "To have standing to assert a [UCL] claim, the plaintiff must '(1) establish a loss or deprivation of money or property sufficient to qualify as injury in fact, i.e., *economic injury*, and (2) show that economic injury was the result of, i.e., *caused by*, the unfair business practice or false advertising that is the gravamen of the claim.'" *Cornejo v. Ocwen Loan Servicing, LLC*, 151 F. Supp. 3d 1102, 1118 (E.D. Cal. 2015) (quoting *Kwikset Corp. v. Superior Ct.*, 51 Cal. 4th 310, 322 (2011) (emphasis in original)).

PWLS argues that Plaintiffs lack standing to bring a UCL or FAL claim because their claims are based not on unfair business practices, but on personal injury. *PWLS Mot.* 24; *SAC* ¶ 61. Plaintiffs argue that they have economic losses stemming from "the costs incurred enrolling their children in tackle football programs and purchasing materials and/or equipment." *PWLS Opp.* 25. But Plaintiffs did not allege this economic loss in their SAC; rather, they claim economic losses resulting from personal injury, including loss of income, emotional distress, and death. *See SAC* ¶¶ 196, 215, 220. The Court agrees with Defendant that no economic injury occurred within the meaning of California's UCL or FAL statutes.

UNITED STATES DISTRICT COURT
CENTRAL DISTRICT OF CALIFORNIA

CIVIL MINUTES - GENERAL

Case No.	16-CV-6603 PSG (PLAx)	Date	October 20, 2017
Title	Kimberly Archie, *et al* V. Pop Warner Little Scholars, Inc. *et al*		

Defendant PWLS's motion to dismiss the Business and Profession Code claims (Sixth and Seventh causes of action) is **GRANTED**.[1]

vi.   Leave to Amend

Whether to grant leave to amend rests in the sound discretion of the trial court. *See Bonin v. Calderon*, 59 F.3d 815, 845 (9th Cir. 1995). The Court considers whether leave to amend would cause undue delay or prejudice to the opposing party, and whether granting leave to amend would be futile. *See Sisseton-Wahpeton Sioux Tribe v. United States*, 90 F.3d 351, 355 (9th Cir. 1996). Generally, dismissal without leave to amend is improper "unless it is clear that the complaint could not be saved by any amendment." *Jackson v. Carey*, 353 F.3d 750, 758 (9th Cir. 2003).

The Court concludes that Plaintiffs' insufficiencies might very well be cured through amendment, and it does not believe that Defendant would be prejudiced if leave were granted at this time. The Court therefore GRANTS Plaintiffs leave to amend.

Accordingly, the Court **GRANTS** Defendant PWLS's motion to dismiss Plaintiffs' Sixth (UCL) and Seventh (FAL) causes of action **WITH LEAVE TO AMEND**. It **DENIES** Defendant PWLS's motion to dismiss the First (Negligence), Second (Fraud), Third (Fraudulent Concealment), and Fourth (Negligent Misrepresentation) cause of action.

B.   NOCSAE's Motion to Dismiss

NOCSAE moves to dismiss Plaintiffs' SAC in its entirety based on (1) lack of personal jurisdiction under Fed. R. Civ. P. 12(b)(2), (2) timeliness, and (3) improper venue. *See generally NOCSAE Mot.* Because the Court finds the personal jurisdiction argument dispositive, it need not reach NOCSAE's second and third arguments.

1.   Personal Jurisdiction

a.   General Jurisdiction

Plaintiffs do not assert that the Court has general jurisdiction nor do they address this issue in their opposition; they argue only in support of specific jurisdiction. *See* Dkt. # 97 ("NOCSAE Opp.") 4–10. Plaintiffs thus effectively concede that no general jurisdiction exists

---

[1] PWLS also seeks to have the Medical Monitoring Class dismissed as a matter of law. *PWLS Mot.* 25. Because that is a purported class and not a cause of action, the Court notes that class certification is the proper stage to address this issue rather than in a motion to dismiss.

UNITED STATES DISTRICT COURT
CENTRAL DISTRICT OF CALIFORNIA

CIVIL MINUTES - GENERAL

Case No.	16-CV-6603 PSG (PLAx)	Date	October 20, 2017

Title	Kimberly Archie, *et al* V. Pop Warner Little Scholars, Inc. *et al*

over NOCSAE in California. *See Ramirez v. Ghilotti Bros. Inc.*, 941 F. Supp. 2d 1197, 1210 (N.D. Cal. 2013) (deeming argument conceded where plaintiff failed to address it in opposition); *Qureshi v. Countrywide Home Loans*, Inc., No. 09–4198, 2010 WL 841669, at *6 (N.D. Cal. Mar. 10, 2010) (deeming plaintiff's failure to address, in opposition brief, claims challenged in a motion to dismiss, an "abandonment of those claims") (citing *Jenkins v. County of Riverside*, 398 F.3d 1093, 1095 n. 4 (9th Cir. 2005)).

Thus, the Court turns directly to the question of specific jurisdiction.

        b.   *Specific Jurisdiction*

        1. Minimum Contacts

The Court again applies the Ninth Circuit's three-part test (the "effects test") from the Supreme Court's opinion in *Calder v. Jones*, 465 U.S. 783 (1984), assessing whether Defendant "(1) committed an intentional act, (2) expressly aimed at the forum state, (3) causing harm that the defendant knows is likely to be suffered in the forum state." *Picot*, 780 F.3d at 1214 (quoting *Dole Food Co., Inc. v. Watts*, 303 F.3d 1104, 1111 (9th Cir. 2002)).

        a. Intentional Act

Plaintiffs allege that NOCSAE committed an intentional act by "creating standards for various athletic equipment," *see SAC* ¶ 18, and by licensing the use of its logo, on a sticker that indicates a "helmet has been tested for safety and protection against injury." *Id.* ¶ 24. This is sufficient to meet the "intentional act" prong within the meaning of the *Calder* test.

        b. *Expressly Aimed*

Plaintiffs allege that sufficient minimum contacts exist because NOCSAE has "licensing agreements with football helmet manufacturers who buy and sell goods throughout the state of California." *SAC* ¶¶ 92, 93. Further, they allege NOCSAE receives revenue from football helmets sold, reconditioned, and distributed to California players. *See SAC* ¶¶ 99, 104. Plaintiffs also note that NOCSAE's website refers to California's reconditioning law and also allows California residents to apply for research grants. *Id.* ¶ 108.

In its May 12 Order, the Court stated that "mere licensing of NOCSAE's logo to manufacturers who place helmets into the stream of commerce in California is 'not an act purposefully directed toward a forum state.'" *See* Dkt. #72, quoting *Holland Am. Line Inc. v. Wartsila N. Am., Inc.*, 485 F.3d 450, 459 (9th Cir. 2007) (citing *Asahi Metal Indus. Co. v.*

UNITED STATES DISTRICT COURT
CENTRAL DISTRICT OF CALIFORNIA

CIVIL MINUTES - GENERAL

Case No.	16-CV-6603 PSG (PLAx)	Date	October 20, 2017
Title	Kimberly Archie, *et al* V. Pop Warner Little Scholars, Inc. *et al*		

Superior Court, 480 U.S. 102, 112 (1987) ("Even a defendant's awareness that the stream of commerce may or will sweep the product into the forum state does not convert the mere act of placing the product into the stream of commerce into an act purposefully directed toward the forum state.")); *Bancroft & Masters, Inc.*, 223 F.3d 1082, 1086 (9th Cir. 2000) (finding a "handful" of licensing agreements with California entities insufficient to confer personal jurisdiction over non-resident defendant). The SAC contains no assertion that NOCSAE has licensing agreements with California-based manufacturers, and none of the licensing fees collected by NOCSAE are determined by the type or number of helmets sold in California. *NOCSAE Reply* 3. Plaintiffs allege that NOCSAE has reconditioning agreements with two entities in California, but allege no facts indicating that such companies recondition youth helmets or any equipment for Pop Warner players, nor that they sell or redistribute helmets back into the stream of commerce in any way (in fact, they are reconditioned only at the owners' requests). *Oliver Dec.* ¶ 20. Furthermore, Plaintiffs allege the existence of California-based reconditioners for the first time only in its opposition, not in its SAC. *See NOCSAE Opp.* 7.

As to the facts alleged regarding NOCSAE's website, Plaintiffs have failed to amend their SAC in light of the Court's prior Order. The Court determined that the "non-commercial, information-based website . . . [was] insufficient to show activity 'expressly aimed' at a forum state simply because it is accessible by California residents." *May 12 Order*, Dkt. # 72 at 12; *SAC* ¶ 108. *See Callaway Golf Corp. v. Royal Canadian Gold Ass'n*, 125 F.Supp.2d 1194, 1204 (C.D. Cal. 2000) ("Simply by maintaining a Web site accessible to California users and including information on the site ... [defendant] has not purposefully availed itself of this forum."); *Pebble Beach*, 453 F.3d at1158–59 (declining to exercise specific jurisdiction over a passive website). The Court also found insufficient the allegation that NOCSAE's funding of a single research grant in California conferred jurisdiction, noting that Plaintiffs had failed to describe the research, to claim a nexus between that research and youth football or to connect it to Plaintiffs' injuries. *May 12 Order*, Dkt. # 72 at 12. Plaintiffs have alleged no additional facts about this grant in their amended complaint, but rather have relied on identical wording. *SAC* ¶ 108; *FAC* ¶ 51.

What Plaintiffs have added is a claim that in 2004, NOCSAE voided a manufacturer's certification of lacrosse helmets for non-compliance with NOCSAE standards. *SAC* ¶ 105. Presumably, Plaintiffs include this incident to illustrate that NOCSAE could have similarly voided certification of football helmets had it chosen to. However, this action cannot establish conduct "expressly aimed" at California as it is not alleged to have taken place in California, involve football helmets, or have any other connection to this case. Plaintiffs also add that in 2011, the Federal Trade Commission began investigating NOCSAE for its refusal to allow youth football players to use a Guardian Cap. *Id.* ¶ 111. NOCSAE stated that the use of a Guardian Cap would void the certification of NOCSAE compliance. *Id.* ¶ 113. It was Pop Warner who

UNITED STATES DISTRICT COURT
CENTRAL DISTRICT OF CALIFORNIA

CIVIL MINUTES - GENERAL

Case No.	16-CV-6603 PSG (PLAx)	Date	October 20, 2017
Title	Kimberly Archie, *et al* V. Pop Warner Little Scholars, Inc. *et al*		

chose to include the NOCSAE stickers on its youth helmets, however (indeed, as the Court noted in its May 12 Order, "NOCSAE's contacts with California depend entirely on California manufacturers and football leagues *choosing to* adopt its safety standards, and as such, fall far from asserting that NOCSAE engages in any affirmative activity that is purposefully aimed at California." *May 12 Order*, Dkt. # 72 at 10, (emphasis added); NOCSAE did not require any such certification. Even if it had, Plaintiffs fail to allege that any conduct giving rise to the FTC issue took place in California, was aimed at California, or is related in any way to this case.

2. Arising Out Of Forum-Related Activities

Even if Plaintiffs had sufficiently plead minimum contacts, they have not cured the problems that plagued the FAC regarding the second prong of the jurisdictional analysis: that its claims arise out of NOCSAE's forum-related activities. The Ninth Circuit applies a "but for" test under which the Court must determine whether the plaintiff would not have suffered injury "but for" the defendant's forum-related conduct. *Shute v. Carnival Cruise Lines*, 897 F.2d 377, 385 (9th Cir. 1990), *rev'd on other grounds*, 499 U.S. 585 (1991) ("The 'but for' test should not be narrowly applied; rather, the requirement is merely designed to confirm that there is some nexus between the cause of action and defendant's contact with the forum.").

Plaintiff SAC alleges that NOCSAE failed to promulgate standards specifically tailored to minors. *SAC* ¶ 149. As Defendant notes, Plaintiffs' complaint would necessarily be exactly the same whether or not NOCSAE had any California contacts. *NOCSAE Mot*. 14. Pop Warner could have continued placing NOCSAE stickers on its helmets, NOCSAE could have continued promulgating its safety standards from its headquarters in Kansas, players and their parents could have continued to have a false sense of security, as Plaintiffs allege, from NOCSAE's stickers and Pop Warner's "safety first" message. None of these things implicates any action whatsoever taken by NOCSAE that was directed at California.

In any event, Plaintiffs fail to respond to any of Defendant's arguments about but-for causation in their opposition. Instead, they mistakenly name Pop Warner, not NOCSAE, in their heading, and then merely state the rule established in *Ballard. NOCSAE Opp*. 9. As Plaintiffs have not addressed Defendant's arguments, the Court takes them as conceded.

Plaintiffs have failed to amend their complaint to meet the requirements of the first and second prongs of the specific jurisdiction analysis. Based on these considerations, Plaintiffs have failed to establish the Court's personal jurisdiction over NOCSAE. Therefore, NOCSAE's motion to dismiss for lack of personal jurisdiction is **GRANTED**, with prejudice.

IV.   <u>Conclusion</u>

UNITED STATES DISTRICT COURT
CENTRAL DISTRICT OF CALIFORNIA

CIVIL MINUTES - GENERAL

Case No.	16-CV-6603 PSG (PLAx)	Date	October 20, 2017
Title	Kimberly Archie, *et al* V. Pop Warner Little Scholars, Inc. *et al*		

In conclusion, the Court:

- GRANTS Defendant NOCSAE's motion to dismiss WITH PREJUDICE;

- DENIES Defendant PWLS's motion to dismiss for lack of personal jurisdiction;

- GRANTS Defendant PWLS's motion to dismiss for untimeliness as to Plaintiff McCrae, WITH PREJUDICE; and DENIES as to Plaintiffs Cornell and Archie;

- GRANTS Defendant PWLS's motion to dismiss for lack of standing as to Plaintiff Barnes, WITH PREJUDICE; and DENIES as to Plaintiffs Cornell and Archie; and

- DENIES Defendant's PWLS's motion to dismiss Plaintiff's First (Negligence), Second (Fraud), Third (Fraudulent Concealment), and Fourth (Negligent Misrepresentation) causes of action; and GRANTS its motion to dismiss the Sixth (UCL) and Seventh (FAL) causes of action, WITHOUT PREJUDICE.

Plaintiffs may file a third amended complaint ("TAC") by **November 20, 2017**. If a TAC is not filed by this date, causes of action Six and Seven will be dismissed WITH PREJUDICE.

IT IS SO ORDERED.

UNITED STATES DISTRICT COURT
CENTRAL DISTRICT OF CALIFORNIA

CIVIL MINUTES - GENERAL

Case No.	16-CV-6603 PSG (PLAx)	Date	October 20, 2017

Title	Kimberly Archie, *et al* V. Pop Warner Little Scholars, Inc. *et al*

ACKNOWLEDGMENTS

This project began more than two years ago and has taken on a life of its own. This book wouldn't have been possible without all of the contributions made by each of the chapter authors and their friends and families who helped with memories, dates and details. Every author poured out his or her heart and soul to help prevent even just one child from being exposed to unnecessary brain damage and disease.

Special thanks to @ConcernedMom from Twitter, and Kent Johnson for all of their feedback during the process. Big ups to USC Law School Professor Jody Armour for all his help in understanding civil rights and tort law.

To our book cover designer we're grateful for your vision and professionalism during the process. Kudos to Heather UpChurch our book designer who literally saved the day, as well as our website designer Tiffani Bright. You guys produced miracles.

We couldn't have done this project without the help and backing of all the attorneys, including those who volunteer at the National Cheer Safety Foundation. The families are forever grateful for your time and dedication to this project.

Thank you to parent advocates Crystal Dixon and Greg Ransom, who also paid the ultimate price. Your support is greatly valued and your efforts ensure that the legacy of your sons, Donnovan Hill and James Ransom will live on. We also want to thank the Hilinski family for their hard work with Hilinski's Hope and changing the narrative and stigma surrounding mental health for athletes.

To Brenda Easter and Allison Epperson, your vision to carry on Zac's last wishes through CTE Hope is commendable. We are so glad you're a part of our group.

To the Matin family, we are honored and grateful that you choose to donate your beloved Andre's brain to science as the first brain from our group to go to Mt. Sinai brain bank. You truly honored his love of Science and helping others with your enormous gesture.

We are forever indebted to the Institute on Violence Abuse & Trauma. Words don't do justice to express our appreciation for your dedication to preventing child abuse.

A huge thanks to Austin Murphy for inspiring us with your 2016 article in "Sports Illustrated," *End Game* and giving us the confidence to make this project happen.

Shout out to the source of our strength, faith and hope for seeing *Brain Damaged: Two-Minute Warning for Parents* to completion.